Chained Melody

Debbie Martin

Pen Press

First published in Great Britain

All paper used in the printing of this book has been made from wood grown in managed, sustainable forests.

ISBN13: 978-1-78003-547-5

Printed and bound in the UK
Pen Press is an imprint of
Indepenpress Publishing Limited
25 Eastern Place
Brighton
BN2 1GJ

A catalogue record of this book is available from the British Library

Cover design by Jacqueline Abromeit

Foreword

'For such as we are made of, such we be.'
William Shakespeare – Twelfth Night Act 2 Scene 2 line 3

This story is written with no bias – hetero or homosexual, gay or straight. It is written because not every experience is possible in our lives, but the power of the written word is to allow the imagination to experience what is not possible in our personal reality. In this story, experience what it might be like to live and love as a transgender in a gender specific world.

Please read it with empathy, because it is empathy that makes love able to make the world go round.

Thank you to those who read, checked and corrected facts in order for it to be 'real'.

Prologue 1995

The door in the gate shut firmly behind me; but it shut me out this time – not in. I stood for a few moments savouring being on the other side of it, hearing the buzz of the traffic at the end of the road, noticing the litter blow across the pavement. It had always been squeaky clean inside. Littering had been an offence and privileges got withdrawn if you were caught – a way of ingraining principles in the *deadbeats*, the failures of · humanity. I had failed, but my failure was personal. I hadn't failed any more than mankind in general but when you're labelled a killer, outwardly what else are you?

I picked up my bag and walked to the end of the street, leaving the HM Prison sign behind me, but unsure of what came next. The letter, with the diary, was still in my pocket. It was the last thing to arrive before my release, and it posed a difficult question for me; THE question, in fact. I'd put off deciding until I was outside the prison confines, thinking maybe when I was free again, I would know – as if physical freedom would also free me from the past and indecision too. It hadn't, so I made my way to the café I spotted on the corner of the street where it joined the main road, and entered it. It smelt of coffee and sweat, but I wasn't choosy. I sat at a table far into the back of the room and ordered an espresso. Its bitter taste should help clear my head. In the background the radio was playing. I half listened as my mind wandered.

My last view of myself in the misted glass that passed for a mirror before leaving my cell was of a man now in his late thirties, dark hair lightly tinged prematurely with grey but still thick and curling at the ends, tucking itself around my shabby collar as if playing with it. Penetratingly blue eyes looked back, judging and finding myself still wanting. I tried to remind myself that no-one else was judging me now. That was past and done, but I couldn't quite convince myself the past was the past yet. The waitress would probably have called me broodingly handsome – fit – but she would surely know from the clothes and the look that I must have just got out, so she wouldn't be going there, no matter how attractive I still was. I fiddled with the salt pot in the centre of the red plastic table and waited for my coffee to arrive, ruefully laughing at myself for the ridiculously romanticised inner picture I'd created until the song on the radio drew my attention like I'd been punched. I couldn't help but listen to it, my body feeling oddly vacant. The radio presenters' voice cut in before its conclusion, brash and over-enthusiastic. I disliked him intensely.

'Now guys, when was that a hit from? Shall I give you a clue?'

In the gap between the presenters' question and the answer, I wanted to reply out loud but I knew that would make me look odd and I didn't want to draw attention. I answered in my head instead.

'I don't need any clues, thanks. I know.' The radio presenter ignored me.

'Unchained Melody' – May 1995 – in the charts for seven weeks now, from the awesome...'

The voice rambled on, reeling off names and facts, but I'd tuned out by then, thinking only about the melody and the memories it revived with it. There was only one person it meant for me – and that was the crux of the problem. It was as if the radio presenter had read my mind.

'Unchained Melody' had finished now and the presenter was onto some other modern junk, but it's haunting strains remained in my head, going round and round like I had done over the years – never finding an ending. I wanted to turn the radio off, not be influenced by anyone's thoughts but my own, but it was out of my control. It was a 'greatest hits' show, and ironically, although initially I'd wanted it to shut up, as I was forced to tolerate it, it started to create an odd interface with my life. Outside it was grey and dismal. Inside I felt that way too. It was odd that the lyrics of a song had stayed with me so strongly, even from childhood, and had been so relevant in so many ways.

Suddenly it struck me then that I had gone through my whole life half-listening to songs which defined it and me, and yet not paid enough attention to them at the time. I decided to listen carefully now, as if irony would also make the asshole presenter find the right melodies to play to encapsulate the meaning of my life until then. A stupid idea, maybe but what else could I do to while away the time whilst I made this decision?

I thought about the lyrics of that, so specific song, and how they applied to me. It had been lonely, and yes, time had gone by slowly – eight long years of slowly slipping time. Now the diary and a single song were bringing all those years flooding back as if they were yesterday; thirty-eight years, and so many mistakes. My life had gone from being rhythm-less and lyric-less to the overwhelming swell of the full melody of love and then back to solitary silence after the death. Now I had the chance to turn on the volume again, but I was afraid – like I had been so many times. The fear of uncertainty and confusion I, the teenager, had thought being able to conquer pain would conquer too, had never left me. Courage was nothing to do with facing the fist or the barrel of a gun without flinching. It wasn't about facing pain or death, it was about facing life. In all of those thirty-eight years had I found that courage to face it now? Free and unshackled by society or others expectations, I still couldn't decide – about that or the letter.

I listened to the medley of songs as they flowed on the radio, following the first espresso with several more as I allowed them to define the past in my mind. As the afternoon wore on, I knew I couldn't avoid the diary any longer. Eventually I pulled it from my pocket and flattened its spine. Initially I opened it half way through, the page already marked with a folded corner, but then duty overtook inclination and I went back to the start, right to the start. By the time I drained the last cup, the waitress must have been starting to worry that I was going to be a problem, and wouldn't leave. You're all wrong; we were all wrong, I thought. I left without trouble, tossing the right money from the meagre amount I'd been given on leaving the prison on the table without looking at the bill. I'd read the diary from cover to cover and it pointed my steps only one way – a way I'd trodden before. The answer would finally be there.

Chapter 1:

Boys, 1964 to 1972

The lyrics of that first song coiled the bitter sweetness of nostalgic regret round my brain, like chains anchoring me to the prison of my past. Securing me to what could have been, not to what was. What could have been.

Not only the year of its fame but its theme, yearning for a lost love, brought back the strongest memories of her. Yet it pulled me back further even than then to the time I'd first heard it, years before when I was a child – maybe seven or so, on my mother's Righteous Brothers album that she played interminably when Dad was away. I was at primary school, and for me it was just a mournfully sad song, preceding the appearance of my mother's equally mournful face. It signified time to get out of her way quickly before she picked me up on some minor misdemeanour because she was miserable and wanted to make someone else feel the same way.

I remember, as a boy, thinking about all the things I found most disgusting, and wanting to talk about them to the other boys to see if I could think of something more foul than they could. It was a challenge to be best – or worst, really. And that was where it had all started, with a song and one of my earliest memories. It was when I was about seven too that I remember having had a particularly bad cold. My nose was running like a tap and as I ran up to Will in the school yard, aiming to tackle the football off of him. I could feel the smear of snot gathering under one nostril, but ignored it in my enthusiasm to get the ball. My nose was so cold it was almost numb anyway.

'Hey, ball's mine!' He shouted as I approached. I snorted in response. I didn't know the snot had blown out into a balloon, dangling precariously from my icicle nose, but one of the other boys did and pointed to it, laughing.

'What?'

'Bogies and snot!' The boy shouted. 'And you're making a bubble with them.'

Some of the other boys came up and laughed and pointed too. I was centre of attention and wanted to see what was so funny, so we all piled into the girls' loos. They didn't put mirrors in the boy's ones.

'Wow!' I stood in front of the mirror and created another snot globe and then sniffed it up again before blowing it out as if I was chewing bubble gum and blowing bubbles.

'Do another big one,' urged Ted.

'Yeah, and then a long stringy one…' said the boy who'd noticed it first. I performed with gusto until the bell rang and I had to hurriedly wipe my nose on my jumper sleeve, leaving a slimy trail like a snail had slivered along it. I was supreme snot champ.

Will didn't say a word, just looked at me. I didn't like the fact that he disapproved, because that was what his look said to me. For some reason, just the look made me want to win him over, like he was important to me in a way I didn't understand, even though he always only stood at the back of the gang of boys, observing. I caught him as we went back into class.

'Hey Will; ever been apple-nicking?' He looked surprised and unsure by my attention.

'No-o.'

'Wanna come with me after school today?' He went beetroot red and grinned.

'Oh yeah,' and then shyly, 'you 'n me?'

'Yeah, you 'n me.' The snot was dribbling down again and I did a catarrhy snort, but he didn't look disgusted this time.

'Ok,' casually, but his face was a beacon of pleasure. I remember that look so well. It was the day we became best friends, even though we didn't know that until much later.

Later on when we were in our early teens, we still used to go apple nicking after school. For Will, I think it was just something he always did with me because he knew I wanted to. For me it was another kind of best-worst challenge.

That raid was the first of so many they've coalesced into a composite in my memory now, so what I remember is probably a melee of all the times we robbed and ran. I can still hear old Mrs Jones shouting as she watched Will and I scramble back over the fence from her tiny orchard, our jumpers full of apples. We didn't really want the apples. What the fuck were we going to do with all of them? We'd have bellyache for days if we ate them all. It was for the sheer hell of it and being able to creep in, grab the apples and get away with it, hearing Mrs J shout ineffectual curses after us as we ran off laughing, our jumpers stretched round the apples like we were pregnant.

'You little buggers!' We'd wave back at her, laughing rudely.

'If I get hold of you, you little bastards,' the curses faded into the distance. We kept running as fast as we could in case she for once found the ability to follow through with one of her curses and cane the hide off us. We ran side by side until we were in the alley that ran behind the terraced houses in Tanners Row. We had to slow down there because it was cobbled and difficult to run without risking a twisted ankle. By the time we got there, though, we knew we were safe. Old Mother J wouldn't follow us that far. She'd have a heart attack before she got anywhere close.

We eased up our speed and slowed to a stop behind the row of bins that belonged to numbers 6 to 9, Tanners Row. They ownership of them was firmly stated by the numbers painted on the lids.

'Ok?'

'Yeah!' gasped Will.

'Good haul!' I laughed.

'Yeah!' Will loosened his knotted jumper to reveal the extent of his swag. I did the same. He had less than me – he usually did.

'I got more.'

'Yeah – I know. You're better at it 'n me…' He smiled at me admiringly.

'Well,' I felt slightly awkward suddenly. A small part of me wanted to make him feel better, not like I'd beaten him. 'I probably just got lucky with my tree.' A fly buzzed past my face. I waved the fly and the feeling of being sorry for him away.

'What shall we do with them? Mrs J was pretty fumin' this time, weren't she?' I laughed at the memory of her flushed face and the roll of her massive breasts as she struggled after us.

'Perhaps we better leave them here – or maybe take them back to her?' Will peered at me, worriedly.

'Take them back? Shit, are you mad? She'd flay us alive.' I thought for a moment, searching for the best solution. 'We'll leave 'em here… In the bins!' I roared with laughter. 'If she flays anyone then, it'll be bins 6 to 9!' Will laughed too, but hesitantly. I felt as if he was humouring me more than laughing *at* the humour. It took the edge off the joke for me and my laughter dried up, only to be rekindled by the thought of old Mother J lolloping after us, stockings wrinkling at her ankles and boobs swaying.

'Hey Will, have you ever noticed what huge tits she's got?'

Will looked at me; a sideways look. 'Ye-es.'

'Well, I wonder what they feel like? I got a feel of Susie Evans' tits the other day, but they are tiny, like little bumps with a zit on the end. I wonder what really big ones feel like?'

Will carried on looking at me through slitted eyes. He had unusual eyes for a boy – almond shaped with thick dark eyelashes, and a deep hazel brown. He was good looking, no doubt about that. Sometimes I felt jealous of his deep eyes and the way the girls looked at him, but we were best buddies so I didn't hold it against him for long. I'd noticed how he always stood aside for me to take the advantage if there was ever advantage to be taken, so I assumed he thought of me as the leader of the two of us.

He didn't comment, just shrugged his shoulders and bit into an apple, making the juice spray out and dribble down his chin. He wiped it carefully away.

'I've never really thought about them,' he said eventually. I had. Quite a lot by then, in fact. I thought that maybe Will thought about other bits of girls bodies the way I thought about tits, and bit into an apple myself. We remained companionably silent after that and I carried on thinking about old Mother J's big tits and Susie Evan's tiny ones. I wondered which were better. Probably Susie's, despite the size.

I didn't think that summer was anything other than another summer at the time, but I see now it had started to define us a people without us actually realising it. In the background was my mother's romantic sentimental music interspersed with joyful times when my father was back home and they gave me enough money to take myself off to the flicks or just down the road to the café so they had the house to themselves. In the café I would use my hush money to buy cokes or the odd beer to swig back if I could get away with it, and I learnt that girls' tastes ran more to the sickly sweet of milkshakes. The juke box would be playing all the time, dance and popular hits that were the number ones of the time, arriving within days of hitting the charts. Rod Stewart wearing it well, which was on the edge of being slushy for me, but just ok, or the more acceptably male 'Mouldy Old Dough' or 'Schools' out'. That was my favourite at the time, especially as it came out in the school holidays when I was an even more frequent user of the café whilst Dad was home on leave. I looked at Will in surprise once when he said his favourite single was a Don Maclean ballad about Van Gogh.

'But that's a girl's record?' I'd exclaimed, taking a mental step back from him.

'Just because it's sentimental, it doesn't have to be a girls' record.' He retorted. 'It's expressive and where would we be without any expression? No Mona Lisa, no Shakespeare, no Beethoven, no comic books. They're all art and writing too. No records in the charts because they're all music,' he stopped to draw breath and I stepped in.

'Whoa there!' We looked at each other as if momentarily seeing each other for the first time. Slade's claim that we were all crazy rooted and tooted in the background and that seemed quite apt. As I observed Will's flushed cheeks and eyes sparkling with animation as he pressed his point home, I thought maybe we *were* all crazy in our own ways.

'Rant over!' I laughed.

At fifteen I was already a typical boy, testosterone-driven and looking for the immediate response, the rush. I didn't have the time or the finesse to wait for anything to develop, or the inclination to think about it more fully, but I could also see that Will was right. More than that, I found I admired the fact that he had the maturity to have already thought it through and come to a far more adult view of the world than I had. He didn't respond to my 'whoa' straightaway, just carried on looking at me, deep-lashed almond eyes intent on my face until I felt vaguely uncomfortable. I elaborated as that was plainly what he was waiting for.

'I get what you're saying. It's not just a girly song, ok? It's just I don't really go for it, that's all. It's not my style.'

'Why isn't it?' He asked. 'What's wrong with it?'

'Well, I ...' I was stumped. Why didn't I go for it? I liked the melody; the singers' voice was alright, it was just it was – actually I realised then that I didn't know what it was because I wasn't sure I understood the song or what it was saying. I could get 'Schools Out!' The meaning of that was obvious, but these more ambiguous notions, these deep and meaningful comments – well, I was confused by them. I finished off the sentence awkwardly, 'I suppose I actually don't really understand what it's about – really. I mean I know it's about Vincent Van Gogh, but,' I trailed off, and shut up. I felt stupid. I made a grimacing face and shrugged my shoulders. Will burst out laughing.

'Oh Tom! It *is* about Van Gogh, but how he saw things differently, more intensely, more dramatically than most of us do, but maybe just as confusingly as we all do too. Sometimes things are confusing and then we don't know how to deal with them so it is easier to not deal with them – and run away.' He looked at me with a sideways grin, 'or say we don't like it,' and then mischievously, 'or they're girly.'

'How did you get so smart, and me so dumb?' I asked incredulous at his grasp of what seemed like sheer mystery to me.

'You're not dumb. We're just different,' and again the smile. I couldn't help but smile back, whilst still wondering how he and I could be such best buddies and yet so unalike. I've listened to the album that song came from many times since, and the empty chairs he sings about too. One day they became a reality for me and I understood, but I didn't get it then; didn't get it at all.

That summer was a summer of discovery in so many ways for me – and maybe it was for Will too. When we went apple nicking and ran away from old Mother J, my heart pounded with excitement. The raids made adrenalin surge in me and I felt powerful and invincible, running away from her irate aged frustration. Young and strong and callous. Once I disconcertingly found myself semi-erect as I plopped down next to Will, heaving and puffing when we'd eventually found a hidey hole. Was it rebelliousness, or the thrill of maybe being caught one day? I understand that boys never talk about how they feel to each other. They catalogue their escapades, their conquests – their claimed expertise, even, but never describe how they feel. Scared, exhilarated, anxious; unsure. They're all too weak and wet to admit to. Hour-long erections, the way they'd poked this girl or that, and how the girls had squealed when they'd done it – that was all normal. Feelings of tenderness and, God forbid, *love* – that was taboo.

Ironically, although they represented little more than simple boyish mischief to us, another discovery about me and Will presented itself during one of those raids, and led me on to the next stage in my life. It was one of the last raids we did when we were mid-teens and I suppose our hormones were really starting to race then. We were still jumping the wall into old Mother J's puny orchard and shinning up the nearest trees as usual, but less from childish exuberance than adolescent bravado by then. I still had the knack of picking the best laden trees so my crop was always the better of the two. As we shook the tree branches it was as if Old Mother J detected their trembling like seismic activity because it was always at that point that she would loom over the fence, red faced and angry. We'd leap nimbly down from our perches, and run like hell. We knew she'd never catch us; she knew she'd never catch us, but it was our comical routine, just like in a farce. The only real danger was if her son was home on leave and appeared at all the hullabaloo. Then of course he would give chase on his mam's behalf and we WERE in trouble because he was fit and hard and toned from a life on the drill ground.

It was odd that I almost had a hankering to actually get caught by Old Mother J's son. I was fascinated by the army. It was Dad's way of life too, yet he rarely talked to me about it and that just made me more curious. I knew one of the reasons my mother was so besotted with him was his lean body. I wondered what it felt like to be so toned, so strong, so apparently oblivious to physical pain. Was that something you controlled by an effort of will, or did the hardness of the body act as the armour against it? It would almost be worth a beating to experience what it was like to be on the end of the pugnacious determination to pummel someone into oblivion, to see if I could withstand it. Was I my father's son? If I had the ability to go through the pain barrier like my father seemed to be able to, would it make me more able to cope with life and understand some of those things that were so confusing to me now? I equated it with courage, not understanding the difference. That very male and aggressive world held a fascination for me but I knew instinctively that Will wouldn't accept, condone or understand it. It divided us completely and yet ironically was maybe also what defined the doubtful link between us, although I never shared any of those odd un-boyish thoughts with him then.

This time our luck was out and Old Mother J's son was actually home. He appeared sullenly and dangerously behind her at her first shouts of protestation.

'What's up, Ma?'

'Oh shit!' I exclaimed on seeing him. 'Go Will, fuckin' go!'

Will didn't need any urging – he'd seen the monster at exactly the same time as I had. He skidded down the trunk, landing hard on both feet. It must have jarred his back, but he was almost immediately springing back up. Lucky for him sprinting was easy. He was light on his feet – 'a lightweight', my father called him when he wanted to be particularly scathing, but being a lightweight today was definitely a bonus.

He took to his heels and fled, leaping the rickety fence at the far edge of the orchard in a single fluid cat spring, barely touching the ground on the other side before taking off again. I laboured behind him. I was a much heavier build than him and not anywhere near as fast. I looked over my shoulder once I drew near the fence to see Old Mother J's son gaining rapidly on me.

'Come on!' Will shouted at me, his voice taking on a wild shrieking element with the 'on'.

'Fuckin' come on yerself,' I yelled back and cleared the fence, just as Old Mother J's son reached for me and grabbed me by the shirt collar; but I wasn't stopping. I bolted forward with so much force that all the shirt buttons popped and the shirt disintegrated round me like a piece of soggy tissue paper. I laughed wildly and thought I'd got away, but I hadn't bargained for Old Mother J's son. The disconcerting thought that this must have looked like a slapstick comedy routine distracted me momentarily from applying full speed. My face turned from victorious laughter to surprised confusion when Old Mother J's son crashed straight through the wooden fence, sending pieces of it spinning in all directions. Bellowing with rage, he lunged forward and grabbed me by the hair instead. I jerked backwards, face crumpling as my hair was torn from the roots and Old Mother J's son reeled me in, spun me round and sent an iron fist straight into my nose. Blood spurted out in a spray.

The moment of impact has no pain. It is as if the blood vessels and pain receptors all cower and cover their heads with their arms when the fist collides; flesh on flesh, bone on bone – crushing, grinding, pounding. 'So this is what it's like!' The thought flashed through my head in surprise and relief. 'I can cope with it!' But it was replaced equally rapidly by the stinging of capillaries and vessels released from pressure as the blood coursed back through them, whipping the nerve endings into action. My head throbbed and my ears sang. The sheer agony in my face made my legs turn to jelly and my stomach lurch. My shout of triumph turned to a howl of pain and I crumpled into a pulped heap, shirt trailing around me. It made no difference to the pain, but instinctively my hands flew to my nose to protect it as I whimpered like a child.

'Now yer leave me ma's apple alone, yer little sod, or I'll do more damage next time,' the thug warned. 'And yer – sonny Jim; yer want some too?' He pointed at Will with his bloodied fist. Through the haze of pain I saw Will shake his head vigorously.

'Right, then piss off and take yer mate wiv yer...' He pushed me forward with a rough shove behind the head. Will looked as if he was frozen to the spot as I stumbled towards him, still clutching my nose.

'Pah! Yer little sissies,' he spat at us and turned away, stepping over the shattered remains of the fence this time, and kicking the sprayed bits of splintered wood out of his path. 'Yer need a new fence, Ma,' he called, almost conversationally to her.

For a moment I swayed as I stood, unsure whether I was going to cry or throw up. I hoped it wasn't cry. Luckily the pricking tears and the lump in my throat rapidly subsided because the throbbing pain took over instead. Will rushed over to me as Old Mother J's son moved away across the orchard.

'Shit! You ok?'

I pulled my shirt back over my shoulders and tried to stand up straight, concentrating hard to control the dizzy feeling that was still trying to override the tears.

'Yeah, thanks.' My voice was nasal and muffled from behind my hand. 'Got a hanky?' I coughed thickly. Welts of iron tasting mucus slid down the back of my throat, and the need to retch overcame me again. Will fumbled in his trouser pocket for a hanky. It was a bit grey, but it did. He handed it over and I gingerly mopped myself up, wincing as I touched my nose to wipe the blood spatters away. It was hot and swollen and my head ached as well now – a dull buzz settling behind my eyes and in the bridge of my nose.

'Is it broken?' He seemed anxious, hovering around me. Suddenly I felt strong and male, despite being the injured one. He reminded me of the way my mother fussed around my father.

'Nah, I don't think so, just bruised. Hey, I'm going to have one hell of a shiner tomorrow!'

An odd sense of well-being was flooding through me as I straightened up completely. I found myself grinning, albeit slightly lopsidedly as my nose was already starting to swell.

'You're already getting it,' commented Will, examining me. Pride swelled through me. I'd come through it. I'd hit the pain barrier and come through it. Will had a look of horrified

fascination on his face, and I sensed he was a little afraid –
probably at the thought that it could have been him that got
the bloodied nose, not me.

That afternoon stayed with me for a long time. It was the
second time the difference between us had been sharply
defined, and I suppose, it was the first time I was able to
actually document that difference as if we'd just taken part in
an experiment. I was the archetypal male, and happy with it.
Will, he was different.

Chapter 2:

From teenager to the divide, 1972 – 1973

I didn't give it even a passing thought then, but now I wonder how the months and years went so fast. Our apple nicking days continued as a theme as we barely noticed moving through the summers until we were past mid-teens, and apple nicking became a thing of the past. We had more important things looming – GSE's for one, and girls...

Girls certainly loomed large in my mind, whatever Will thought about them. My early mornings were characterised by a lump in the bed clothes and it was a regular occurrence to wank myself off before heading for the bathroom to brush my teeth, like it was part of the getting up routine that everyone must have, or so I assumed. It's an odd fact of life that whilst women talk about everything to each other, men seldom discuss innermost thoughts. Will and I were no different, even though we were closer than most boys of that age. I didn't ask him about his thoughts and he didn't ask me about mine. Mine were lurid in the extreme at times, one girl, two girls – many girls. I doubt I would have handled it if it had ever happened but my precocious teenage sexuality gave me an imaginative presumption that I was the world's most excessive lover, and that was how I set about my teenage years. Hormones were rampant. No girl was safe around me. I prided myself I could get to their knickers in just half an hour and through them in another. I built up quite a following amongst my year at school – both of other admiring teenage boys, keen to know how I did it, and a steady group of budding nymphomaniacs. Girls who were suddenly aware of their bodies and the spark had been awakened, inexpertly maybe, but awakened nonetheless, by me.

'So you fancy the flicks tonight, Susie?' I cruised alongside Susie Evans in between history and double science. Susie's budding breast bumps with the little zits had developed into generous handfuls. I, for one, was definitely keen to get my hands around them again now, but Susie was proving hard to handle these days after her early enthusiasm to display her wares. I knew she'd say no; she always did, that was why I asked her now – it was expected.

'The flicks or a fumble?' She retorted.

'Aw Susie…' I smiled charmingly at her, 'you know I really like you. Won't you give me a chance?'

'The last time I gave you a chance, you took more than that!' She flicked her long blonde hair at me, catching me in the face with the ends of it, like the whip of a lash, and strode off. Her long legs swung under the too-short shapeless grey school skirt, that couldn't ever be shapeless with her in it.

I looked after her, tongue metaphorically lolling, knowing I was going to have to use a lot more than charm to get anywhere near her knickers, let alone into them. I suppose Susie had already worked out what it takes some women many years to learn. After her early easy attitude, she'd quickly realised that the way to power over the opposite sex was not by impressing them with her skills, but by simply implying she had those much sought after skills, whilst steadfastly withholding them. She was out of my league now and that was why I didn't even try any finesse with her – it was a foregone conclusion that she'd say no to me so I might as well needle her a bit anyway. Ah well, I'd fill in the time with easier prey. I remembered that Lucy James was in my science class, and she wasn't likely to be as hard to persuade. I followed in the wake of Susie's soft floral perfume which lingered in the corridor and followed her to double science, like Hansel following the candy trail to the gingerbread house. Lucy was sitting alone in a double seated desk when I got there, and I slipped smoothly in beside her, flashing my best rake's smile at her as I did so.

'Ok?' I asked casually, deliberately leaving it unclear whether I was questioning whether she was ok, or whether it was ok to sit next to her. She looked at me uncertainly. We'd had a run in once before and I'd breached the defences as far as the underwear and then she'd shouted stop. Being the gentleman – and also because her little brother was playing in the room next door, and would have told on me, I did. We'd eyed each other ever since with her no doubt wondering what would have happened if she hadn't said stop, and me anticipating – far more lasciviously – much the same thing.

'Yeah, 'spose' she said. She feigned indifference to me as I arranged my books and pens on the desk top. The inky blob stains spread across the centre of the worn wooden desk and underneath I could feel the nobbly moulding of chewing gum that had been stashed there by some previous occupant. It rubbed against the tops of my thighs as I shoved my long legs under it. I played it cautiously – keen to win the prize this time.

'How did you find that last homework?' I asked genially. I sensed her relax a shade.

'Not too bad, but I didn't understand the thermographics bit, did you?' I hadn't understood most of it – but then neither had I bothered to listen to much in class. I'd been daydreaming about girls and bikes and when I'd be able to blag my way into the pub for a first pint. Lucky for me I had a quick mind and a ready tongue so I could talk myself in or out of most situations, homework problems included.

'No,' I looked studious for a moment, as if considering how difficult the thermographics problem had been. 'Hey, as we both found it difficult, we could have another look at it together, if you like?'

'Well...' she was hesitant, obviously remembering our last encounter.

'Look Lucy, 'I broke in, 'this is awkward, and I feel stupid, but... I shouldn't have jumped all over you last time – I'm ashamed of myself, really. I guess I just really like you and I got carried away but I didn't respect you, so I'm really sorry about that, and if you'd give me another chance...' I'd been talking quietly, almost intimately to her, so none of our classmates nearby could hear, and I let my voice trail away at the end of the plea, intending it to sound slightly pathetic but not completely so. I already knew girls responded well to the penitent and lovelorn. She looked uncertainly at me, but my expression must have been suitably hangdog and sincere and I saw her visibly soften. Jeez, I was getting good at this!

'Oh, ok, we'll start again,' she smiled at me and I knew I was in.

Lucy was small – about five three, and very slim, with a short sleek dark bob, delicate features; smart, but naive. Actually it was true; I did like her – but not in the way I lusted after Susie Evans. She was a pretty girl, generally kind, and intelligent. In fact, she was probably quite sharp under her *nice* manners. When we'd had conversations in the past, I'd unaccountably stopped concentrating on the curves of her figure under the routine navy school jumper and engaged in the debate instead. The first time I did it, I'd not realised I had until we'd almost finished the conversation and I suddenly noticed she'd taken her jumper off during it, pulling it roughly over her head and leaving her slightly ruffled in an appealingly vulnerable kind of way. Whilst I'd been aware of her doing it, I hadn't focussed on the action itself. I'd not tried to define the swell of her breasts through the thin cotton shirt. Instead I'd remained engaged in the discussion. That was odd for me...

We left the arrangements loosely made as the class teacher arrived – it was Mr Williams and he was a bastard. There was no losing concentration in his class otherwise you'd be in trouble – and not just detention. He'd been known to let rip with his blackboard rubber before now and that could leave a hefty bruise where it landed. I thought ruefully that if he'd been teaching the lesson the other day, I'd be able to shine like a professor to Lucy – I wouldn't have dared miss a word. As it was, I was obviously going to have to do some private study on the subject after all. The lesson droned on through two periods, with Lucy and I sharing snatched smiles between laborious note-taking. Williams liked to give such copious ones. I reckoned if I bothered to check it out, I would find them lifted straight out of a text book, but I couldn't be arsed trying to catch him out. Instead I just scribed, biding my time until the end of the lesson when I could progress things a stage further with Lucy. Eventually the lesson end bell went and we hastily shuffled books, pens, paper together, and scrambled out of the room in a great flood of raging teenage hormones, powdery make-up, heavy black mascara and sweaty boy armpits. Lucy moved ahead of me and I had to strain past others to drag at her arm before she disappeared in the midst of a gaggle of her girlfriends.

'Lucy?'

She half turned at her name. I raised my eyebrows at her questioningly.

'Yes?' Somewhat off-putting that she'd tried to head off so quickly at the end of the lesson but there was an expectant tone to the question.

'Do you want to meet up later?'

'Umm, well... Ok,' but she couldn't disguise the smile. 'Where?' Now she was taking the initiative; good.

'The coffee shop in town?'

'Ok, when?'

'Straight after school?'

'Ok.' And then she was swept away in the gaggle of chattering girls, but it didn't matter, I had my date.

Will slipped in beside me as we hustled along the corridor, and surprised me as I was so immersed in self-congratulation for swinging the date.

'So you look pleased with yourself...' he said, leaving the question hanging for me to answer.

'Huh?'

'You – you have a grin like the Cheshire Cats on your face.'

'Ah, uh-huh! I've just got myself a hot date this evening!' I angled my head smugly to one side to allow Will to join in the celebration by clapping me on the shoulder. He didn't. I looked at him. This was something to congratulate me on, why didn't he? Was he jealous? Did he fancy Lucy too? Then I realised that was a stupid idea – he didn't even know who the hot date was with.

'Oh.'

'Well, don't you want to know who with?'

'Who with?' he asked dutifully. His face was a mask. I wondered why he was so subdued.

'Lucy.' I replied, then, 'what's with you?'

'Me? Nuthin'. Why?' He added.

'Well I thought you'd be a bit more interested.' I was more than a bit pissed with him by then.

'Well, so you've got a date with Lucy – good luck...' he sounded short, and I was confused by the testiness of his reply, but the mask stayed in place and I just shrugged my shoulders.

'Ok, thanks,' I flipped back at him, impatient with this odd response, and 'I'll tell you about the first lesson in seduction tomorrow...' I added cockily. I threw my rucksack full of books over my shoulder and marched away from him down the corridor. Moody bastard, I thought – as moody as a girl sometimes. I felt as if Will's almond eyes were boring into me as I strode off and that made me feel like squirming, but I wasn't one for setting store by instincts and feelings. Life was about doing it, not thinking it, as far as I was concerned, yet something about his reaction had made me uncomfortable, almost oppressed. I wanted to get away from him for once, not fool around. I dismissed the feeling as I made my way out of the main school door and down the road towards the bus stop. Will would normally catch the bus with me and we would hang around the bus stop together, me making cheeky and crude remarks to the girls who I knew would blush or shout back at me, or horsing around with some of the other boys, as we kicked rucksacks into the road, and swopped football tales. Will was usually quieter, joining in intermittently but more likely to talk to the girls than cheek them and retrieve the rucksack from the road than kick it there. I suppose we were rather an odd couple. He was not the run of the mill teenager – shy and deferent even at times. I knew that made him popular with the girls but still there seemed to be no specific one that he latched onto, despite the flirtatious and encouraging glances that came his way. He was only medium height, if that, about five foot eight – and lithe; a bit like a dancer. He'd even taken some ballet lessons at his mothers' insistence at one stage. I think she'd wanted another girl, not a boy. She'd got a notion he could be the next Nureyev, maybe? I'd called him that recently as a joke, when we'd been talking about the school prom, and he'd said maybe we should learn how to dance properly. But I'd only said it once, because he'd rounded on me angrily and told me to 'piss off and shut up.'

'I'm not a poof.'

'I didn't call you a poof, what are you getting so pissed about?'

'He's a poof, that's what you're trying to say,' he retorted. 'I'm not a poof!'

'Oh shit, man – what are you going on about – I called you it because of the dance lessons, ok?' I emphasised the 'ok.' Jeez – he could be touchy these days.

'You got a problem with me?' It was Will, coming up behind me as I sauntered towards the bus stop.

'Hey, man – I thought you were working tonight.' He had a job at the local supermarket, and usually worked the evening shift stacking shelves on a Thursday evening. I hadn't really walked off and left him on purpose.

'Swapped shifts with Jack,' he explained. 'Sorry Tom, I meant to say good luck with the date, not sound pissed. Just some stuff on my mind.' The tone was conciliatory.

'Ok, no prob,' I responded, punching him on the shoulder – we were mates again. 'What do you reckon?' I was keen now

29

to ask Will's advice because all the girls seemed to like him so much. 'Should I be the good guy, or go in for the kill – the long slow build-up or the quickie approach?'

Will's face took on the masked look again and then almost immediately seemed to relax, as if he was making a conscious effort to join in with my mood.

'Do you like her or do you just want to poke her?'

'Well, both I guess.'

Will looked at me with an expression that said 'you arsehole' and then burst out laughing. I joined in – I was really.

'Well if you like her then maybe you ought to be nice to her,' he suggested. 'She is actually a person,' he added pointedly. The comment was barbed and I did note the sharpness under the exasperated smile he directed at me. It was a double edged look and comment, and once again I wasn't sure what was going on behind his deep eyes.

'Yeah.' He was right though – I was being an arsehole. I would be nice to Lucy. She was a nice girl. I studied Will's expression again.

'No dates?' I asked offhandedly.

'Nah,' he dismissed the idea – 'I've got stuff to do.' Stuff, I guessed, meant studying. I knew he wanted to get to university. He was smart, and I was smart, if I tried. The difference between us was that he wanted to work and study and get on, I wanted to play around; have adventures. It was the reason I had always wanted to go apple nicking and had initiated the raids. Will was always given the job of planning the escape route. He was thought; I was action. I knew he would get there, but I had other plans. The army – that's was what I wanted to go into. Action, travel – 'see the world, and shag it!' That was what I said in my cruder moments. Will just visibly cringed at that. 'You really are an arsehole!' he would reply, but laughing all the same.

'Your loss, buster.' I commented as the bus arrived and we shoved to get on it and bag the back seat or the seats upstairs. The girls giggled and hustled in front of us and we let them go, I and the other boys threatening to pinch their bums. One or two of them shrieked satisfyingly even though we didn't even touch them, and we all eventually crammed onto the bus, joggling and pushing the slower ones along the gangway until we were all wedged into seats.

As soon as the bus moved off and the driver couldn't police us the boys got up and moved around upstairs. The driver couldn't see but he could hear the high jinks.

'Sit down up there, you boys!'

It made no difference to us – he was downstairs and driving the bus. He wasn't going to stop us larking around that easily. The girls were pestered and jostled, boys squared up for mock fights, and ties and rucksacks were tossed up and down the gangway.

'You boys up there,' thundered the driver, 'sit down or I'll be up there and 'ave you off!'

'Yeah, right' noses were fingered and 'wanker' gestures were made towards him downstairs but we piped down knowing that if we carried on too much longer, he really would be up to 'ave us off', and then it was a long walk home.

I could see Lucy sitting sedately up the front of the bus and wanted to move up there and make sure our date was firm still but maybe that wouldn't be cool – and in any case too much more moving around might get me thrown off so I stayed where I was. Will sat quietly alongside me until it was time for him to get off. His was the stop before mine. He shouldered his bag and swung out of the seat as the bus slowed.

'Good luck,' he said as he moved away. He gave me a serious look – as if challenging me. I looked curiously at him, but then the expression faded from his face and he grinned.

'Don't be an a-hole,' he added and was off. I watched him move swiftly and lightly down the bus and disappear down the stairs, head dropping out of view within seconds. He was often an enigma to me now – yet he was my best friend. Odd that. Were friendships always like this; sometimes with a stranger, sometimes with someone so familiar they might actually be you? I spent the rest of the journey home wondering about friendship, but it didn't last all that long – only the one stop – after all, action was more my style – not thinking.

Dad was home on leave so of course he and Mum were keen to see the back of me. I noticed he looked less solid, as if the hard man was starting to lose his edge but I barely gave him and my mother more than a thought because their keenness for me to go meant I had money in my pocket to use on Lucy. I changed out of my school uniform and into a white tee shirt and jeans, which emphasised my broad shoulders and slim hips, and swaggered off down the road ready to treat

Lucy to as many ice cream cola-fizzes as it took to soften her up. The music blared out in the café as usual. Slade imploring everyone to 'skweeze' them should have told Lucy what I was up to, but luckily she seemed more naive than I thought she was and I suppose she was thinking more 'Young love' – which suited me because that made her easily gullible. We ended up smooching in the corner as far away from our other classmates as possible. They sniggered and pointed at us from time to time. I walked her home about 9.30 when it was getting dark as she said her mum insisted she was home by then. I was going to try the trusted Tom Cat – the nick name I'd given myself – tackle when we got to her back door, but Will's words nagged at the back of my mind, 'she is actually a person,' and annoyingly I didn't feel like I wanted to push it with her.

He appeared from nowhere beside me the next day as I sauntered towards the bus stop.

'Good evening then?'

'What?'

''Your date.'

'Ah yeah, well it was ok. She's nice, you know.' I knew he was sounding me out to see how far I'd got and a bit of the usual bravado reared up, but looking down into Will's almond eyes, it was tamed like the horse-whisperer quieting a wild horse.

'Aw, I was ok with her – alright? I thought about what you said and, yeah – she's a person and I just walked her home…' I paused, and then added mischievously,

'...don't mean she won't be fair game further down the line though,' and then winked at him. He was unusually quiet for the rest of the route, not expounding any of his theories on why exams were necessary evils and why we should eat vegetables as well as meat – some of the more weird things I usually ribbed him about, but had come to accept as just Will. Looking back, we were almost children of the sixties and one of us had to have some radical ideas, I suppose. The bus ride took the normal course with hollering from the driver, horsing about from the boys and coquettish preening from the girls as they patted their flicked hair and straightened wide hairbands into sleek swathes across the top of their head. We teemed off at the school gates, swarming up the drive and into our respective classrooms like an army of ants, small and scrabbling in our dark school uniform, school bags flung over shoulders like our allotted daily work burden. I glanced at Will a couple of times towards the end of the journey as he sat silently by the window on the seat we'd nabbed on getting upstairs. Eventually I couldn't stand the silence any longer.

'What's bugging you?'

He swung round immediately to look at me as if he'd just been waiting for me to ask.

'Do you really like her?'

'Who?' I asked stupidly.

'Lucy, of course.'

'Oh, yeah – of course, sorry, I wasn't really thinking about her but, yeah, well...I suppose I do. I've not thought about a girl as a girl before, but she is nice.' I thought he would be pleased I was actually treating a girl like she was part of the human race for once – he so often ranted at me about my bad attitude where girls were concerned, so his response completely floored me.

'Ok, right!' and he virtually turned his back on me, twisting as far round in his seat as he could towards the window.

'What now, man?' I asked. His reply was muffled, but unmistakably pissed off with me.

'Nothing, great – have a good time with her.'

I couldn't ask any more as we were pulling up at the school and the jostling to get off started in earnest. Will flung off the bus behind me but as I hung back to walk alongside him up the drive, he ducked into the middle of a group of giggling girls, and they surrounded him with a solid wall of curls, eyelashes and overpowering perfume that I couldn't get past. Will melted into it – almost as if he became subsumed by them. That was the last I saw of him for the rest of the day. He didn't catch the bus home and at the last minute I remembered he'd said yesterday that he was swopping shifts at his part-time job so I guessed he'd gone there straight from school. I had no idea why he'd seemed pissed with me in the morning. I'd done what he was always urging me to and been nice to Lucy – but it was as if he didn't want me to be nice to her now. Like he was jealous? No, that was just too weird. 'You're going weird too!' I made fun of myself. Forget it – it's not important. What's Lucy up to tonight, anyway – maybe the Tom Cat tackle could take a step forward tonight if she was free, and I would tell Will about it all tomorrow and he *would* admire my finesse this time …

But I didn't see Will for the rest of the week, his mother was ill, someone said. I knew his mother often came off badly when his father had too much to drink. I wondered if it was that. What was worse – a father who beat your mother up so she was perpetually avoiding any form of trouble, so never stuck up for you, or a mother who was so besotted with your father, and a father that was so disinterested, that they both ignored you? Between us Will and I could compare both and yet never did. Was it the same unspoken rule as talking about emotions?

Exams were coming up fast and the timetable was underway for some of our year already. Mine started in earnest the following week, as did Wills. To get into the army I had to at least try to get some passes in my basic subjects and I knew all my recent time at the café and behind the bike sheds with whoever I could persuade to join me had meant that grades in mock exams for me were dismal. My father for once showed an interest in my performance and stood tight lipped and folded armed whilst I sat at the kitchen table and slogged at maths and English and tried to make head or tail of French verbs. I guessed Will would be studying too because he'd talked about university, but of course his absence meant I didn't see him on the walk to the bus stop or on the bus, and Mum and Dad refused the phone to me. I was on a curfew – one that started and ended with the school day, and that was all that happened for a while.

The exam weeks passed in a blur of confused text books, invigilators saying 'put your pen down', or 'you may start writing now' and unsuccessfully trying to escape Dad and his folded arms. I would occasionally see Will in the distance; head down, set-faced. The only times I got off were Saturday nights and I tried cultivating Lucy then, but never got past the back door. Ironically just as I gave up on Lucy – just too nice a girl, another local siren, Tammy Johns, showed signs of thawing towards me. Maybe it was the idea of me being in the army that nudged under her armour. The break-through came one Sunday afternoon when we were all down at the local Lido. Brighton eat your heart out; this was Wilverton-on-sea and it was steaming. Tammy was with all her gang at one end of the pool, dangling long brown legs into the water and affecting being uninterested in the boys at the other end all farting around and trying to show off their rippling torsos and athletic abilities. Will was significant by his absence as he was most of the time that summer, but I didn't ask, just assumed the reason. Apart from that, there were times when he was becoming just too complex and confusing for me and all I wanted to do was GET LAID. I was sixteen, going on seventeen after all. That's what I should be doing wasn't it?

I performed a disastrous dive-come-back-flip into the water, ending up as a belly flop with a massive impact splash. It made everyone stop and look and although I surfaced wanting to sputter and heave at having been winded, some male instinct told me to appear sinuous and toned, cutting through the water like a sleek torpedo instead. I did, quelling the desire to go 'ahhh-hurgh!' in the same way that I'd controlled and withstood the pain of the punched nose when old Mother J's son's fist had collided with me. I opened my eyes to see the distinct expression of appreciation on Tammy's face, before she carefully closed it off by putting her huge rimmed sunglasses on again. 'No fooling me lady; I saw,' I thought. I swam the length of the pool to her and appeared dolphin-like by her trailing foot, artfully brushing the water with her toes.

'Hi, are you a mermaid or am I?' I asked cheekily, shaking the water from my face.

'Ooh, you're making me all wet,' but she was playful despite the complaint. She slipped her glasses off and looked me full in the eyes, bold and challenging. 'Who do you think?'

'Oh, you: definitely. Didn't they lure men to slavery? You can lure me anywhere.' I winked at her and she giggled. Definitely thawed and it wasn't the sun that had done it!

'Maybe I will,' she winked back.

'Tonight then?' I pulled myself up out of the water, displaying my tensed pecs and taut stomach. I hardened them more and strained to bring myself as high out of the water as possible in order to get mouth level with her.

'Could be,' she responded coyly.

I'm lured then,' and I made a final supreme effort and lunged for a kiss. She didn't evade it; she caught it, full on her lips. The promise in them was more than a lure, but she didn't keep it later. She kept to the Susie stance of tempting and promising but never quite giving. I was hooked for the rest of the summer, though, trying to get past the 'promising'. Lucy became an almost forgotten part of school. Maybe she never forgave me that rejection? You can wish many times over with hindsight that you had behaved differently, but the fact remains that you didn't. Immersed in pursuing Tammy, who I never quite won then, I almost forgot Will. Or maybe I just wanted to steer clear because I couldn't figure out those strange eyes and those even stranger looks he gave me at times.

Finally that summer came to an end – one of the most enjoyable but frustrating ones I remember from my childhood – if you can call sixteen your childhood? It was tinged with regret for many things, but mainly now, Will's absence from it. I suppose it was really the end of my childhood because the week after the exams finished, Dad had asked if I still wanted to join the army. He promised he would take me to the recruitment office the day after my seventeenth birthday in early September if I did. It was like recognition by him at last. All of my childhood had been spent being ignored by him or being given money to get rid of me so he and my mother could be on their own. To be allotted his time to actually accompany me to the recruitment office was like all my birthdays and Christmas's rolled into one. Ironically it didn't occur to me that it was simply a more conclusive way of getting me out of the house than giving me money to go down to the café.

I signed up for six years initially and my basic training started one month later. By the time I was due to leave for the basic training, there was an 'understanding' between Tammy and me, and I found myself being described as her 'almost' fiancé. The night before I was due to leave some of the other guys met up with me at the café and Joe the proprietor turned a blind eye to our ages and allowed us to drink Watney's out of six packs. We'd never drunk that amount before – only ever small amounts of filched cans when parents weren't counting what they had in the cupboard, so by the end of the evening we were all well worse for the wear. Jimmy was outside puking when Will arrived but Johnny and David were still propping up the juke box as I draped myself over a chair. I was pretty much blind drunk by then and all I could say was, 'oy there Will me mate, long time no shee…' before suddenly feeling like the Watney's was about to revolt. It did, and I was heaving up five cans of it outside the café shortly afterwards. Will sauntered out to see how I was doing when I'd reached can four. I spewed can five onto the grass verge and then lolloped back to prop myself against the wall he was lounging against.

'All done?' There was a vaguely sarcastic note in the query but when I looked at him his expression was sympathetic. He looked fresh and attractive in his white 'T' shirt and faded blue jeans, our uniform of the time: hair neat and eyes clear. So unlike me, who was distinctly worn and foul-smelling from vomit and spilt beer. I felt at a disadvantage and wondered why I'd got into this state.

'I think I need to go home,' I said in a weak voice, and Will, my mate, helped me home, with me, so much bigger and bulkier, draped over his shoulder like a sack of potatoes, lurching alongside his neatly contained figure. He saw me into my house and upstairs before my mother or father could see the state I was in. I knew my father would bawl at me and question whether I was fit for the army. I didn't want that to happen. Coward, was I? Probably. I flopped backwards onto my bed like a rag doll, stretched out in full, arms akimbo and slurred at Will.

'Wh-why did I drink sho much?'

'I don't know but you're going to have one hell of a hangover tomorrow.'

'Yesh – I – uuu-hhh-mmmm ' I found myself drifting into a haze of nothingness punctuated by the sensation that the room was spinning dizzyingly around me. Nausea assaulted me again.

'Oh, I'm gonna throw!' A bowl appeared on the floor by the side of my bed and I rolled sideways towards it, letting it all heave out of me and into the bowl. Eventually the contractions of my stomach slowed and the urge to 'uh, uh, uh,' eased off. I flopped back onto the bed, exhausted. I felt as if I was completely empty – drained off all content, both physically and mentally.

'Ooowww. ' I sighed , feeling my face go slack and my mouth slip open, dribbling slightly as alcohol induced sleep crept over me. I heard Will's voice in the wooliness of the background noises: the clicks of the pipes as they expanded and contracted with our archaic heating system, the low hum of the TV and Mum and Dad's voices intermittently downstairs.

'Will you be ok?' It was comforting from him, and ironically although I must have looked a complete prat, he didn't make me feel like one. He didn't fuss around me like he had when I got the bloodied nose from Old Mother J's son, but I felt looked after all the same. Maybe that's the nature of best mates?

'Yesh, I'm fi...' I must have drifted off completely at that point as it was dawn when I awoke, with a crisp clear autumn day, almost as hot as a summer's one. It wafted through the open window, making the net curtains billow gently into the room. As they shifted I caught glimpses of the bright aquamarine sky between their slightly opaque grey-white. The noises of autumn-summer were already underway, even though it was only just dawn. Birds were busily calling to each other, 'wake up, wake up: tick-chirp, tick-chirp: new day, new day...' and I could hear the hum of the bees nest outside the window where it a swarmed into Mr Hunnet's hive next door. The name made me smile inconsequentially – so close to being 'honey' it was especially evocative – and yet so distinctly not. Will and I usually made fun of him – 'funny honey Hunnet' we dubbed him. I felt a surge of homesickness at the silly name, and realised the true significance of today as I remembered who I made the joke with. Today I joined the army. Today I left home completely for the first time ever. Today I started on the road to real manhood. Today, I said goodbye to my mate Will, although thinking of the latter, I suppose I'd said goodbye to him last night as I sunk drunkenly into oblivion, or maybe even sometime before then. I was ashamed now as I realised too that I'd abandoned him to whatever bad shit was going on with him all summer because it had been easier to, whereas he'd made the effort to seek me out on my last night even though I'd excluded him from it. I wondered if that significantly also delineated the difference between us. Will, smart, compact, neat, *sorted*. *Me*; drunken, sprawling and about to pitch himself into the alien world of aggressive male supremacy that the army presented in an attempt to find himself. I wished I had as much confidence in myself and what was right to do as Will seemed to right now. Will already seemed to have much more manhood about him than I did.

Chapter3:

Soldier boy, 1973 – 1980

That first army day passed in a blur. I was still hung over so my stomach was lurching and my head fuzzy like cotton wool was padding it out. The grogginess didn't go away until I was in barracks, allocated a bunk and with a neat pile of uniform including the boots piled on the end of it, all papers signed. I'd just promised six years of my life to the army to do what they wanted with it, including give it away if my country called upon me to do so. I'd been carried along by the excitement and the sheer need to keep going despite the hangover until then but reality sunk in as I sat there, fatigued and unexpectedly homesick.

The barracks were austere. Cool grey walls with 10 bunks in this dorm, neatly spread in two rows of five, with small iron grey lockers squat to the beds, and full length hanging next to it; a place for all my worldly possessions whilst here. I sat next to the pile of uniform on the bed and observed my companions – occupants of the same dorm, and who I now had to live my every waking and sleeping moment with for the next however long, before our passing out parade when we were posted. We were the battalions' new intake and comrades in arms for the foreseeable future.

During our first eighteen weeks there we had to make it through training in fitness, weapons, map reading, camouflage and concealment, NBC (chemical warfare) and drill. We were 'beasted' to test our character. Beasting was having you, your kit and your bed thrown around or out of the window to test your persistence and strength of character as a soldier, or being punched, kicked doing press-ups, and running for hours with your SLR (rifle) above your head. It was exhausting physically and mentally because the days were long too – starting at six am and ending at midnight. One day, as a punishment for getting pissed out of our heads the night before in town, we were woken at five o'clock by strident shouting and being booted in the ribs by the Sarn't Major and his cronies as they tore through our dorm like a hurricane. We had to stand outside in the freezing cold in just our PT kit. Shorts, tee shirt and plimsolls are bloody cold on an icy winter's morning. We were made to do bunny hops and press-ups by the hundred until the Sarn't felt he'd impressed on us sufficiently how stupid it was to be hung over when we might be needed to go into battle the next day. I suppose he had a point. Our final test was a twenty-six mile tab (march) back to camp with full kit – including toby (helmet), rifle, ammo, webbing and full pack all in all weighing about sixty-five pounds – around four and a half stone; like carrying around that schoolboy I'd been once, all day, as well as myself. It was all done on an empty stomach to mimic battle conditions. By the time we got back, I was almost delirious with exhaustion, but I made it through. When I 'passed out' – luckily it wasn't literally that day – but at the end of my training time, I was a full artillery soldier.

When I looked at my dorm companions I had no idea how gruelling it would be for us. I wonder now if I would have still completed it if I had? Yes, I think I would.

Jim, opposite me, was short and squat with spiky short sandy hair and a snub nose which made him look pugnacious. Ironic because he wasn't – he was probably the deepest thinker of us all but that face got him into scrape after scrape when the locals started the argument.

'Oo yer lookin' at squaddie?'

'No-one.'

'Oh yeah? I think yer lookin' at me? Wanna prove me wrong, *squaddie*...' and so the skirmish would start. Jim would be needled and niggled until sheer frustration had its way, and we'd all pile in and bail him out. Fists flying, boots kicking and elbows slicing into stomachs, as noses splintered and spurted blood, teeth were shaken loose and ribs pounded until one would break and the irritator bent double with agony, retching and vomiting with the pain. One quick kick up the jacksy and he was through. Job done. We usually came off best and the local talent got a thorough beating ... but we were always labelled the aggressors; the initiators of the fight, and they the victims.

Next to him to the right was Mike. Mike was an annoying little shit. There's always one in any troop. Mike was ours. Always arguing, always commenting on what you were doing and how he wouldn't do it that way. He was short too, and appeared slight but he was wiry – that kind of hardened body that bent like a green twig and never snapped, however hard you pushed it. I'll give him his due; he was pushed to the limit many times without breaking. I had to admire him for that. When he was killed in the fiery ball of the Lynx that plummeted to annihilation one day during our tour in Germany, annoying as he was, I wept with shock. The sickening lurch of realisation that I would never again be able to say, 'shut the fuck up,' with irritated familiarity made me realise then that it was actually affection I felt for him. It was the first time I'd really thought about never seeing anyone ever again. It was unreal. Was he really part of that firebomb that dropped from the sky and landed in a shower of still flaming ashes and twisted metal on the plain ahead?

'Jesus Christ! Mike's on there!'

'Fuck me.'

We stood together, the weight of our packs forgotten, a clod of mud and khaki, watching with horror as we thought of Mike, now consumed in the furnace. The rest of that day we could do nothing. We were stunned by the closeness of death. We were supposed to be on patrol, but anything could have got past us. When we got back to barracks that evening, and showered off the grime of the patrol, no amount of washing could wash off the sense of vulnerability which suddenly hit home. That could have been anyone of us – it was simply the luck of the draw which of us had been allocated to the Lynx that day. It might have been me, no longer here in this cramped dorm, lying on the hard bunk and thinking when his

47

next leave would be, or wondering if Tammy Johns was still waiting for me – Tammy with her brown curls swinging across her cheek, her sparkling eyes and her firm apple-breasts pressing against the flimsy stuff of her psychedelic peasant blouse. None of that would figure anymore. It would be black, just black and empty. Or would there be anything at all? What was death? Was it nothingness or was it that rosy heaven that the Church primed us with – all angels and harps and the white frothy shit that my Mam believed in? I'd never thought about death before. It was cold in the dorm anyway, but I felt chilled to the bone as I wondered where Mike was now.

That was all further down the line. Here I was just meeting the men who would figure in my life for the next six years; strangers in an increasingly strange world. Next to Mike was Jack. Jack became my best buddy; never quite the same best buddy as Will was, but it was different. In this environment, there was no-one I would have trusted more than Jack. He had a shock of black hair that grew long and thick when it was left, but we were virtually shaven-headed on entry, so it looked now as if he just had a fuzz of black covering his head, like iron filings on a magnet. He had a wide grin on his face most of the time, with a slight gap between his two front teeth, which gave him the charm of a schoolboy to the girls, apparently. No wonder he scored so often – more often than me even, despite my normally greater efforts. He grinned across at me as I sat there, muddle headed and fuzzy.

'Hey,' he said, grinning inanely. It was friendly and made me want to smile back.

'Hey,' I grinned back at him.

'Sure is shit, isn't it?' He gestured to the hard narrow bed and the austere lockers.

'Yeah!' I grimaced ruefully. We both laughed and the bond was created.

The other side of Jim was Steve. Steve and Jim became best mates while we were there. Steve was quiet. I guess that was why he and Jim became best mates. They understood each other, but he didn't have a pug face, he had a 'don't ask me…' kind of face – almost shy, but he wasn't shy, just kept his thoughts to himself. He had a kind of quiet determination to him. If it needed to get done, Steve did it. The number of times we were nearly up shit creek without a paddle because someone's boots weren't shined to mirrors you could see your face in were far less for our dorm because Steve would see to it we got it done. He was a bit of a mother hen in that way, and we all needed one at times. I wonder who his mother hen was. What kept him in check? Funny how you can look back years later and see all the things you didn't then: youth makes you blind, but age makes you see. I saw so little about those guys then, but I see it all now – I should have been able to see it then and I could have made so much better use of the knowledge I was gathering about them; about everything – than I did at the time. There was Steve next to Jim, anyway, and next to him to complete the row was Bad Bill.

Where Jim had the pugnacious face that said 'wanna fight?' even though he didn't, Bill wanted a fight all the time – even with us, his dorm buddies. Barrel-chested, broad shouldered, built like a brick shithouse, no one argued with Bad Bill. We learnt that by the end of the evening. Everyone else learnt it by the end of the next day – even Sarn't Major. We lived with him on and off for over six years, but I never got to know the guy. He got married just before we all got discharged or signed up for another tour – and I wondered what his wife was like. It was idle curiosity really, nothing more, as I didn't like him or want to like him. She was a tiny little thing it turned out, and already six months pregnant by the time we saw her at the passing out parade on my last day before I finally left the army. He dwarfed her, yet there was something between them that told me that she was the officer and he was still the squaddie where they were concerned. I was fascinated but that was the last time I ever saw him as he walked away from the parade ground. I wondered what life would hold for them. Bad Bill was the reason we got into so many fights – more so even than Jim's pug face, and then there was always bad blood between the aggressors and the responders when he was around.

Drink was often the precursor to the fights – too much of it – and drink has a habit of turning the innermost characteristics of a person outwards and exacerbating them. There was no need to look too far inwards with Bill, the characteristics were all very apparent outwardly to start with, but a few too many pints of courage and he was well off the radar.

'Watcha looking at ya bastard?' to the barman. The barman wisely walked away, but that wasn't going to stop Bill once in belligerent mood, and he turned to whoever was closest to him next. 'And you?' The guy next to him had already had one too many too, and jostled against him angrily.

'Piss off squaddie!'

'Who you callin' squaddie?'

'You – you ugly fat bastard!'

'You ain't no Miss World yerself. Want me to rearrange yer?'

'Wanna try it bastard?'

The boys had to pitch in too at that stage – it was expected. We might all sigh inwardly and think, 'shit, here goes our night off again. I wanted to get laid tonight, not laid out,' but the boys had to stick together, and so we did. In with the fists again – with less sense of comradeship than if it had been Jim, but Bill was one of us nevertheless and so we had to do our duty for him too. Once in Germany I even ended up on a charge for taking the rap for Bill. It held up any chance of promotion for me, but it was the rules. We covered for each other and Bill had already been in the shit too often by then to take another charge. Luckily I got off with a warning and a fine. I would have liked Bad Bill's summary justice even less if I hadn't. Someone else would do it for me in the future, anyway, I hoped.

Moving along the rest of the bunks on my side were Gary on the end – I'll come back to Gary – and then Don between Gary and me. Don's full name was Donald, so of course it produced raucous and crude plays on Donald Duck – fuck. Don was used to it, even played on it by then. He'd obviously suffered since childhood and decided the only way to put up with it was to actually become what he was being ribbed about. Don was a fuck machine. There is no other way to describe it – and even I'm amazed at the antics he used to get up to. I'd become a randy little sod as a teenager, but Don put me to shame. He was a good looking guy so that helped to start with. He had fine features and deep brown soulful eyes. Even I could see if he stared at a girl with his puppy dog eyes, her heart would melt – and with it her resolve to say 'no'. Crisp white tee shirt and freshly pressed faded blue jeans were our 'out of uniform' dress code then and he made a habit of manipulating it to his benefit, fitting his clothes like a glove around his V shaped torso when we went out to town. He was the perfect specimen of manhood, and with the soulful eyes, good looks and a slightly pushy but always charming manner. He asked, and he got more often than not. His worst scrape was when he chatted up the landlords' wife whilst we were keeping the landlord busy. How the hell did he manage to pull her to go upstairs for a quickie whilst her husband was pulling pints for us downstairs?

We'd spent most of the early part of the evening steering Bill out of a fight and then realised that Don was already well on his way to scoring with his target. It was only at that point that we realised who his target was.

'Oh man, can't he keep his prick in his pants just for once and let us have a night off?' Jack exclaimed exasperatedly to me.

'Seems not,' I responded and swung into action with the landlord, starting a fresh discussion about Spurs and *that* goal to steer him away from where Don was leaning hungrily over the bar at Mrs Landlord, and Mrs Landlord was making sure her breasts were as close to Dons straying hand as possible.

The rest of our dorm was Dave next to me and Chas next to him. Chas 'n Dave – of course that became their nickname – they were both cockneys and best mates by the time the Chas 'n Dave 'Gertcha' came out. Courage was our normal tipple anyway, so it produced a lot of rowdy 'gertcha's', whenever we were out, mimicking the advert, and Chas and Dave played along with it, clinking pints and letting rip in their cockney slang. They were nice guys. I'm sorry now I didn't get to know them that well as they became such close mates, but I liked their company generally. They were easy to get on with, always tried to do their bit to keep us out of trouble. They took their share of the blame for the rumbles, and you could trust them to watch your back on patrol in Ireland – which counted for more than almost anything at the time.

This was army life, close-knit camaraderie, living in each other's pockets; no peace, no privacy. There was never solitude because we were always together during training or out on the town; privacy just did not exist unless you went to find it. When you had a shower it was with a bunch of men, all surreptitiously looking to see who was big, who was small – where were you in the order of dicks. You got used to it and after a while stopped looking. Your dick was your dick, and no amount of looking was going to make it bigger or smaller.

53

Anyway, wasn't it what you did with it that mattered – so they said? There was at least macho support from those in charge, and that's what we gave each other too – the best buddies. As much as I confided in anyone then, I confided in Jack. Moments of homesickness, the fear of being unable to keep up physically, the cutting disappointment when Tammy wrote me the 'Dear John' letter we all inevitably got at some stage from our girls: sorry met someone else, too long to wait, lonely, want some fun of my own, and I expect you're having a whale of a time with all the girls in all those places...

'Actually Tammy, I'm not. Shall I tell you what I did this week?' That's what I wanted to answer back. I wanted to tell her how it really was.

'This week we fucked up on parade and the drill Sarn't gave some of us in our dorm punishments. Not the ones who fucked up – the ones who didn't. The bastards' twisted logic was that he would come down hard on the non-fucker-uppers and then we wouldn't allow them to fuck up again in the future. Jim's was to report to the guardroom in full battle order to be checked 6 times across the day, after which he was given tasks to do. They varied from scrubbing the kitchens till they sparkled to mopping the floors, to running with a fire extinguisher held out horizontally in front of him for half an hour. Do you know how heavy they are? About thirty pounds, so imagine carrying about fourteen bags of sugar straight out in front of you and running with full battle pack on you too – about another sixty-five pounds or thirty bags of sugar – behind you. No wonder he could barely stand when he got back to the dorm, and was shaking so much with fatigue he simply lay down in full kit and then puked all over the floor.

Jacks was to sweep the parade square with a scrubbing brush and each troop that came across it had been out on a forced march and were covered in shit and mud from the march. There was a steady scattering across the square at least five times that day, each time when Jack had just completed it so he had to go back to the start and do it all again until it was swept clean again. By the time he finished it his knees were raw and his arms were so stiff he could barely move them the next day without wincing, but he still had to go on parade and present arms.

And me? Mine was to clean the toilets with a toothbrush. Maybe that doesn't sound so bad until you also know that the Sarn't set up as many of his buddies to go in there during the day and take a dump, leaving shit splattered up the sides and round the rim, sticking to the pan, wet and foul-smelling, and then piss all over the seats and the basin too. Imagine trying to stop yourself from retching at the stench all day.

Yes, I'm having such a whale of a time here – thanks so much for dumping me whilst I'm having it...' But I didn't of course. I just didn't reply. I kept the letter with the others she sent me, and all of Wills' replies to mine. They were strands still linking me to the life I'd known as a child, not this gut-wrenching adult world of physical toughness and emotional turmoil. I suppose it helped me to grow strong mentally as well as physically, and there was nowhere I needed that more than during the tour of Northern Ireland. I told most people very little about that tour – except Will, and even he knew only some of it. I talked about things occasionally with Jack and wrote a few times to Will. The rest just ingrained in my mind like a movie screen in the background replaying silent clips from the shadowy memories that still haunt me, just as surely as she does.

Northern Ireland was the worst experience of my soldier days. When you went to Northern Ireland, none of the finer points of the argument were explained and we didn't do anything to find them out for ourselves – stupid schmucks that we were then. We were ostensibly just going to maintain law and order on the streets – and that's what we facetiously told ourselves we were doing. I felt big and tough being posted to NI and it didn't register to begin with that people, including soldiers – not just the IRA and its antagonists – were getting shot daily on the streets there. I somehow thought the army uniform made me invincible.

When we first arrived at 6am on a dreary ice cold morning, I thought, 'what the fuck is this place?' It was damp and grey and miserable. I was just an army ant in amongst the swarm of others being loaded onto four ton lorries and shipped off to Belfast. Seeing Belfast for the first time was also the first time since the Lynx had exploded that I thought again about not making it back home. The place felt derelict, and the people watched us pass with guarded eyes. I thought, 'Christ, I want out of here...'

There were three main duties a day; guard duty, stand-by, and patrols. Stand-by was generally an easy job. There were three kinds of stand-by; immediate, ten minute and thirty minute. Immediate stand-by involved eight people, all fully kitted out and ready to go out to support the patrols. Ten minute stand-by was to provide cover for the immediate stand-by, should they be called out. You would have to be dressed for action but you could relax, watch TV, sleep, read, write home, go running or practise with your weapon, but you could also get sent out to cover the immediate stand-by, so you couldn't relax completely. Thirty minute stand-by was like a day off – you could even stay in bed. No beer was allowed on immediate or ten minute stand-by, but on thirty minute stand-by you were allowed to drink up to two cans – almost off duty, and we all relished this.

For guard duty you had to be up for 7am washed shaved and dressed to go on duty at nine. You only spent an hour in the observation post before getting moved so you couldn't relax too much, and you spent the lonely day watching apparently nothing happening on housing estates. The only source of relief in them was to read porn mags or sleep in the brief times you were relieved over the course of your twenty-four hour shift. The guard post was a mix of boredom and hard-on. I'm not sure which was the more frustrating.

Patrols were also twenty-four hour duties, but when you were on patrol you were on show too, so we would be inspected before leaving and also briefed on the task we were completing. Patrols generally lasted two hours unless something happened. You covered a small area at a time, stopping and searching some people. Some would be silent, some slag you off. The hardest thing was when a child spat in your face simply because of what you were wearing and what you were doing. The only way to get past that was to remind yourself that they weren't spitting at you the person, but you the representative of the British Army who was interfering in their lives. Whether the party line was that you were keeping peace on the streets or not, you were also definably adding to the sense of animosity too.

You never knew whether you would encounter animosity or pleasantries, but the atmosphere could change dramatically from time to time, especially at nights if something was going to go down. In the Murph we 'cross-grained'; that meant we never went down the streets in case we were picked off by snipers. If there was something suspected of going down, or a particular sniper was being flushed out, a patrol of four men as 'bait' might be sent out. The first patrol/search I ever went on was an eye-opener for me. I went in the back door of the flat we'd targeted and we were bang in the middle of the kitchen. It was austere, didn't even have a proper sink – a stained plastic bowl served. A woman came into the kitchen to rinse a mug out. She saw us but didn't bat an eyelid, just went back into the other room. In full combat kit and rifles out, we were just part of the scenery to her; a part to be viewed with disdain.

I was on patrol the day Gary was shot. It was my last patrol for a while, and I knew I was due to go on thirty minute stand-by next. I hadn't exactly relaxed, but I was winding down and looking back, I'm aware of that now – even if I denied it to myself then. Not that it would have made any difference if I hadn't. We'd progressed down the street cautiously as there had been reports of movement here and we were part patrol, part bait that day. Gary was directly in front of me as we moved in a gang of four along the hedge at the front of the neat row of terraces. This area was actually better class than many and it was surprising the action was reported as being here. It was quiet and calm on the street so we moved further along and started to relax a little, yet with that insidious sense of 'don't relax too much, this is too easy.' There was a shout behind us. I swung round and so did Jack, elbow nudging mine. We had our SLR's poised ready but there was nothing to be seen. Gary and Jim were two abreast ahead of us and swung round at the same time too, so we were all facing the same way at the same time. It was bad practice, but it just happened that way. It felt like a breeze shifted the air by my cheek and I stepped aside instinctively and swung round, realising we were all looking the same way and shouldn't be. Gary made a strange face at me like an 'ooh' then stumbled backwards.

A gunshot wound looks ok at the point of entry but high velocity bullets are incredibly destructive to internal organs. They may enter the leg and exit cleanly in the chest, but they shred everything in their path. This one entered Gary's throat – just above where the body armour ended. As he fell backwards, rifle splaying out from one hand – thankfully with the safety on otherwise his involuntarily twitching trigger finger would have let off a volley of ammo at us – a neat red-black hole appeared just below his Adam's apple.

'Man down!' Jim shouted it faster than me, and Jack and I leapt to attention, swinging round and round in a circle to locate the sniper. There was no-one in sight. Of course there wouldn't be – not if they were aiming to pick us all off one by one.

'Get down, you assholes,' he hissed. 'Do you want to be next?'

Jack and I flung ourselves to the ground to join Jim and Gary, the hedge providing a small amount of cover on one side, but we were totally vulnerable on all others. The sniper had obviously fired from behind us.

'Shit we need to move, we're sitting ducks!' Jack made a move to stand again.

'Stay down, you stupid bastard!' Jim hissed. 'Look, the aim was from over the hedge – he must have got him as he was turning around.' Jim indicated Gary's half twisted body position as he'd fallen, and now lay semi-supported by Jim, one hand under his head. Gary's eyes stared back at us helplessly, imploring us to help as he gurgled indecipherable words, slowly drowning in his own blood.

'I can't help you mate,' said Jim. I could see tears sparkling in his eyes, 'I can't help you...'

I knew I was holding my breath, stunned by the way everything had so dramatically changed from routine alert to imminent tragedy. That pleading look suddenly got to me, like he was a small wounded child, and I wanted action – to do something, no matter how helpless the situation was.

'Fuck it, help him!' I shook at Jim's shoulder, as Gary's eyes shut.

'Stop it!' Jim shrugged my hand away and lowered Gary's head gently to the ground.

'He's shot to hell man,' he said quietly to me, 'remember what those bastard bullets do?' The hand he withdrew from behind Gary's head as he rested it carefully on the pavement was covered in the blood I could now see oozing steadily outwards in a pool.

'He's gone,' said Jack.

'Fucking hell! Bastard! Fucking bastard!' Rage flooded me. If I could have got hold of that sniper right then I would have torn him limb from limb. Just as quickly the rage was replaced by bitterness. 'He was a good guy!' Shocked, we stayed huddled around Gary's body until training kicked back in and I radioed in our report.

'Man down.' I relayed our position and an armoured patrol vehicle with a med team arrived within minutes but it was too late for Gary. It had been too late for him ages ago.

It is particularly difficult to see someone die when you have spent a lot of time with them, even if you weren't that close. At first there's just shock, freezing you almost emotionless; the grief comes later. It didn't hit me until we were back at barracks, showered and changed and sitting on my bunk, trying not to look to my left where Gary's empty bunk was. Strange how we'd kept the formation we'd first started out with, despite the friendships and alliances we'd forged over the years. Eventually there was no avoiding it – it was like a black hole just on the periphery of my vision and I had to look and I had to acknowledge. Looking at that empty bed, neatly folded and tucked, the emotions raged through me like a storm – disbelief, anger, horror and finally sadness and regret. Regret for a life wasted for no reason other than prejudice. Regret I hadn't been able to help him – and a sense of failure with that too, and finally regret I'd not known the guy better. Hadn't made the effort to in all the time I'd bunked with him. He'd been part of my team ever since we'd joined up. I should have known him better. I should know all of them better than I did.

We'd lost Mike in only our third year and now we'd lost Gary. Two out of ten: one fifth of us. Life shouldn't be so cheap. My tour was almost over and I think it was that which finally decided me I'd had enough of the army. There were other things too. The close call with death twice now had got me thinking seriously about whether there was more to life than this – and how important it was to experience life to the fullest. I'd now known two guys who hadn't got beyond their twenties – what life had they experienced? I wrote to the only person I instinctively knew would understand how I felt – even more so than Jack who both knew Gary and had been there at the moment of mortality: Will.

'...what am I meant to be doing with my life – what are any of us? These people here live a life of hatred and fear and I am steadily being sucked into it – for what? Am I helping their

troubled life become less troubled or am I just part of the movement that unwittingly fans the flames so that I will eventually get burnt by it myself? I think I'm lost here – lost and afraid now – and I'm a soldier – I shouldn't be afraid ...'

That was precisely it – the incident of Gary dying had finally instilled in me an understanding of fear. I'd thought being hard and strong and able to withstand physical pain and discomfort – the type I'd withstood with vigour in my first eighteen weeks of training – and beyond, made me a hard man, able to withstand anything that life threw at me. I was now just starting to realise that not all that life throws at you is outward physical struggle, much of it is inner turmoil – mental: emotional. Where does the strength to withstand that come from? He replied.

'Understanding that you have fear is in itself strength. How stupid is the man who has no fear and blindly walks into a dangerous situation that he could have avoided if he had listened to the instinct of fear because our instincts are what tell us what is right and wrong. If your instincts are telling you this is no longer the way to live your life, listen. It's not failure or giving up; it is moving onto another part of your life to enable you to experience other things that are right for you now.

And do not think you are to blame for Gary's death. Were you the sniper firing the bullet? Even if your vigilance had been 100% would you have known where that sniper was and where he would fire the bullet from? Sometimes terrible things happen and you have no choice but to cope with them. You cannot influence or stop them but you can learn from them. Maybe this is your chance to learn about another way in your life. Return home proud of the service you have done for our country and make the next part of your service for yourself...'

He was right. My hearing was already bad – not caused directly by bomb blasts or combat, but in that there were no ear defenders used then. When I was working with the artillery and they were firing their massive guns it was deafeningly loud. If I was at the receiving end, albeit within a safe distance, my ears were being continuously pounded. I had to regularly fire a rifle to practice shooting – no good being a squaddie if you can't shoot. The crack next to your ear hundreds of times a day, plus the noise of everyone else shooting alongside you eventually takes its toll. If we had worn ear defenders, it would not have been a problem but cotton wool or 4x2 – the rag used to clean the weapon after shooting – stuck roughly in your ear is more or less useless. Health and safety was definitely not around then. Add to that driving clanking armoured vehicles day in and day out with the radio noise crackling intermittently through the background drumming of the track that reverberating continuously in your ears often resulting in it taking several minutes to be able to regain sufficient balance to even stand properly at the end of the day. Over a number of years I and my mates had steadily been worn away in many ways – good hearing not being the least of them. Hearing impairment didn't affect us all, everyone has a different vulnerability. Mine was my bodies' inability to tolerate and withstand the impact of intense noise, year in year out. When I was discharged they gave me some money to be fitted with a hearing aid, but no matter how good it purported to be, it did not replace natural hearing.

At twenty-three, I knew it was time to move on, but that old fear kept me there. Fear of myself, and of not knowing what to do. I was still outwardly perfect, but inside, the damage was done.

Chapter 4:

Different worlds, 1973 -1977

Whilst I went off to the army sick to my stomach with too much beer, Will went his own way to complete A' levels and then to university. We wrote to each other in an on and off kind of way and I knew a little of his life there – so different to mine, but it wasn't until I read the diary that I got a true sense of the absolute difference between us and our ways of life. Oddly I thought despite him sometimes being so different to me, I felt I knew him well – well enough to be the only one I wrote to about my fears from Ireland. Maybe I never knew him at all?

I'm not sure he'd meant me to read the diary, or whether that was his sisters doing but there it was on the table in front of me, picking up where my memories had just left off. It started the week I left for the army. I read it in snatches, there in the grimy café and my understanding of the past gradually became complete, like a kaleidoscope slowly revolving to reveal all its patterns before you, and how they transformed from one to another. I'd never asked. Never dared to, because knowing how little I had control over, how little I'd had a hand in creating brought back that old fear; the fear of not being able to face pain and withstand it. Yet how crazy was that?

Each moment I'd lived, I'd lived through fear and pain and here I was looking back on those moments, still alive, still in one piece and now with a choice too. The problem was, now I was afraid of that choice as well.

***

6th September 1973

Tom went off this week. I'd been wondering what I'd feel when he went – my best friend. Odd how he went and life carried on really. Mine is full of text books and study, his full of guns and war. I often wonder how two people so different could be friends. I do feel a vague lurch of fear when I think of him being posted somewhere like Ireland but I know I can't do anything about it so I have to accept it somehow. Strange to realise how little control we have over our lives – we can choose our path but what happens once we're on it, well that is of other peoples making too.

I'm putting Tom out of my head as much as possible for the time being – he confuses me anyway – has done for a while now. I know we think differently about so many things, not least girls. In fact girls are a confusing thing all of their own. I know I'm attractive to them because I see their sly surreptitious glances at me, even though I pretend not to, and the way they edge closer to me in class or at the café, their arms brushing mine, and then that *smile.* Tom called it the 'come and get me' and used to complain I got more 'looks' than he did. Why the hell didn't I do something about them? I suppose the reason is that I didn't want to – still don't, I don't think. I mean, I like girls, they're good company. I like the way they smell, dress, talk. I'm often more interested in their conversation than what the guys have to say, but of course I can't join in; just listen and observe. And I find I do that a lot – look at the way they move, flick their hair back, look at me from under their eyelashes – that looking down, but up as well look. I stood in front of the mirror and tried it myself the other day. I think I did it quite well after a while, but I had to stop when Fran came home and pitched in with her usual tart comments.

'Who you trying to impress then, little bruv – finally got a girl now Tom Cat's out of the way?'

'Don't be stupid!' But secretly I didn't know which part of her comment I was referring to as stupid – that it took Tom to not be here for me to want to get a girl, or that I should get a girl at all. I retreated to my room and shut the door, hanging my 'studying – GO AWAY' sign on it first. That should keep her out.

29th September 1973

I got a letter from Tom today. It sounds like he's going through it there. He described the drills, and the physical regime and beasting to me. It sounds awful but he seems to thrive on it. He mentioned a guy called Jack and I wondered who Jack was. Were they becoming friends? I felt a tinge of – I suppose its jealousy – when I read the name and wondered about the relationship. He seems very far away from me. He's in there for six years minimum; that's a long time. I wonder if we'll still be friends when he gets out eventually. Gets out – I've just re-read that bit – makes him sound like he's in prison. I suppose if it were me that *is* how it would feel. I re-read Tom's letter twice and wondered about Jack. Perhaps he'll not mention him again or his name has just casually cropped up this time.

22nd October 1973

George Barrows called me a girl today. I could have beaten him to a pulp, but I've never been any good at that. God knows I've wished I could be at times – then Dad wouldn't have been able to hit Mum so easily. She hides the bruises well, but I know they are there. I wonder if Fran does too, but she says nothing. I hate that, and I hate him. I hate myself too, I suppose, for being such a wimp – and Mum for putting up with it. It makes me feel even guiltier, and then still I say nothing *because* I feel guilty. That's what George Barrows is – a bully like my father is, and I'm a coward. I wish Tom had been around. George would have shut up then. I'm going to avoid him, the asshole. He's only around in my free period on Mondays. I'll go the library then in future. I know Tammy Johns goes there too, and I don't much like her since she and Tom got too friendly last summer but he's not around and although she tells everyone she's his girl, he hasn't mentioned her to me in his letters so I think that's all talk from her now.

21st November 1973

Another letter from Tom: and more references to Jack. Who is this Jack? Tammy Johns was boasting about how Tom writes to her every week, but I've only had two letters from him in two months. I fumed at the smug little bitch but of course I couldn't say anything because George Barrows was hanging around like a dog after a bone. I know he fancies Tammy. Now that would be a nice little set up; George and Tammy – made for each other, a bastard and a bitch. I have to admit I feel a secrete admiration for Tammy – she has beautiful auburn hair and it tumbles over her shoulders – in the way they describe them in those romantic novels the girls all read avidly. If I was a girl, I would want hair like that. Mine is a similar shade actually and although I wear it longish, because that's the fashion, it doesn't have the same effect as Tammy's because of the length of hers – and of course, she's a girl. I sometimes think that even though I hate it when George Barrows makes his sly 'girl' comments to me like, 'oh hanging out with the girls again,' and 'oh yes, Will's definitely one of the girls too...' maybe he's more right than he knows. I definitely feel more of an affinity with them. I feel at ease around them whereas with guys, I feel as if I'm about to be challenged at any time. 'Are you meant to be here? You don't belong with us...' I even felt that way with Tom a few times. I particularly remember one time when he was comparing Ma Jones's and Susie Evan's tits. To me the idea was just gross but I couldn't say so. What is the fascination with women's breasts? I don't see it at all. I don't want to feel two lumps of flesh on someone else. Maybe it would be different if it was my body they were on, but then that's just weird. It's times like these that I wonder about me and who I am. Do I feel the same way as other guys or do I feel differently?

Tom's the only guy I've ever talked to about feelings, ever – and then I had to be careful as I could see that blank look come over his face, but Tom's feelings about women and himself seem quite different to mine. That much I did work out. I do get a stiffy sometimes in the morning, but not every morning like Tom. I'm far more likely to get it from imagining someone touching me – I mean touching me all over, than from sticking it in some girl. In fact the thought of that actually turns me off. Maybe there's something wrong with me? Some mysterious illness no-one has discovered the name of yet? And another thing, I'm hiding this diary because Fran keeps snooping around, teasing me that I'm lovesick now 'wonderful Tom' is in the army. It's really starting to piss me off, so the last thing I want is for her to find this – nosy cow. She'd be better off helping Mum than snooping in my room.

21st December 1973

Thank God it's the end of term. I'm getting so sick of George Barrows and his stupid quips. Tammy still preens and talks about Tom. I haven't heard from him in weeks even though I wrote back to him straightaway after his letter to me in November. I suppose the tempo is stepping up there as they approach passing out parade, but still Tammy goes on and on about her letters, and that jealous feeling I had a while ago keeps coming back when I hear her. I've taken to walking away rather than risk letting that odd twisting get to me, but it does anyway.

She's already started boasting that he will be inviting her to the parade and her girlfriends are all huddling around her and saying how romantic it is, just like some slushy war drama with her as the heroine waiting for her man. I try to ignore her as much as possible. To think I used to like girls and even felt sorry for them – like I did for Lucy James when Tom first tried to take her out because I thought he was going to just try to lay her and she deserved better than that. It's like Tammy knows she's winding me up whenever she talks about 'her Tom.' I just want to shout at her, 'he was *my* friend before he even noticed you, sly little bitch,' but what's the point? And more to the point, George Barrows would just have a field day. So I keep my head down and out of the way of all of them and study. It'll get me out of this shithole, if nothing else.

January 19th 1974

I know Tom passed out from training today but I didn't get invited – well I didn't expect to, but I did think I'd hear from him. I had to hear it all second hand from Miss Supercilious Tammy, so up herself because she got invited. Actually I don't know how she has the gall to parade herself around as his girlfriend because I know she's been hanging around with

George for weeks now. She was grumbling about how boring it was never having someone around to take her out whilst Tom was away. I overheard him ask her if she wanted to go to the local Friday dance and she was all Miss Simpering Tammy instead. I felt sorry for Tom being made a fool of behind his back, but a bit of me also felt satisfied that she was making a prick of him. If he can't be bothered to even write to me – and I'm loyal to him – then he deserves a bit of come-uppance. Yeah.

June 7th 1974

I'm disappointed with myself for not having written in here for so long, but somehow I've just been too busy, although fuck knows what with. It's hardly exciting here. Dad still knocks Mum about, Fran and I pretend not to notice – or maybe she really doesn't. She bugs me, I ignore her, and life just grinds on. I miss Tom, hate Wilverton, and often look at myself in the mirror and wonder who the hell the stranger is. End of year exams are coming up but I'm not worried. I've got the hang of this now. I've found I can really study when I have no distractions – I mean *really study*. I got 98% in my mock English paper. I think I'll be ok. It's only the first year anyway; next year is the real thing. It made me laugh inwardly when they read out our marks in class. Prissy Missy Johns only got 52% and George Barrows failed. Asshole – serves him right for all his piss-taking remarks. Now they all want to be friendly and borrow my notes – well suck up assholes!

I smiled at this. I remembered George Barrows now Will made reference to him. Sandy-haired and sweaty, George was big-built, and with great ham joints for fists. Pig-headed and pig-faced; so he'd been Tammy's new squeeze? He was welcome to her. I didn't read all of the entries from this period in great detail. Maybe I should have done but there was a lot of the same and Will obviously became more and more immersed in his studying as the two years progressed so the commentary was more about themes and topics he'd noticed in the books he was reading than on the people with whom he was living. Maybe that was his form of escape? Certainly the entries slowed down significantly too. He didn't report on Tammy dumping me – it was as if she didn't mention it. She'd made me feel small even though I didn't care about her by then, and I suppose that was what I was in reality to her – insignificant. We still like to think we are of importance in the lives that are important to us at the time, even if we know we aren't. It begs the question of our belief in ourselves when we find we didn't really figure at all.

The entries reappeared when he started university, and that did interest me as it seemed to be as much the starting point for Will's journey as the army had been for me. And I was curious about university life too. I couldn't even begin to imagine it; this totally alien world to the one I'd known. It seemed to me to be a life of decadence compared to mine of restriction – although ironically some of my leaves and nights out had a hundred times more free love and decadence in them than Wills comparatively frugal existence in that department, it seemed.

***

Wednesday 6th October 1976

I've now been at university all of 2 weeks. I'm not sure whether I like it yet, but at least it's not Wilverton. I've escaped the shit hole at last!

It was Fresher's week the week I arrived; a chance to socialise with all the other first year students and I used it as the opportunity to size them up. I wanted to pinpoint the George Barrows of this world as soon as I could so I could give them a wide berth. I wasn't going to spend the next three years here with the same crass attitudes as I'd spent the last two. There was only one guy I decided to avoid by the end of that week. Strangely enough he reminded me of Tom – but I suppose it was the physical similarity rather than the personality – initially at least. He was broad shouldered and narrow-hipped – like Tom. He even had the same light brown slightly curling hair that Tom had, close cropped to his head and coiling around it like a Roman God's would have. In a moment of fancy I imagined ivy leaves encircling it as he was holding court to three girls over by the Student Union stall at Fresher's week fair. His name was Dan. Dan, Dan – the man who can. That was how I dubbed him in my head. I haven't spoken to him since that first week.

I have made some friends early on though. Some of the more avant-garde in the music and art departments – that's where I seem to fit best, but not first years. Katie and Ella are the two girls I prefer from them all. Ella is a determined feminist and makes me smile at how deliberately masculine she appears even whilst parading her womanhood like a Botticelli Venus. She is a cross between the archetypal fortune-teller, with her long flowing skirts and trailing beads – a sixties throwback already – and a skin head. Under the floating skirts and tumbling golden locks are jackboots. A soft outer and a tough interior – is that what she's trying to portray?

Katie is all girl; little, feminine and very effusive. I like the way she looks, but she seems to like me too – and that makes me feel uncomfortable. Sometimes there seems an edge to her feminine exterior too, which I can't define so I'm still a little anxious around her. I'm not sure if I like that or loathe it. I don't have any interest in shagging her but I suspect that's where she's going with this. I suppose I'll have to try it sometime though and perhaps it could be with her.

The guys are an indeterminate bunch. Joe and Paul are a pair of reactionary nuts, but that's just plain funny a lot of the time. They drivel on with their *ban the bomb* and *get the troops out* slogans, and I wonder if I should tell them about Tom being in the army, but then they don't even know who Tom is and I don't want to bring him into this life. I haven't heard from him in months, anyway. This is my life now. He's living his – well fuck him, let him live it. This is mine.

Freddie, I'm sure is gay. It makes me feel uncomfortable when he looks sideways at me, and smiles – in the same way that Katie does, but in a way that makes me want to question the feeling and why I feel it at all. He's not bothered me yet though, so it's no hassle, but I've seen him 'look' – that 'come and get me' look again, at me so this sex shit is going to hit the fan sometime here. Maybe I should have experimented a bit with the girls at Wilverton High – but then if I had it would have been all round the school if I couldn't get it up and that is the thing I wonder about most. Can I?

For all that, I like it here. At last I feel like I may find out who or what I am – at last.

Saturday 12th February 1977

The first students union bar disco here tonight. I went – it felt like a milestone I should mark. I've been here a whole term and started a new one and life has a routine now. I can't say the Students Union bar is the most romantic of places for a Valentine's disco but that's what it was meant to be tonight. They'd spent all day sticking lurid paper hearts all around the walls and it was plastered with them. They even hung them on strings from the ceiling, twisting like coiling snakes whenever anyone walked in the doors and brought a draught of cold air with them. The disco was set up the far end – away from the bar. Fluorescent flashing lights pulsing with the beat as would-be lovers gyrated on the sticky dance floor that was awash with spilt beer and fag ends by the end of the night.

Freddie asked me if I wanted a splif. I wasn't going to try it but I thought hell, this is what it's all about here. I slipped into the office where Freddie was beckoning from to join the circle of tokers. There were seven others crammed into the tiny room and I could see Katie wedged into a corner in between a big fat guy I knew was the SU Sec and a skinny girl with large heavy spectacles and lank hair hanging either side of her pallid face like curtains. She looked like Nana Mouskouri did on my mother's album covers and so incongruously out of place I wanted to laugh, but their faces were so earnest, I knew my giggling would be taken the wrong way.

'Have you got the shit, man?' asked Freddie of the fat guy.

'Yeah, close the door.'

Freddie pushed the door shut and the disco sounds were muffled in the stuffy office. It was dark in there and the faces of the others were like the shadowy forms of the face in Munch's 'Scream', I felt uneasy now I was in here and shut in with them all. It was stifling and I felt trapped. I wanted to ask to leave but somehow didn't dare. I'd been invited into the inner sanctum. How many other guys got here this quickly? Normally it took you into your second year to be invited in the SU office to smoke. I was there in only my second term. Katie and Freddie were second years already – it was probably because of them I was here and I didn't want to queer their pitch – again the temptation to giggle at my quip as it related to Freddie hit me but I stifled it – it was just nerves I told myself. I stayed stumm.

The joint was ceremoniously rolled and passed along. I watched what the others did. Inhale deeply and then hold your breath. Let it out in a long trail of smoke and a deep 'ahhh'. The joint moved around the circle and the faces of the tokers were beatific with inhaled peace. It was my turn next. I took the joint nervously. The end where the roach was had become soggy from somebodies over-enthusiasm – or maybe their inhaled peace had just made them dribble. I didn't really want to put it to my lips but Freddie was watching me with interest so I did. I took a long drag and the smoke hit the back of my throat, harsh and burning. I wanted to cough but knew I had to follow the routine – hold it in your lungs as long as possible before exhaling. It felt like someone had turned on a hot air blower in my chest and it ached from holding my breath but as I let the air out thankfully, the buzz hit me like a juggernaut.

My head swam like I had been put on a rollercoaster and it was just in mid-swoop, then the rollercoaster swept up the incline to the top of the rails and far below me was the rest of the earth, floating away in a spiral of blue and green and brown. I lingered there at the top admiring the beautiful pattern the world made and then just as suddenly swept down the slope into the roar of the worlds' noise and bustle.

'Pass it on man,' someone said irritably and I felt the joint whipped out of my paralysed fingers as I banked up the incline again ready for another pass into the deep blue-green-brown. The joint came round again and this time there was no hesitation. I tugged at it and swallowed down the smoke enthusiastically, feeling the same head-spinning rush. Man, this was great. Then just as suddenly I felt overwhelming nausea. I was wedged in next to Freddie and he must have seen my face turn as green as the green in my earth patterns. He propelled me out of the chair I was in.

'Get some air, man.'

I lurched outside and propped myself dizzily against the wall at the back of the SU building, dragging in the cold fresh air and praying for the nausea to fade away. It didn't and I doubled over, puking violently. Someone had thought up the bright idea of making blue heart shaped jellies for sale on the evening. Jelly and ice cream had been the latest craze in the SU bar – there was a new one every week. Obviously the jelly had gone down as well with someone as the joint had with me. It lay in a little pool on the ground in front of me, spikes of grass sticking through it and my puke mixed with it in an interesting variation on the green-blue-brown earth pattern on the roller coaster ride earlier. I watched it for some while in fascination, unable to move. Katie appeared by my side at some stage and gradually I realised what she was saying,

'Will, you ok?'

'Oh, yeah.' I smiled stupidly at her. I couldn't do anything else. Nothing seemed to be working the right way.

'Come on, I think we'd better get you back.'

'Yeah.' I continued to grin. She took my arm and dragged me along behind her like a tender behind a train. I followed meekly, still vaguely nauseous and concentrating on not puking again. We tumbled through the door to her room and I collapsed flat out on my back on the bed. An odd memory slipped through my mind as I flopped there. This was what Tom did on his last night before joining up. I'm Tom. I must be Tom. I giggled. Katie giggled too and lay alongside me.

'What's so funny, silly Willy?' she asked still breathless from exertion.

'Me – me – I'm a Tom, a Tom Cat...'

'Miaou, and I've a pussy,' she declared. All of a sudden she was on top of me, kissing me hard; tongue deep in my mouth. I felt like I was going to suffocate at first, but then the sensation was nice; exciting. I let her tongue slide around in my mouth and I wrapped mine around hers. They flowed together and I felt as if molten lava was gathering in the pit of my stomach and seeping down my legs, making me feel heavy and languorous but energised as well.

'Mmm, more,' she said.

'Mmm, more,' I mimicked, and we both laughed. She reached down and covered my crotch with her open hand, cupping my genitals through the material of my jeans. The sensation was explosive. I could feel myself harden as she held me. Much nicer than holding myself as I'd done all this time, wondering what it would be like with a girl – a real girl...

'Ooh, nice,' she whispered in my ear and followed the words with her tongue. Instinct seemed to take over and relieved that my body seemed to know what to do after all I rolled over with her still attached to me like a limpet and straddled her. She tore at my jeans belt and stripped it from the loops of my jeans in one smooth movement. Then she moved up to my torso and pulled at the tee shirt I was wearing. It was only at that point that I realised I'd left my jeans jacket at the SU bar. She pulled the tee shirt upwards and it slipped neatly over my head as I ducked slightly to let it. She ran her hands flat-palmed over my chest, stopping to pinch and squeeze my nipples as they roved up and down. My nipples hardened immediately and tingled like electricity was sparking through them.

'Shag me.' She commanded, and pulled off her own top revealing two rolling round breasts with tight buds thrusting up at me.

'It's now or never!' I thought incongruously, and wanted to giggle at the song line as it ran through my head. I rolled off her and shed my jeans. She raised her hips off the bed and wriggled out of her skirt and panties, flinging them with a whoop onto the floor.

'Go tiger, fuck me,' she urged again. I suppose it was because the physical urge was so strong that I was able to ignore the fact that the moment was the least romantic one of my life for a first experience of sex with another person. Maybe it was the worst possible way to be introduced to sex? I wondered how many other guys this tiny little ultra-feminine doll had urged to 'fuck' her, and at that all urge to do so went, but I knew I had to try. The erect penis I'd wondered about for so long was still there, like it had been glued into position, and she wriggled her open legs and pubic mound obligingly at me. I fell back into position and my cock slipped neatly into her waiting receptacle, but that was all it felt like to me, like fitting something into a waiting spare part. The sensation around me was hot and wet and exciting in an immediately gratifying way but there was no enjoyment to it. It was like a volcano boiling up to eruption point and I knew I would come. When I did it was just a physical release, like the top blown off the mountain to allow the lava to cool. As soon as it happened – all of two minutes later I would estimate – I wanted to escape, run away, far away from her. I felt stupid and out of place. She tried to hold me tightly in place by hugging her arms around me afterwards, making little mewing sounds like a cat who'd licked a pot of cream but I lay rigid, unable to relax but unable to escape either.

The sensation of nausea rose up inside me again, and I dismounted roughly.

'It's the joint – it's got to my guts – got to go!' I dragged on my jeans and tee shirt and almost ran out of the door. I just about made it out of the building before heaving again.

So, I know I work ok then, but do I want to do it again? I'm not at all sure about that. Yes, it's been a landmark night tonight – but what kind of landmark?

February 17th 1977

I'm avoiding Katie. She keeps pursuing me and calling me Tiger. I hate it. It's given me a bit of a reputation, and one or two of the other girls have eyed me with renewed interest. That's the last thing I want. That night is a bit hazy now, but I still remember the feeling of embarrassment. Now I can't decide whether it was with Katie or myself. I heard from Tom today, out of the blue. He has a leave coming up before his next posting but it's right in the middle of exams for me. Its mid-week and I have them on all the days he's home – which is only three anyway. He mentioned Tammy Johns again, although I thought she dumped him in favour of George Barrows at one stage, so I guess I wouldn't see that much of him anyway even if I did manage to get home. He's another life, and I don't want to think about it or him unless I have to. This is my life. I've got to work out how to live this one first before I work out anything else. I'm not going home.

Easter 1977

I'm home for Easter holidays. I hate it. Uni was getting to me – well Katie was, so in the end I thought going back to Wilverton would be welcome, but it was like walking back into the same suffocating cocoon. The same old faces, the same old boasts, the same old gossips. Mum still thinks Mrs Andrews is shagging the postman, and that old Fred the barman in the Rose and Crown is a druggie, as she puts it. That made me want to laugh and I wondered what she would do if I told her about my first experience of a joint. Probably have a stroke. I'll just enjoy the incongruity of the idea of Fred toking – or maybe shagging Katie – no, that's really sick. What's the matter with me? Fran seemed nicer when I first got home but soon the old sly quips about Tom started when she thought I was off-guard.

'So you missed lover boy, then?'

'Lover boy?' I knew who she meant but I played dumb.

'Tom, Tom, the piper's son...'

'Oh.' I said nothing more.

'Didn't you want to see him?' She was obviously niggled she hadn't managed to irritate me.

'Well we were school buddies but he's gone his way and I've gone mine – I had other things to do.' I sounded off-hand and for the first time I must have sounded convincing too because she gave me a quick scrutinising look and then just left it. I thought I'd got away with it until she followed it up with, 'who's Katie?'

'Katie?' I whirled round. How would she know about Katie? I said nothing.

'She rang for you when you were down the shop getting Mum her fags.'

Damn. Was she not going to leave me alone even here? Fran plainly wanted to know more but I walked away resolutely and went upstairs to my bedroom and hung my old 'GO AWAY' sign on the door. She stayed away. I'm going to have to do something about Katie when I get back.

I had a dream the other night and they say you should write them down. I suppose it was born out of general emotional confusion and the turmoil that always seems to settle in me when I'm back here in Wilverton. I fell asleep looking at the old school photo that is still propped up on my shelf. I couldn't sleep so I lay there picking out most of my old classmates faces and giving them names. There were only a few who'd faded totally into insignificance, and one I felt sad about – Andrew Berry, who died the following year when an electric heater in the bathroom fell into the bath and electrocuted him. I remember him as a quiet teenager, slightly otherworldly. Maybe he was. Maybe he wasn't meant for this world like Maclean's Vincent wasn't?

Fran had been out with her new boyfriend, Joe, that evening and I'd been distracted in her room when I was dropping the pile of magazines and scarves Mum had asked me to put in there as she tidied the debris Fran left behind her like a trail to say *I've been here*. She'd obviously been undecided over which dress to wear out with Joe and the runner-up was abandoned in a disappointed tangle on her bed. It was a pretty sheath with a slash neckline, generous and forgiving of unbidden lumps and bumps as it wasn't close-fitting like the tight psychedelic whorl she'd chosen instead. I straightened it to stop it creasing. The material was silky soft, a jersey which draped elegantly, making the soft blue of it appear like velvet as it folded. I held it to me, stepping almost automatically in front of Fran's long mirror to see its effect. I hadn't done this in a long time. I felt guilty and jumpy in case Mum came up stairs. I heard the TV volume go up and knew that was unlikely. She was deep into Corrie and wouldn't emerge for another half an hour at least. I'd thrown off my shirt and jeans and slipped into the blue sheath before embarrassment stopped me. It wouldn't zip up fully, but I pulled the zip far enough for the dress to slip mainly into the right places. My hair had been steadily growing longer over the last year. How could you be a student and have a short back and sides? Now it framed my face and was comfortably to my chin, softening the harsher edge to my jawline. The person who stared back at me was disconcertingly feminine – in the same way I'd seen myself the last time I'd been tempted to do this. I smoothed my hands over the soft folds of the dress, a small shiver of excitement travelling the length of my spine and ending in my groin. I felt good. I wanted to stay like this, felling warm and soft and comfortable for once. I must have stood there like that for almost the whole half hour that Corrie was on, just looking and lightly stroking. I was shocked into action by my mother's quavering voice and her footsteps stomping slowly and heavily up the stairs.

'Will, the TV's on the blink. Can you fix it? Where are you?'

'It's Ok Mum, you stay down there. I'll come and sort it out.' I tugged the dress roughly over my head, its zip catching momentarily in my hair and taking three dark russet strands with it. With relief I heard her acknowledgment.

'Alright, but I'm missing the end, so hurry up please.'

My heart was pounding and my breath coming shallowly in waves at almost being caught. I hastily slipped back into jeans and shirt and went downstairs to fix the TV. She didn't comment on my flushed cheeks. She probably didn't notice. She was more often in her own world now than in ours. I went back upstairs hurriedly once she was back engrossed in her mindless entertainment and carefully unsnagged the caught hairs, then spread the dress back over Fran's bed in a semblance of how she'd left it. My sister had sharp eyes. I wouldn't give her any ammunition to use against me. The dress was still in my mind when I drifted into sleep and an anonymous face and the blue dress were the only part of the figure I could see shifting in and out of focus in the dream. It was one of those frustrating ones where you almost grasp the meaning or the plot and then it fades away like mist burned off by the sun. The last shifting image was of the person wearing the dress turning round to face me. It was me, but me fully female, and yet still undeniably male too, like the sense of confused identity Ella gave out when I studied her. I woke with a lurch and a sickening feeling in my chest; like I'd been there before.

June 15th 1977

I never realised how hard end of year exams would be. I must have been coasting until now.

Life has got to get a lot more serious. Freddie and his toke parties have got to stop if I don't want to be thrown out. One good thing about exams is that Katie has been leaving me alone – probably for the same reason as me – needs to actually learn something to be able to do an exam in it. It's stiflingly hot at the moment and I'm sitting at my desk, facing the wall and my mosaic of Pink Floyd and art deco posters, and trying to make sense of what Donne and Sheridan were saying about social satire. It's all about appearances, but what's underneath?

Nothing is making sense. Maybe that's it? Nothing makes sense because it's all appearance?

I have a lifetime already of just appearances. Mum so 'respectable' and always having to hide her ugly bruises, Dad a bully. We kept up appearances all through my childhood with that.

Dad would roll in drunk every Saturday night. I used to hear him clomping up the stairs, cursing and stumbling. The door would creak as he went into their bedroom. There would be the high pitched sound of my mother, cajoling, then pleading, and finally crying out in pain. I knew he would have hit her by then, but didn't want to think what led up to it or from it. There would be low sounds after the cries; murmuring, the bed creaking, and his heavy breath and almost animalistic grunting. I guessed he was forcing himself on her and she was giving in – what else could she do?

She'd be downstairs in the morning, trying to seem blithe and as if there was nothing wrong. He would sit, heavy-lidded and silent across the breakfast table. Fran and I had long-since learnt to say and do nothing out of place at those times. He never so much as raised his hand to us, but then he never had anything good to say or do with us either. All he ever said to Fran was to not part her legs for any bloke until she was married or she would prove herself to be as much of a slut as the others. What others? Me, I was just a nonce, with my head stuffed full of stupid university ideas. I barely even warranted acknowledgment. I suppose by the time we were in our teens, Fran and I preferred it that way rather than get the same attention Mum did, wrapping her brightly coloured silk scarfs neckerchief-like round her throat to mask the hand marks, or letting her fringe drop loosely over one eye to cover the swelling there. I assume Fran has worked it out too, but I'm not sure. We've never talked about it. The only time we were about to get close as siblings, she made some joke about Tom and I thought, 'fuck you then,' and left. By the time I was fifteen, we were both grateful the booze had released us from him when he fell down the stairs one night, paralytic from too much whisky. Mum claimed she didn't even know he was home until we rushed out at the dull thuds as he somersaulted down the stairs – but she was at the head of them before we were, and our bedrooms were closer.

He'd knocked a bowl of fruit off the hall table he crashed into at the bottom. Its contents were scattered all across the hall; oranges, lemons, a flattened, browning banana and a solitary apple. The apple appeared completely intact when we tidied up after the ambulance had been, but later it developed a dark brown bruise that rotted to juicy pulp within a day. I always remember the odd way the fruit splayed across the floor – like someone had picked up a handful of paintbrushes of different colours and flicked them so the colour had spattered everywhere. In the middle of the splatters was my father's twisted body, head at an unnatural angle, eyes staring in surprise and hand flung out and almost touching the perfect apple. He looked like a bowler just letting go of the ball in a cricket match, and watching to see whether it made contact with the wicket. My mother, the batsman; just waited at the top of the stairs.

We never said anything to her. Why would we? The escape was more hers than ours. She went back rapidly to her maiden name after the funeral. She'd had a habit of telling us and everyone she met, that we had proud origins, but always mutedly when Father was around. He still left his mark on her even though he'd gone. I could see it in the absent-mindedness she displayed, like she'd slipped into another room without us noticing it. At least the forced smiles she plastered over the ugly bruises when he was alive were replaced by the previously rare happy ones I'd seen at times when Tom's father was home on leave and had been round to help replace a shelf fixing here, or carry something heavy out to the shed for her. He'd be hurriedly leaving as I and Fran arrived home from school. Of course I knew why she smiled so happily then.

Maybe it was what made me disgusted by sex, with the relationship between men and women? My thoughts wondered on from there. That first sexual encounter with Katie keeps coming back to me. I haven't repeated it. I don't want to face that strange sense of distaste it roused in me. In fact I've been almost monk-like since.

I don't like my body. I don't even want to look at it in the shower or the bath. I've put on weight over the last few months and whilst I do actually like the softer feel to me– that I'm rounded, cushioned, not lean and hard anymore – I still don't want to look at myself. I feel like an alien in a body suit.

Like in one of those stupid films they have on a film club on a Wednesday night. I've got to concentrate, to study, but all I think of is me in that alien body suit. Last night I even dreamt about it and in the dream I peeled it off – the suit. I peeled it off and suddenly I knew I was real, that I was going to see the real me. I ran to find a mirror but couldn't find one anywhere. I was frantic. Weird that I was also back home in my dream, wearing Fran's blue shift dress and it wasn't until I'd run all over the house and started shouting to find me a mirror that Fran suddenly appeared out of nowhere, with Tom, and handed me a small fragment of broken mirror that was just big enough to see myself in if I held it out far enough away. I tried to, but my arm wouldn't lift it. It was paralysed, like it was glued to my side, so finally I had the mirror and I could see myself if I could lift it up – but I couldn't. I cried out in frustration and woke, drenched with sweat. The temptation to look at myself in the mirror on the wall was too much and I got out of bed in the half- light and stood in front of it. I was still Will; still in the alien suit.

I shall be glad to get away from here, but I dread going home for the summer too. I'm lost wherever I am.

July 8th 1977

I'm saved – I've escaped! I'm not sure Freddie is exactly what you would call a saviour but he does have a spare room in his flat in Golders Green and I'm staying there this summer. No Wilverton, no sanctimoniously correct mother, or nosy Fran.

No complacent Tammy Johns, full of who she's dating now – but at least it's not Tom any more – or that bastard George Barrows eyeing me like he knows what I'm thinking. I've got a job in a small boutique off the Kings Road. Completely gay – it would be – Freddie found it for me, but they seem to like my looks and that got me in there. I don't care. I'm fascinated by the clothes the women wear and the way they style themselves. Anything is better than Wilverton. And better still Katie has dropped out for her final year and gone travelling. Life is looking up. Even the alien dream hasn't bothered me for over a week now.

August 14th 1977

Freddie is actually quite a good guy, now I'm getting to know him more. He hasn't bothered me at all even though I'm still disconcerted by the way his gaze lingers on me just slightly too long sometimes. He took me to a club his friends go to in town last night. It was such a beautiful place – all mirrors and mosaics and white and silver. It was like a harem but with men and women – all beautiful. The lights were eastern in design, hanging elegantly on long slender silver chains, their cutwork design allowing the light to shine through in a pattern spilling onto the floor and pooling into shadows in the corners of the room. The walls were uneven matt white as if built of squat mud blocks rendered over. It gave a sense of solidity strangely incongruent with the delicacy of the eastern lights and silver mosaics, yet comfortingly masculine against the femininity of the rest of the interior design; I liked it.

We sat in an alcove full of plush cushions and Freddie ordered champagne. I'd never tried champagne before but I liked it immediately – the way it rushed intoxicatingly to your head whilst the bubbles fizzed at the tip of your nose when you swallowed. I knew after two glasses that I was getting pissed but what the hell, it was cool.

Freddie was dressed in one of his favourite djellabas, and had his toy dog perched on his shoulder. It has become a recognised part of his style to parade the pretend dog – a soft toy like a mini Chihuahua – on his shoulder and invite everyone to say hello to Mimi. As far as the gay community is concerned, it certainly sifts the girls from the boys – the girls being the gays who take on the female role and the boys being, well, the boys. I wasn't sure which Freddie was going for – maybe none of them, but he was definitely sifting. I could already tell that from his systematic approach. He approached me.

'Say hello to Mimi, Will.' He commanded. I had no idea what to do but the champagne was buzzing in my head already and I patted the toy dog on its head and obediently said it.

'Hello little Mimi. Good girl.' Freddie nodded his head at me and moved on. What did that all mean? The rest of the evening passed in a champagne blur and I found myself safely home and untouched later on in the early hours. I vaguely remembered Freddie putting me to bed but doing nothing other than remove my clothes, leaving me lying completely naked on my bed. He looked at me appraisingly before drawing the bedclothes over me and saying, 'night, night little Will, good girl,' and clicking the light off. My head swam for a while as I tried to get my eyes accustomed to the dark but then I gave up and just let the dark envelope me completely. I woke up the next day with a most god-awful headache. I had to go into work anyway so I wore sunglasses to try to ease the glare of the sunlight.

'Oh darling, so cool, so stylish,' an over-dressed man-woman figure loomed over me. Babs was a cross-dresser who swanned in and out of the Kings Road boutique in a blaze of flamboyant colour. Maybe a peacock would be a better bird description for her than swan; swan was too understated and elegant. I liked Babs, but she was too vibrant for me on this day when my head felt like it was exploding every five seconds. I retired to the relative peace of the back room, hoping Babs wouldn't try to follow me as he was wont to do sometimes. The back room contained the expensive evening dresses so generally only drew in the richer clientele, who were more subdued. Predictably Babs didn't follow me in there and I settled down by the gloves drawer to make sure they were all paired and ticketed. A good twenty minutes passed quietly that way until a woman came hesitantly through the door, as if she wasn't quite sure whether she was in the right place.

'Evening gowns?' She asked when she spotted me. Her voice was unusually deep and husky for such a feminine woman, but nevertheless it was sexy. I looked at her with a different level of interest. She still didn't arouse me. I was becoming used to that lack of response to women now, but I appreciated her attractiveness.

'Yes, that's right.' It struck me that the timbre and resonance of my voice wasn't that dissimilar to hers as I replied.

'What size?'

'Gosh, I don't really know – I've lost so much weight recently.' She hesitated, 'what do you suggest?'

I sized her up – I was becoming practiced at doing that now with dresses and jackets. Women's underwear was still a closed book to me and I held back from examining any of the delicately laced items in the rest of the shop because of the uneasy feeling it awakened in me touching something so intensely feminine. It seemed like opening Pandora's box to get that close to women's essential femininity, but I was good at deciding what matched, what suited, what would work best with this jacket, this skirt – these gloves, that colour. It seemed natural for me to be able to do it.

'About a 16 I reckon.'

'Ok, let's try that first.' It was unusual for anyone to come in to the evening dresses back room and not know their size – they were such expensive things in here – and even more so for them to ask for my suggestions. That made her a curious customer and I surreptitiously looked her over again as she moved towards the rail of dresses. She seemed to sense my look and glanced back at me so I quickly turned my attention to the task. My headache started to resolve as I considered what would suit her. I knew already. I picked out two beautiful dresses, sleek, but with a waterfall of chiffon and sequins, and offered them to her.

'How about starting with these?'

'Ok.' She smiled and it was like the sun coming out. Her jawline was firm and slightly squared but the strong look it gave her was exotic. Ridiculously I felt in awe of her. She had the same sense of authority that I had felt with the deputy head teacher at school. Unusual to have a female deputy head then but you knew why she had the job. There was an indefinable something to her – precisely what I never quite put my finger on, but it implied 'power'. This woman also had it, despite her uncertainty over her dress size. She took the dresses from me and disappeared into the changing room. She was in there for a while as I waited patiently outside, wondering if I should call one of the girls from the front of the shop to help – or one of the gays. It didn't seem quite right for me to be helping her – too intimate, somehow. It didn't feel the same as helping one of the TV's as they selected their next outfit or commenting on how lovely they looked when they came in, all 'girlish' charm, and asked me my opinion.

'What do you think, dahhling? Do I look better than *she* does?' The companion would mimic a flounce and walk away, denouncing 'her' under her breath.

'Bitch!'

I would have to hide a wry smile that these men could be so girlishly spiteful to each other. It was the main thing that put me off cross-dressing myself because if I was absolutely honest, it *was* tempting. I'd secretly tried on Fran's clothes from time to time as a teenager at home. Of course they don't fit – despite my small frame I'm still broader-shouldered than her and my shape is inherently wrong, but the high-waisted, empire-style dresses generously hid my narrowing hips and flattered even a male body shape. I looked feminine in them, even with the zip only half done because my back was too broad to pull it all the way up. The effect was odd. I looked back at an almost-woman. The soft feel of the silky material used in women's clothing, the drape of it over breast or curving hip and the smell of women – the perfumed, summers day scent of them – intoxicated me, even though it didn't make me desire them. I'd rapidly pulled the dress off me that first time, disconcerted and confused by the way I looked – but even more so by the way I felt. I hadn't done it again for a long while afterwards, and then only a few times more – like an almost-addict sneaking a fix when they thought it wouldn't matter. The silky blue-green sheath thrown carelessly onto Fran's bed the last time I'd been home had been one of those times; too much of a temptation to pass up. That was probably why I liked the back room here so much – in amongst the sheer glory of the sequins and lace, but secure from the garish onslaught of the TV's and the other cross-dressers who made that part of me who'd enjoyed trying on Fran's dresses squirm in recognition.

The woman reappeared from the changing room, pulling the curtain back with a flourish. She looked utterly beautiful –

stunning in fact. The colour suited her to perfection – a deep peacock blue, offsetting her platinum blonde hair and softening her slightly angular shoulders.

'Wow!' I exclaimed; I couldn't help myself. 'That's the one!'

'Do you think so?' She did a half turn in front of the full-length mirror in the middle of the room, admiring herself from the rear and then flashing me a smile over her shoulder. Something about the way she did it made me want to store it up and try it out myself in front of a mirror when no-one was watching – like I had with those coquettish under the eyelashes looks the girls gave back at Wilverton High. I remembered the odd feeling I'd had when I'd first looked at myself in Fran's dress, but dismissed it uncomfortably.

'Definitely,' I replied admiringly.

'Well in that case, I'll consider it but I'll try on the other one too.' She swept back towards the changing room like a duchess and the curtain swished behind her. I waited outside, off-balance. My headache had gone now but I felt nervous around this woman. Suddenly the fire alarm bell jangled, setting off my headache again. There was no immediate reaction from behind the curtain so I waited awkwardly. Chrissy poked her head round the door leading to the front room of the shop.

'Come on – get a move on!'

'I can't.' I gestured to the drawn curtain of the changing room. 'Someone's trying on.'

'Well get them out – this ain't no drill.'

I tugged at the curtain.

'Excuse me miss.' There was no reaction. 'Miss?' I rustled the curtain again. Now I could hear the fire engine bells in the distance too and panicked. This was real. There was nothing for it but to go in there and get her out myself. I yanked the curtain back.

'I'm really sorry, but…' She swung round to face me, in only her bra and panties. The bra was a pretty pink and black lace affair and her breasts swelled out of the top of it. I couldn't help it. Curiosity to see what this imposing woman looked like in her underwear, and to feel I was on the same level as her, as I would have liked to have done with the deputy head – got the better of inherent courtesy. I dropped my eyes down the length of her body only to stop in shock at her panties. My face flushed red. The swelling bulge of a penis was as unmistakable in the panties as the swelling breasts were in the bra.

'Oh shit!' I stepped back in surprise.

'Oh my God!' She exclaimed at the same time. Our eyes locked on each other as it slowly dawned on me she was half man, half woman – a mythical creature. Not like the TV's and the cross-dressers who frequented the front of the shop, but someone, something quite different.

'Don't tell anyone.' She asked me imploringly. 'I've only got three weeks to go to the op and this was to be my celebratory dress for afterwards.' I was completely uncomprehending.

'Op – what op?' The strident sound of the fire engine siren broke through my confusion as a whiff of smoke hit me too.

'Shit – we need to get out – the place is on fire!' I grabbed her clothes as they hung over the back of the chair in the changing room and thrust them at her. She took them mechanically, eyes never leaving my face as she quickly dressed in the psychadelic swirl of her patterned dress and abandoned the evening dress in a pool of glorious seawater blue on the floor.

'Come on, come on, for chrissakes!' I urged her, him – Oh I dunno what!

She pulled up the zipper on her dress and followed me swiftly out of the changing room still clutching her white Peyton boots in one hand. As we ducked through the doorway the noise from the fire bell became deafening and the smell of smoke acrid and choking. The shop swum round me in a blaze of colours as we now ran for the front door. I was clutching her hand and dragging her along behind me. There was crackle and snap as we got level with the front door, followed by a great bolt of flames from the corridor running along the left hand side of the shop and leading to the kitchen and loo the staff used. The heat was immense, scorching our backs and sides of our face.

'Christ!' She screamed and I yanked hard on her hand, catapulting her though the open doorway like a stone from a slingshot. I wheeled after her as if on the other end of a rubber band attached to her and we collided together outside the door. A burly fireman grabbed us both and hustled us to safety as the flames burst through the shop front.

'You're bloody lucky,' he said, 'you only just made it – would've singed your balls good and proper!' This addressed to me, and then 'sorry, miss – no offence,' to her. We said nothing to each other and she just shook her head at him as if forgiving him the crude remark as only a lady can. He moved away from us onto other duties taming the now raging fire.

'Thanks for saving my life.'

'I didn't.'

'Yes you did, I owe you.' She took my hand. I didn't know what else to do, so I let her. She smiled and then I remembered again what I'd seen in the changing room.

'Are you a guy or ...' I stumbled to a halt – how on earth could I ask?

'... a girl.' She finished it for me. 'It's a long story,' she said, but after a brief pause, 'I'll tell you it if you like?' Part of me wanted to say no thanks and walk away – as far away as possible, and another even more confused part wanted an explanation. In the end the part that wanted the explanation won and we both walked away to a coffee shop further down the road. She gave me her explanation, which actually only made me want to ask more questions.

She was a boy by birth but had always felt more like a girl. The irony was that at school she'd often been given the female parts in school plays. When she'd been at college in her teens, they'd staged a drag beauty queen contest for fun and she'd looked more glamorous than most of the real girls. She'd tried to ignore it but the feeling that she was in the wrong body had plagued her more and more until one day –

and married by that stage, trying to be the normal man everyone expected her to be – she'd tried on one of her wife's maternity smocks whilst the wife was out shopping. The feeling of suddenly being in the right skin and looking the right way was indescribable. It became a regular routine to try on her wife's clothes when her wife was out, and eventually she developed her own wardrobe, hiding it behind the panel over the side of the bath. Her wife worked evenings on telesales so she would be left at home, with the children, and once they had gone to bed, she would lock herself in the bathroom and recover her treasures. She experimented with make-up too after a while, and found the transformation it completed to her face was the last piece in the jigsaw. I couldn't help laughing along with her as she told me how she hadn't known about make-up remover to begin with and had regularly scrubbed off the make-up with soap and water so that one day her wife came home and accused her of going down the pub and leaving the children because she had such a red shiny nose and smelt so clean. As if she was trying to get rid of the smell of beer and fags, not lipstick and foundation.

The years went by and her secret life continued, but becoming more difficult to pursue as the children grew up and so couldn't be trusted to stay in bed, like babies or toddlers would. After a while the wife gave up her telesales job too, so all of the secret evenings were curtailed. She became resentful, and irritable. The relationship suffered and gradually, she also started to realise why sex didn't feel right with the wife either; why it never had – and why she felt so different all the time. Even the other men around her seemed alien. Finally she reached the inevitable question – do I feel like a man or a woman inside? The answer was most definitively a woman. Since then she'd travelled the long and difficult road towards gender reassignment. It hadn't taken ten years, far less in fact, but the op she referred to was the final stage in transforming her outward appearance from male to female.

I listened, mostly dazed, occasionally laughing because amongst the pathos of the tale, she also displayed an ironic sense of the farcical. Because of where the shop was in the Kings Road, its clientele was hugely varied. Tom Petty immortalised exactly what the Kings Road was like in his hit of the same name a few years later. The people who came into the shop were just people; you took them at face value. When she'd come into the back room at the shop, I'd simply assumed her to be a well-off woman looking for something a little different. I'd got used to a daily parade of all walks of life. I was surrounded by TV's and cross-dressers, gays and the ones who thought they might be gay, and accepted all of them without assigning them to any particular group. It was just a morass of emotional and gender confusion, but somehow to my indeterminate sexuality, it was entirely appropriate, and made it unnecessary for me to have to face any conclusions about myself. However, I'd never really thought about anyone bridging the gap completely and transforming from one sex to another.

'Will you keep this to yourself?' She asked at the end of the tale. 'I told you because I owed you that for saving me from the fire. I've managed to be quite credible as a woman, obviously from your first reaction to me – you didn't even begin to suspect, did you?'

I shook my head, not absolutely sure which question I was really answering in doing so – but no, I hadn't even suspected.

'Shit,' was all I could eventually think of to say. I did agree to say nothing and she left, telling me only her chosen first name: Suzanne. She scribbled her number on a scrap of serviette. I watched her walk away, down the street and out of my life, but I remained haunted by what she'd looked like in the changing room: like an alien half–transformed. Half man, half woman. I realised that was the alien body I'd seen once before in my dreams, but it had been faceless then. I wondered whose face to put on it now.

Chapter 5:

Fire damage, 1977 – 1980

I was pretty different by the time I made my way back to Wilverton. Will was too – although he hadn't appeared that much different at the time – older, more refined, more knowledgeable, but Will nevertheless. The almond shaped eyes still observed me more than joined in with me, but then he'd always done that. It was disconcerting to now see life through them. I didn't want to read on, but I had to.

***

August into September1977

I'm writing in retrospect now as it is almost time to return to university and I've left this diary alone for a while because I haven't known what to write in it. We parted at the coffee shop. She said that when one saves a life, that life is then owed. She owed hers to me. I said that was nonsense but I took the number she offered me on a scrap of paper torn from the café serviette although I then promptly lost it when I washed my jeans without emptying the pockets. The image of the mythical creature stayed strongly and disturbingly in my mind.

The boutique was closed for two weeks. The fire was put out quite quickly with minimal physical damage but of course a lot of smoke damage. For the first week we couldn't get in whilst they did their safety checks and then the police checked for arson. All that time was mine to spend how I wanted it. I walked for a while through Green Park. It was cool and expansive there. Somehow it let my thoughts expand beyond the boundaries that seemed to confine them most of the time. I'm not sure what I thought during those walks. I just remember that mythical creature roaming the grassy places of the park with me. When we were allowed back into the shop again, there was a lot of work clearing, airing and sifting through what could be salvaged and what had to be thrown away, then listing it for the insurance claim. I spent a lot of my time just shifting things around and putting things away. It was fairly mindless and my mind remained engaged on the same walks as I'd been doing in person through Green Park, and immersed in the same thoughts.

I know Freddie noticed my immersion. I don't think anyone else did really. They were too busy trying to get the boutique back open again. On the night of the grand re-opening we all went to the beautiful white night club again. Freddie ordered champagne and so did Miriam, the boutique owner. I thought I saw the woman-man in the crowd, and then chided myself for being ridiculous. She would have only just have had the operation that was to finally transform her. How would she be up to being out and about – let alone at a night club? It was just my fanciful imagination. I was becoming obsessed. *Put the idea aside, you idiot*, I told myself. This time I didn't drink too much and Freddie didn't need to put me to bed. I felt as if a part of me was starting to stand aside and observe. What was it I was observing – them or me?

The summer finished in a blur of avant-garde parties, colourful characters, and more of an insight into the young and trendy artistic scene. It was only a snapshot I was being lent because in reality I am no more than an impoverished student, hanging onto the extravagant coat-tails of Freddie and the like, and enjoying the privileges their moneyed backgrounds allowed.

My bags are all packed up now and tomorrow I leave the flat and Freddie's overwhelming bonhomie. I return to university. Back to the plain and basic halls of residence, the routine of lectures missed and hurried note swapping so essays and dissertations can be finished on time despite absences from study; back to the next intakes' Fresher's week, the rowdy disco's and drunken first years. Shit, I'm only just going into my second year yet I now feel like an old lag, as if I've been there for ever. Freddie will be back for his final year, but luckily not Katie. I feel so much more relaxed about that. Freddie has never said anything more to me since that night he put me to bed, but he still sometimes looks at me appraisingly. I'm not even going to think about that or girls or how I feel about them or sex or anything. I'm simply going to study this year. Study and find my way towards that privileged moneyed background that Freddie has, and the champagne and the silver white nightclubs and the trendy boutiques in Kings Road. Once I get there, I'll figure the rest of it out.

* * *

The entries over the next two years were patchy, more notes about events he had to go to, lectures, dissertation and essay deadlines and academic submission dates. More of a calendar than anything; like Will had indeed submerged himself in intellectual minutiae and avoided the emotional maelstrom even I could see developing. I was surprised since he'd poured out such a wealth of disturbing experiences over the last few years, I couldn't understand how he could have turned off the tap, once full flow, to now just an occasional drip of information. I skimmed the pages. The rag ball and the annotation 'watch Freddie', 'final dissertation' a few weeks later, 'CD pub crawl' and a series of question marks after it one Saturday in June, 'library interview' ringed around in the middle of the summer of 1979, and I knew of course that had been the interview for his job, but they were mere snippets of a life, not the inner framework. Just two events seemed to warrant comment from this mysterious Will during that time; my letter from Northern Ireland – the cry for help in the midst of confusion after Gary died, and then Easter 1980. My last Easter in the army before I was discharged and the Easter Fran got married too. We saw each other face to face then for the first time in all those years. I had no idea what he'd been doing or what he'd experienced then. There was none of it in his letters – just comments on how hard he was studying and how beautiful places like Green Park were, his current favourite music from the charts and oblique questions about how life was for me. It was perhaps significant there were no girls, no romances, no relationships, as I might have expected there to be. Why hadn't I noticed that? When I'd replied, I'd not once wondered in reality how worlds apart we were. I was too immersed in my own one. That gap was desperately important to me now, and who Will had become in that blanked out time.

I remember seeing him that Easter was odd for me too – like going back in time, but yet also just part of the place that was firmly rooted in my teenage years so he wasn't out of place, he wasn't seemingly different, he was just where he should be; how he should be. I'd been not only deaf, but blind too.

***

Maundy Thursday 1980

I had to go back to Wilverton. Mum insisted I come home this Easter as Fran was getting married just after it. As it happens Tom was coming home on leave at the same time. He was already in Northern Ireland and I'd been thrown by the Tom I hadn't recognised in the letters he now wrote about life and the living death they lived there. He was shaken by death. I'd seen it when he'd written about the guy who'd been killed in the helicopter, but the letters now, when they intermittently appeared, were increasingly sombre. They made me think about death too. It was just a fact when Dad died and we simply got on with it. If anything I suppose our main emotion was relief. That ominous feeling of waiting for trouble to brew when he rolled in drunk was finally gone.

I gave in to Mum's emotional blackmail, and agreed to stand in for Dad, giving Fran away in his place. That was embarrassing. She and I never got on too well whilst we were growing up and I still thought of her as a bitch for all the taunting she put my way. Strangely though, she seemed to have softened – as if falling in love had added a new dimension to her. The night before the wedding she was standing out in the garden looking up at the stars. She'd had her hen night the weekend before and Joe, the bridegroom had done likewise so there were no embarrassing delays at the altar whilst the bridegroom was sobered up or retrieved from Scotland where he'd been left in just his underpants.

I saw her out there and was going to ignore her as usual and go to bed, gritting my teeth for the Dad role I was going to have to pretend my way through the next day, but there was something almost wistful in her posture. Her back was towards me, head tilted so she could gaze upwards. She looked small and vulnerable looking up at the stars, like the little girl she'd once been. It must have been the first time in years that I felt some affection for her. I watched her for a while, and she must have eventually sensed my presence because she suddenly turned and beckoned for me to join her. There was no escape then.

'Thanks for being Dad tomorrow. I know you hate the idea, but I do appreciate it you know, Will.'

I was surprised. I looked closely at her in the gloom. The clouds drifting across the moon slid away at that precise moment, exposing us to its full beam and a tear glinted unmistakeably on her cheek. Like a violin playing a sweet clear high note, a pang went through me. I actually wanted to put my arm round her and without even realising I'd done it, I found her nestled up against me.

'Do you think Dad can see us still?' The question was unexpected too, but it was one that nagged at me from time to time, especially when I wrestled with myself over my own confused feelings. I imagined him talking to me with derision in his voice.

'I would never have believed it of *my* son…'

'I don't know Fran. What makes you ask – do you miss him?' I hadn't thought Fran missed or felt anything much for anyone but herself until now. She always seemed so self-absorbed, so sharp.

'It's just that tomorrow is the day most Dad's look forward to for their daughter, isn't it? I wondered if he would have done that for me. Would he have been proud of me? Just once, I would so like us to have been normal – normal wedding, normal parents, normal childhood, you know.' Her expression was wistful.

It suddenly dawned on me why Fran was always so sharp and self-absorbed. It was her form of self-defence. She'd felt as ill-treated by Dad as I and Mum had. I didn't want to ask her if she knew about the regular Saturday night routine between them. That was sharing too much in this tentative and awkward moment, but I felt sorry for her. We weren't that different after all. I couldn't answer for Dad, but I knew she needed me to somehow – to make her feel like tomorrow was the day it should be for her as a daughter. I took on Dad's mantle properly but with Wills twist on it, and for the first time, my sister and I were in tune.

'What would there not to be proud of Fran? You're fine – in fact you're ok, ok? And tomorrow you're going to make a beautiful bride – even if you are my sister,' and I gave her a gentle nudge in the ribs.

She twisted slightly so we could look at each other; eyes almost on the level. I was only a couple of inches taller than her. Her gaze held mine for several minutes then the corners of her eyes crinkled into a happy smile.

'You're ok too, Will. Thanks.'

We stayed like that for another five minutes or so, not saying anything more, just looking up at the stars, each thinking our own thoughts, but now with a pact between us. The wedding day was fine too. I played my part to perfection, Fran looked as beautiful as I'd said she would, and I also saw Tom again, home on leave.

I knew he might be from the timbre of the letters but I couldn't have bargained for the odd range of emotions he created in me. Tom – the same but different. Or maybe I was different? Maybe we both were. We clapped each other on the shoulder and then lurched self-consciously into a brief manly hug, but I felt uncomfortable. The tails suit I was wearing felt restrictive and awkward. When I gave him the hug, it felt out of place. I'd felt comfortable with the gentle snuggle with my sister the night before. It felt as if the hug with Tom should have been the same, but that was just wrong.

Shit, maybe I *am* gay?

Good Friday 1980

I haven't written properly in here for such a long time and now I can't stop. I'm like a simmering pot left to build up steam and all of a sudden a blast shoots the lid off sky high. The pot boils over and the contents spew over the sides and puddle round the flames on the hob, putting them out and leaving the explosive gas hanging in the air, waiting to ignite ...

Sun 13th April 1980

I've just re-read what I wrote the other day. Fran's gone off on her honeymoon, the wedding guests have all gone home and Mum's retired to bed with a headache. It's quiet now and I can think about it. When I wrote it, I wanted to obliterate it as soon as I'd written the words. Christ – that would make me like Freddie. Am I?

Funnily enough I feel better for having written down my jumbled thoughts. They seem less jumbled. I seem to have had the same thoughts bubbling up so often over the last few years but whenever that alien form appears in my dreams or I wonder what Suzanne is doing, or how it feels to be different to what I am, I ram the pot lid back on. I dare not be engulfed in the steam from the cauldron or I may emerge scarred forever. But now I'm wondering if the time is coming when I actually have no choice but to stir the contents and see what bubbles out.

Monday 14th April 1980

I don't know, is the answer. I don't know if I'm gay. I just know I don't feel and think like the Toms and George Barrows of this world. I suppose I'm going to have to find out now. I've agreed to go for a drink with Tom tomorrow but I feel even more awkward now. Do I fancy Tom, if I'm gay? I'm not sure I can even look him in the eye now I've actually written that down.

Wednesday 16th April 1980

I couldn't avoid the drink with Tom. It wasn't as awkward as I thought it would be, but all the time we were talking those same thoughts were in the back of my head. Do I fancy you? Am I gay?

He talked a bit about the army and how hard it was. There seemed to be a lot of drill work, hard physical exercise, drinking and fucking involved. Well I knew Tom had always had a strong sex drive – that was apparent even when we were first teenagers at school. He was always talking about this girls tits or that girls' ass. I remember when he decided that he was going to go after Lucy James and I'd felt sorry for her because she seemed so, well, vulnerable. I knew that she was far too serious and *nice* to realise what a lone wolf Tom was. I actually gave him a hard time over it – although now I wondered had I been *jealous* then? Had I tried to head him off because I secretly hadn't wanted him to date anyone? Shit, this was becoming really complicated now. I have to admit, uncomfortable though it is, that I *was* jealous over Tammy Johns.

Once I'd started to think about that, I found it increasingly hard to concentrate on what he was saying. Instead I found myself appraising him physically. He'd filled out but it was all muscle. He exuded masculinity from his very pores – like a stallion at stud. Was I attracted to that? His forearms were firm and tanned; a healthy bronze against his white tee shirt, brown leather jacket slung casually over the chair back where he was sitting. I fought off the temptation to touch them as I looked at the dark hairs covering them like fur. There was something exciting about imagining how they would feel if I lightly touched one of them, stroking my fingertips over their soft sheen. Christ, I was getting turned on! I must be gay. I squirmed inwardly. He was telling me about the helicopter accident and I tried to concentrate. His face was taut, a small tic just faintly obvious at the corner of his mouth. Then it was gone. I felt immensely sorry for him. His confusion and pain were evident to me, and I felt ashamed of having been appraising him as a physical specimen when my friend needed *his* friend's sympathy. My attention re-focussed on Tom, my friend. The boy I'd run through Old Ma J's orchards and skinned knees on trees with. His eyes were shadowed and

116

momentarily I sensed a very different Tom to the teenager who'd brazenly fingered the girls and swigged beer from a can until he puked. This man was calmer, with a sense finally of the gravity of life and death – and the depth of loss. I realised my feelings for him were a disturbing mix of boyhood friend and reaching out for something quite different. I wondered if he'd completely identified his yet.

I wanted to get away. I didn't want to feel like this about Tom. I shouldn't feel like this about Tom. He wasn't gay, even if I might be. He would hate me. I wondered if he would hate me so much for having feelings about him, for tainting him with homosexuality by making him the object of my feelings, that he would want to beat me up; obliterate me like I wanted to obliterate the thought when I first wrote it in my diary. Tom must have thought it weird but I engineered a reason to have to get back home to Mum. I think I pretended she was going down with flu or something. He commented that I was such a 'good guy' to her. Fucking ironic to call me a good 'guy' I thought at the time.

Friday 18th April 1980

I've decided not to see Tom again whilst he's home on leave. He's actually home for another four days but I'm avoiding him. I can escape back to uni on Monday anyway if I want. Now I've wondered if I'm gay, I'm scared shitless he will see that physical attraction to him in the way I behave when he's around. I've never fancied anyone in my life before – until now – and Tom I've known ALL my life. Apart from that, I'm not sure if I AM gay or not. Suzanne, that mythical half-man-half-woman I saved from the fire in the Kings Road boutique keeps plaguing my memories, and his/her description of how they felt. There's something familiar to the confusion I feel whenever I open the lid to the box containing my jumbled thoughts and feelings about sex in her description. I'd filed that one and only sexual encounter with a woman in the same box – the fumbled job with Katie, high and drunk. I've not known whether it was unsatisfactory because of the drink and drugs or because of her, or me, and haven't felt inclined to examine it further until now. All of a sudden the issue has turned from one I wanted to avoid at all costs to one I want to resolve at all costs. I've had sex with a woman and haven't liked it. It was comforting to know I could actually perform the deed, even if it did leave me vaguely sickened, but remembering my state of arousal when I'd imagined caressing Toms' very male arms now makes me keen to see if sex with a man is any different. There would be a potentially willing participant in Freddie, no doubt.

April 21st 1980

Back at uni today and the first person I saw was Freddie – like he has sixth sense or radar. I didn't know whether to say something, or imply something but in the end I needn't have worried because his sixth sense set it all up for me. He's invited me to a start of term party tonight. It's now or never, I think.

Sunday April 27th 1980

After the parties over – there's a song about that isn't there? Gran used to sing it – or no, it was to do with after the ball was over. Heart's being broken, or something similar. My heart's not broken but my body feels like it is. I know one thing though – I'm not gay, but I'm going to write the whole thing down so if I ever wonder if I'm gay again, I can read this and know, KNOW, I'm NOT gay.

It was one of Freddie's usual parties; lavish, elaborate and drunken. The guests were from the usual odd assortment of different worlds – art, TV, nouveau riche and students. We appeared in an array of outfits – the garish, the 'different', the pretentious, the cross-dressers, and me – confused and impoverished. I no sooner walked through the door of Miriam's round-the-corner-from-the-Kings-Road-boutique chic pad, than a drink was thrust in my hand and Freddie appeared behind it inviting me to get on down. My mind was so wrapped up in sex and whether I would or wouldn't tonight that for a moment I thought he was actually inviting me to go down on him there and then, but looking into his expansive grin, with Mimi still perched on his shoulder, I realised my potential faux pas before I made it and hastily joined the throng of heaving bodies in the lounge all pumping and grinding away to Blondie and The Jam. More alcohol and more dancing followed, accompanied by the almost obligatory joint sharing, but I didn't want to get smashed, I wanted to get laid. This was the time to find out, really find out. I 'worked my way back' to Freddie with the song of the same name blaring out around me and then wondered how I was going to let him know – without actually telling him – that was what I wanted to happen. Far from the decisive stance I'd taken in coming here, only one thing on my mind, now I was gauche and unsure. What was gay etiquette? Did you ask or imply? Wait or initiate?

Freddie did the work for me in the end. I suppose it must have been somewhat obvious on my part when I deliberately landed up right in front of him again, with what must have been an eager puppy expression.

'Hey, you wanna get outta here?' He drawled.

'Yeah,' trying to sound cool.

'Let's go, babe,' and he was steering me to the lounge door, down the corridor and into one of the bedrooms. There were two other rooms, and the sounds of sex emanating from them were explicit as we passed them. Freddie lingered outside each room, ear to the door, just long enough to determine whether it was occupied before laying claim to the third bedroom. He reeled me into it, shutting the door firmly behind me and we stood facing each other in the darkness. The muffled disco music throbbed away in the background.

'So – at last.' He sounded breathy and excited, but I wasn't so sure now. The remembered excitement that Tom's forearms had elicited in me was nowhere to be found. I was nervous – did I really want to do this after all? Too late for turning back now as Freddie pushed me up against the door and stuck his tongue in my mouth.

The first thing I noticed was how rough his face felt – scratchy and harsh. The stubble on his chin gouged away at mine as he ground his lips and tongue into my mouth. By comparison, although I hadn't enjoyed her slack lips, Katie's skin had felt soft and pleasant, but maybe too soft – undemanding. Freddie was certainly demanding and that was starting to turn me on – the urgency of his lips on mine, his hands roaming over my body – hard and explorative. His hand reached my jeans button, and undid it, then eased the zip of my flies down too. Involuntarily I felt myself become erect. We moved towards the bed and I wondered if I should touch Freddie. I tentatively touched his crotch to find him already thrusting out of his flies. Christ, when did he undo them? He reached down and shoved his jeans hard down over his ass and then pulled mine off as I lay on the bed, legs flailing in mid-air. Ludicrously I remembered the scene in the Disney cartoon of Snow White, where the birds helped the heroine complete her work, clearing away scattered household items and making the broom sweep the floor – *whistle while you work, tararararara!* The cheerful little melody buzzed incongruously around my brain as my tee shirt was pulled over my head and my boxers were slid over my knees as if the same flock of birds were doing the job for him. Instead of doing their innocent little chores, they were assisting in my steady path towards seduction. In what seemed like little more than a couple of minutes we'd gone from the noise and bustle of the party to being stark naked on the bed. I was now very unsure that I wanted this to be happening, but there was no stopping Freddie. In the half-light of the room he waved a tube at me. I couldn't make out what it was and all I could think was *a tube of toothpaste*? What the hell was he going to do with that?

'What's that for?' I asked, astounded.

'Lube, my dear boy – you don't want to do it without, do you?' Then he rolled me unceremoniously on my stomach, plastered me with lube and I felt as if a sword was piercing me and setting me on fire. I couldn't protest – I'd wanted this to happen, hadn't I? I gritted my teeth and just got through it. He grasped my shoulders and thrust harder. The shaft of flame burned fiercer and deeper. Pain surged through me like I was on fire with agony. I held my breath like a child does. *Make it stop, make it stop*. The grunting and thrusting resolved quite suddenly into a long 'ahh' and he relaxed the grip on my shoulders. His nails left small red dents in my skin, like a devils talons had pulled me down into hellfire. I buried my face in the bedclothes, smelling the stale sweat of the previous occupants, grinding my teeth hard to hold back the hot needles of tears in my eyes, willing myself not to cry. *Christ it hurt, oh Christ.* After he'd rolled off and lay flat on his back alongside me, breathing heavily, I put my clothes back on slowly and painfully. Freddie sat up on the bed, lit a cigarette and smoked as he watched me. Eventually his voice cut through the darkness.

'That was your first time, wasn't it?'

I stopped dressing.

'Yes.' It came out harsh and splintered, like I felt.

'You should have said, dear boy – I would have gone slower. Shall we go and do something together tomorrow – a kind of date?'

'I ... no, thanks Freddie, I don't think this is me.' I speeded up dressing; fumbling awkwardly in the dark. Red ants were crawling inside me, nipping and biting. My flesh felt torn and bloody. I wanted to check if I was bleeding, the pain was still so burning, but not with him watching.

'Ok, as you wish. Take care then, dear boy.' He drawled the last words and then leaned over to the ash tray on the bedside unit and stubbed out the cigarette, letting the smoke of his last inhale out in a 'whewww' as he did so. He stood up indolently and started to get dressed himself. I watched awkwardly, unsure what to do now. I was obviously dismissed. It made me feel like a servant who'd just been used for his master's pleasure. I still wanted to cry. I got out of there as quickly as I could, pushing blindly past the waiting couples in the hall.

'About time,' grumbled one guy and barged my shoulder on his way through the open doorway as I exited it. 'Piss off then,' I heard him say to Freddie as he pulled his partner into the room with him. I didn't wait to hear Freddie's retort. Once outside the flat, I tried to ignore the discomfort as I walked swiftly home, struggling with the last few blocks. I hadn't wanted to publically display myself on the tube. I probably looked no different to two hours ago, but I felt like a creature, a foul parody of a human, scarlet letter branded on my forehead – not A for adulteress, like Nathaniel Hawthorne's heroine, A for asshole, like I was.

I virtually threw myself through the front door of my dingy little bedsit. Shutting the door behind me was like shutting out the whole world. At last I could let it all out. Slowly at first, the tears just trickled down my face as I relived the whole scene in my mind, then faster and faster until torrents streamed down my cheeks and my nose ran, sticky and salty into my mouth. I sobbed and heaved, just propped against the front door, barricading myself in. For a fleeting moment, I wanted my sister there, soft and gentle the way she'd felt the night before her wedding; like she cared. Then I shrank back on myself. Who could possibly care about me now?

Who was I? What was I, other than sick and stupid and used? When the weeping stopped, I felt as if I'd been drained. I also felt so dirty, I disgusted even myself. I stood for a long time just running the hot water of the shower over me, standing right under its jet, letting it topple over me and run down my face as if I was still crying. After a while I soaped myself, careful not to touch where I still felt like I was on fire and then just lay rigid on my bed. Eventually I curled into a foetal position and slept. Maybe tomorrow I would awake a different person – one who knew what to do with their life.

Chapter 6:

Two paths meet, 1980-1982

I let my mind travel back to the same time, or thereabouts. I knew that moment of humiliated nothingness too. It was late 1980. I was no longer the callow muscle-bound teenager anxious to prove his virility and manliness through physical prowess. Oh, I could still hold my own. I could fuck and fight with the best of them. I'd just spent nearly eight years doing that. I'd decided at 23 that the army wasn't going to show me any life-truths I wanted to know by then but routine and not knowing what else to do made me hesitant about leaving. It was the downward spiral with my hearing that precipitated the departure for me in the end. When I'd misheard the Sarn't on the parade ground once too often, the barked, 'need your ears testing, boy?' suddenly became a command for a full medical and there was the damning diagnosis on the docs papers right in front of me.

'Moderate hearing loss. Likely to impair ability to respond accurately in noisy situations. Risks associated with this are obvious if in battle conditions. Medical discharge recommended.'

I'd known it was coming. I was aware how often the noise of the world felt more distant to me than it should. Whole conversations often passed me by, or parts of them were deadened or missing, like Mike and Gary. Who wants to admit there is something wrong with them? Especially not when it means their whole life will be turned upside down because of it – even if they are not sure they want that life anymore. All the while I could still hear the Sarn't and his orders I pretended I could carry on, disheartened, disillusioned and disabled. Now of course, it was in black and white. I couldn't. In January 1981 I was medically discharged with bi-lateral hearing loss H4 – noise induced. I was sent home after the med board to wait for the official discharge letter. I waited a further ten months for it to arrive, mooching around home and not knowing what to do with myself. My hearing loss fell short of the threshold for a pension. It was 1dB short of the criteria of 50dB hearing loss. Typical; I'd failed, but not even well enough to be a complete failure.

So I came home from the army with nothing – like I'd joined up – no, actually less than nothing because now my hearing was so bad, at times I struggled to hear any normal conversation. I had good and bad days, but on the bad days, voices were so muffled I had to concentrate hard to make out enough of what they said to reply appropriately. On those days I felt completely exhausted from the sheer effort of prolonged intense concentration by evening. My temper was even shorter than my length of service. The last time I saw Will – that Easter in the diary – was the last time my hearing was normal. The deterioration started not long after that, and in truth shortly after Gary died in Ireland. Someone said to me afterwards that perhaps the two events were linked and it was an emotional response, that I didn't *want* to hear what was said any more. That's just bullshit. Any-one who's ever experienced any form of hearing loss would tell you that the last thing on earth you would choose to do is to become isolated from the world. When you lose one of the main senses – sight or sound – no matter how hard, you are always one step removed from everyone else. You look ostensibly perfect, but when they find out you can't hear, their interest rapidly wanes. I found that a lot with girls. They would be attracted to the physique and the looks – I was good looking then – and then when I explained the hearing loss, I would see their eyes slip away from my face, or look down, and I would know I'd lost them. I got used to it after a while, but it still made me angry – not with the army, but with the shallowness of people in general who equated being less than perfect with less than useless.

Home couldn't really be anywhere but back at Wilverton since I had nothing else. I came back home, but home was very different to the way it had been when I left it. Will wasn't there to start with, and the other lads I'd been mates with were either married; therefore not allowed out with such a bad influence as me, ex-army, and out of work – or they'd long since moved away. The first day back – *home comes the hero* – I wandered my old haunts in Wilverton, even the pub I could now legally go in, and wondered what to do with myself. A couple of week passed and already Mum was getting fed up with me under her feet.

'Why aren't you out getting a job?' She asked me testily one day.

'Can't hear you...' I mouthed back at her pointing to my ears. I could today – perfectly well – but sometimes I could capitalise on it, and when I was being nagged was one of them. No point in nagging if they can't hear you, is it? I rolled off the settee and threw the newspaper on the floor, making for the door. I left before she could complain about the newspaper, already feeling the drag of disillusionment starting to bring me down. There was nothing in the minute Job Centre in town – a token gesture to the town's workforce, pretending the government cared. I strolled into Patel's corner shop to get some fags. The girl behind the counter looked familiar, but I was in a bad mood so I just asked for twenty Marlborough and was about to throw the money on the counter and leave when she called me back. I misheard what she said and replied in a surly fashion.

'Is the change wrong?'

'No, no – it's fine – I said it's Tom, isn't it?'

'Yes,' now I paused and tried to place her. Small, dark haired and with gentle features and a shy air; the vulnerable schoolgirl I'd idly pursued for a while until Tammy had come along.

'Lucy?'

'Yes!' Her response was almost joyful. 'I heard you were back and wondered if I'd see you around.'

'Well, here I am – around – but with nothing to do, but hang around.' Even to me I sounded sarcastic, and I felt ashamed of my tone as I saw her small face drop, and then almost close up like a flower at night. 'Oh, I'm sorry – it's bugging me not having a job – I've been used to being busy, you see.'

'Oh Tom, I do understand. My brother's been out of work for years,' she stopped; obviously realising she'd said the wrong thing.

'It's OK ...'

'I'm sorr...'

We spoke at the same time and the ice broke. The years fell away and there we were at fifteen again, with me trying to persuade her to come to the café or trying to catch her behind the bike shed on the way home again. We laughed and the laughter was warm and encouraging.

'I have a hearing problem,' I said deliberately, testing the water.

'Pardon?' she said and then giggled, 'sorry, that was naughty.' She looked like a cheeky schoolgirl, and somehow, although that response might have annoyed me with some people, it didn't from her. I made a wry face.

'I really do, I'm afraid – it's the artillery fire that damaged it.'

'Oh, Tom, I'm so sorry – I thought you were joking because you misheard me to begin with. You must think me so rude.' She looked mortified and I wanted to make her feel better.

'You couldn't have known. Don't worry, I'm not offended.'

Her face lit up again, like the sun bursting from behind a cloud.

'So, Lucy – how's Mr Lucy?' The old Tom made a reappearance, all charm and swagger.

'Mr Lucy?' She looked mystified.

'Well maybe I should ask "is there a Mr Lucy?"'

'Oh. No.' She looked sheepish, 'I think I'm a bit too serious for the guys around here.'

'Serious? But you've just ploughed straight in with a wicked joke at my expense – how can you be regarded as too serious?' I winked at her.

'Oh, that's because you're Tom, and I feel, well I feel alright with you,' then she cast her eyes down again and blushed. Maybe she didn't feel quite so alright with me after all. 'I mean – I knew you at school, so you accept me as I am.'

"I don't think there's any accepting to do, Lucy, you look pretty great to me.' She blushed even more, so I pressed the advantage home. 'Would you like to go out some time?' The response was just a little too quick, but it was just what I needed. I left feeling like I was riding high all of a sudden, just because I was going on a date with Lucy James.

Things took a turn for the better after that. I found a job at the local electronics factory. It wasn't exactly taxing, but I had one advantage over all the rest, my hearing was already damaged so I didn't suffer from the continual hum of the machines and drone of the equipment. It was blocked out already for me. I suffered the humdrum routine because it earned me enough money, with overtime and extra shifts, to fairly quickly move out of Mum and Dads place and into my own. I was getting under Mum's feet – 'making the house look untidy' was the way she put it, and irritating Dad because for all his good hearing and claimed seniority, he was very aware that as his health failed, so did his strength, and yet mine was still improving. I suppose that element of competitiveness the army ingrains in you dies hard – even in your sixties and ill. Besides, I now had Lucy, and life with her was rapidly becoming all-consuming.

We started off quite slowly for me. I asked her out for a drink, she accepted and after I'd collected her from home, conscious of several sets of eyes watching us as we walked down the narrow path and out of the rickety garden gate, we walked awkwardly down the road side by side. I was starting to wonder if my old style had failed me or whether she really fancied me as she remained so quiet on the walk to the pub, but decided to persevere – well I had nothing to lose currently, did I? We reached the Rose and Crown and I pushed at the chipped paint door, standing aside for her to walk in ahead of me. My gaze flicked upwards to the doorway and the same licensee hovered above us as when I'd been sixteen and regularly barred. I wondered if he would remember me too – me, the cocky little bastard who'd tried it on as a teenager, underage, but swaggering with the self-confidence only a teenage boy can muster, even when they know they are breaking the law. Immediately the typical smells of the pub enveloped me. The lingering haze of smoke hung in the warm air like a heat haze on a dusty day, and the fruity smell of beer slops reminded me of the matey camaraderie I'd shared with army comrades, looking for a promise of more interesting things to plum than the bottom of a beer glass.

A sense of sexual anticipation kicked off in me almost immediately and I ushered Lucy in with more enthusiasm than I'd felt on the way there. She walked hesitantly passed me and as she did so, her very nervousness switched on my automatic pilot inclination to score. I pushed my way confidently towards the bar. You don't argue with the solidity that army muscle gives a physique. There is an almost bestial sense of domination exuding from standing legs astride, chin jutting. Alpha male: leader of the pack. *Wanna challenge me? No, I didn't think so. Move over mate.* I didn't need to say it. They knew it from just one cursory glance at me. The path to the bar cleared and Lucy followed me, mistress with her master.

I looked at her questioningly. She smiled sweetly back at me. I returned the smile and waited; so did she. The landlord became shifty.

'Yes folks, what can I get you?' I raised my eyebrows at Lucy, and she blushed.

'Oh, I see, sorry – I'm not used to ...' I took pity on her flustered red face.

'It's ok – what would you like – he can wait – he's providing the service, not us.'

She threw me a grateful look and hurriedly added her order.

'Cinzano and lemonade, please.' I couldn't quite hide my smile. Such a typical girl drink, I'd bought so many of them over the years, and on the way to a fumble or more.

Somehow, though I didn't want to just fumble with Lucy. I wanted something solid in my life for once. The little embarrassed glance and the flushed cheeks had made me feel protective towards her in the way I'd not felt before. Her face was sweet. The thought crossed and slipped to the back of my mind even before I acknowledged it and then I spent the rest of the evening trying to work out how it made me feel. By the time we walked home, much more at ease with each other after several drinks and an evenings' conversation, albeit at times repetitive because my hearing dipped in and out and she had to patiently repeat her questions and responses when it did, but without any apparent irritation, the sense of protectiveness had acquired an additional dimension of gratefulness too.

I didn't try anything on at all that first evening; I didn't even want to, and that surprised me too. It wasn't that I didn't fancy her and sexual satisfaction could have readily stepped in. It was just that for once I wanted to show respect. As we walked back home, exactly the same route as on the way there and still side by side, our hands brushed and almost as if drawn together by magnetism, her smaller hand slipped into my broader, harder one. It seemed like the perfect interlock between two machine parts, clicked into place like the barrel had clicked smoothly on my SLR; uniform and complete. I suppose our future was sealed at that precise moment, as our hands locked, just neither of us knew it then.

The weeks and months slipped past in a welter of evenings out, small strategic advances on my part, and if I'd but known

133

it, cleverly engineered rebuffs on hers. Ironically I thought she was too naïve to realise how clever a strategy she was unwittingly employing in politely and sweetly putting me off, until the building frustration urged me to reach some conclusion. It was like always nearing a climax and never quite achieving it. Deftly she would bring me on with small encouragements – a deep-tongued kiss full of wayward promise, followed by a demure goodnight, or a chance for hands to slip beyond permitted boundaries into the coveted pleasures beyond the stocking top, or under the soft laced trim of her panties, but then a strident call from her mam would bring the conclusion all too unsatisfactorily quickly with a 'I'd better go, sorry.' Eventually the only way forward was the time-honoured one and I found myself steeling my nerve to propose. Shit was I really going to do that? I surveyed my life as it stood. Good physique, good health and a job, even if it was a mundane and unutterably boring one. Against that, poor school grades, hard of hearing and still in my own backyard. I had a good brain but I'd not used it to advantage until now. Realistically I wasn't such a catch after all. The realisation itself stung. How had I got to here so quickly – stuck in a rut and less than first choice? Actually Lucy was a good option when I looked at it that way – respectable, with a job, sweet-natured and not bad looking. The date was set. By the time I was twenty five, I was married.

I invited all my old mates and so did she – or at least so it seemed as most of Wilverton High came out of the woodwork for the event. My mates were largely those from the army, apart from Will. I wasn't going to ask Will to begin with as somehow I felt less than easy with him ever since I'd last seen him when he'd taken on the head of the family role at Fran's wedding. We'd met for a drink after years of not doing much other than exchange the odd letter and he'd spent most of the evening seeming distracted, not answering me straight away and when he did, it was so obliquely it hadn't felt as if he'd answered at all. I'd started to talk to him about Mike and the Lynx accident, feeling that here was someone who would understand. That conversation about the Vincent song stayed at the back of my mind, but his eyes had become hooded and far away when I looked deep into them for affirmation. I'd clammed up and the conversation between us had slowed to a trickle. Our boyhood friendship suddenly had seemed a long way away and I wasn't sure who I was talking to. I hadn't been surprised we'd not managed another drink before my leave ended. I wondered if being at university made him look down on me. That didn't quite seem to fit the picture but it was the nearest I could come to it. I remembered the conversation we'd had over the jukebox when we were about sixteen, and I'd first remarked on his different attitude to mine.

'How did you get so smart, and me so dumb?'

'You're not dumb. We're just different.' Yes, we were very different now, and however that difference was composed, it set a hefty divide between us. Regardless of that, he was my oldest friend, the person, apart from Jack, who I felt some indistinct but decisive link with. When I'd needed to tell someone about Gary's death, it had still been him. Despite that awkward drink out, when I numbered who I trusted, it was on one hand and two fingers – Will and Jack. I wasn't dumb – far from it. Since my hearing loss had escalated, I'd become more introspective, started to devour books almost voraciously – a chance to live in a world where sight was more important than sound. As a result my vocabulary was now excellent and my understanding of concepts once I would merely have dismissed as 'complicated' was lively and curious, but no-one expected that of a squaddie, so it was easier to maintain the façade of burly thickhead and keep my own counsel unless I thought the listener was truly listening to me. Lucy was one of the few I included in that category currently. I'd thought Will would be too, but our last meeting had made me feel nervous around him. I invited him anyway, and was surprised when he accepted, and pleased when he came, but yet diffident when I greeted him outside the church after the ceremony as the local throng milled around us and the photographer directed this person and that into their set place in the wedding images.

'Hey, man – congratulations.' He clapped me heartily on the back but his eyes seemed to belie the words. Almond blanks, not the warm brown I remembered from our boyhood adventures. This Will was not quite the Will I knew, but I accepted the sentiment and allowed myself to be pulled away into my pre-ordained set of wedding images. It was the brides' day after all, and I was doing my first husbandly duty by pandering to her. I didn't see a great deal more of him until the reception was well-advanced and I and the best man had downed enough pints to make us unsteady, even despite our hardened army training. I briefly wondered, as I noticed from a distance that Will was talking politely to my mam, if maybe the distanced feel had derived from sour grapes – should he have been my best man? When I'd co-opted Jack, it had been because he'd seemed the obvious choice – closer to me, in both proximity and experience. Will was my oldest friend though, and one I felt a strange tie to even if it was diffused by passing years and vastly different lives. Alcohol makes you do and say the things that you should bury deep, deep under the veneer of control you try to maintain, but unfortunately discard too easily when alcohol has stripped away your self-control. The brief thought enlarged into a looming fear, the obsessional paranoia that only a drunk can feel when faced with a relatively minor and unimportant issue. Fuelled with beer, I transformed the idle thought into a self-confessed truth. I should have asked him to be my best man. What could I do to apologise – make it up to him?

Until then the wedding had been a typical provincial affair. Bride and grooms family had sat on the right sides of the church. The ushers had led the guests to the right sides and handed out the right hymn sheets. The choristers had appeared, with freshly scrubbed pink cheeks and tousled hair, and sung the right words, not the school boy substitutions we had all enjoyed so much in our time, 'Father unto wee-wee raise' – snigger, snigger and so on, and now the reception was going relatively smoothly too. The best man's speech had been thankfully short, no-one's Great Uncle Dick had insulted anyone's Auntie Fanny, and the bridesmaids hadn't started bitching yet. As the service wore on the smell of furniture polish had made my post-stag night slightly hung-over state only mildly nauseous but now that seemed to have been completely rectified by the hair of the dog – well, the whole pack of hounds really. I should have left it there, but I didn't. Stupid bastard, I set the scene for the rest of my wedding day and walked onto the battlefield.

'Hey, Will, howsh you doin'?' He spun round and the almond eyes narrowed as he took in my slightly dishevelled and flushed face state.

'I'm good. How's the bridegroom though?' He placed the slightest extra emphasis on the word 'bridegroom' and something in me fired up at it. He was judging me again. *How did you get so smart, and me, so dumb?*

'I'm jush fine, buddy – so don' you worry 'bout'it.' The belligerence was ridiculous. I knew even as I over-reacted that he hadn't said anything to take issue with. Why was I? His manner was mild, to say the least, almost as if he was actually taking a step back from me, even though he stood his ground.

'OK, that's good. You seem to be having a nice time – that's good – it is your wedding day after all, enjoy it.'

'I fuckin' will, *buddy.'* I deliberately clapped him hard on the back, mirroring his friendly slap earlier, and he shuddered at the force. I'd forgotten until then how slight he was compared to me. Will was just Will. I tended to forget anything about him physically except those almond eyes, which now regarded me coldly. 'And don't you be judgin' me.

138

You ain't here and you ain't done none of the stuff I done, in your mimsy university place.' The hitherto unacknowledged sense of inferiority took over, repeating again the dumb connotation to the remembered conversation, and consciously making me emphasis an uncultured accent and attitude I didn't really have. It was almost like sticking two fingers up at him – there you are *buddy* – if you think I'm a different class to hoity-toity you and your pretentious university education, then I will be. Come and live in the REAL world.

He seemed genuinely surprised at the outburst and interjected.

'Tom, I ...' and then shook his head. 'I don't want to fight – I wish you well. I hope you and Lucy will be very happy together – and I'm not judging or, or ... anything.' He took a step back and I immediately felt stupid.

'Oh mate, I've jush had too much to drink.' My head started to swim and my legs lost their solidity. I staggered and Will held out a steadying hand.

'Shall I get you to your bride?' He suggested. 'Mrs should be looking after Mr now, shouldn't she?' Without really registering I'd done so, I found I was clutching the shoulder I'd clapped aggressively and he was guiding me towards Lucy, whose radiant smile turned to dismay as she surveyed my greenish hue.

'Oh dear,' she said ineffectually. To Will, 'what do I do?' He shrugged his shoulders as if to wash his hands of the situation and then obviously changed his mind as he propelled me to a chair and plopped me in it. I wondered how he'd managed to manoeuvre me so easily, given the difference in our stature. I didn't realise then that I was still hanging onto him for dear life. That only dawned when I sat down heavily and pulled him with me. His face ended up within a couple of inches of mine and I found myself looking straight into his hypnotic slanting eyes. The patterns in them whorled and reformed as we gazed at each other, the closest we'd ever been. I smelt the vague scent that lingered on him, musk and something heady yet fresh I couldn't place. My head spun with a mixture of proximity and an odd sense of desire, no doubt prompted by the smell. Apples – apples back in the orchard. That was it. I couldn't drag my eyes away from his as the world spun and the disco noise and wedding guest chatter all merged into a kaleidoscope of sound and colour, mixed with the heavy perfume. Then just as suddenly it all went black.

I emerged briefly from the depths of night to be vaguely aware that someone – Lucy, Jack, Will – whomever, was expertly stripping away my tie, shirt and trousers to leave me spread-eagled, just in Y-fronts and socks, on the giant bed in the honeymoon suite of the hotel the reception was being held at. Voices faded in and out of the background, Lucy's high-pitched and anxious, Jack's rumbling, Will's soothing. I rolled over and reached violently, vomiting beer and wedding breakfast over the side of the bed. When had I done this before? A memory stirred vaguely in my subconscious. Many years ago; many lives ago – I'd done this before with someone who'd cared for me and made me feel safe. Will – it was Will. I wanted the hovering presence to be Will. It wasn't. It was Lucy. I passed out until morning.

The sun streamed through the window in the same way as it had all those years ago when I was about to join up. The same hung over and weak feeling left me wishing the day was anything but dawning. Was I about to join up again? I rolled over weakly to find Lucy fast asleep beside me and the previous day came flooding back. Aw shit, I was married. I remained on my side observing her as she slept, lips slightly pursed and blowing out tiny little 'whooo's'. She was pretty, even with no make-up on, and her face slack from sleep. It could be worse, I supposed – and she was kind – or had been to me throughout the time I'd known her, even at school. I realised with shame that I didn't love her. That feeling seemed to be locked away, just out of reach, but it could be worse. Ok, the next phase of Tom's life was underway; Tom, the married man. I was ashamed of my performance the night before; I would make it up to her. I couldn't remember all that I'd said and done, but I was aware that it was vaguely inappropriate on a number of levels. Maybe it would be forgiven because of the alcohol. I waited for Lucy to wake up, turning over what I could remember of what I'd said and done in my head as I did. The strange moment when I had stared straight into Will's eyes, and felt my head spin, wouldn't leave me. It was that which bothered me most. Oh, what the hell. It was done now. Lucy waking up distracted me from pursuing the memory and trying to categorise it. I had been working my way towards this moment of fruition for months now – had even given up my liberty for it – I wasn't going to waste it on trying to make some confusing notion make sense. As Lucy stirred, so did I, running my hands over the body which was now – according to the church – mine. Finally I took possession.

Married life was a mixture of humdrum and happy. The job at the factory continued, the weekend jaunts to the pub continued and monotony continued too. It was broken by the satisfaction of having my own personal toy in Lucy, always happy to please and always keen to see me happy. That in itself was gratifying. Whoever devalues marriage hasn't taken account of the easy comfort that familiarity lends to two people and how reassuring that can be – even for those who hadn't thought they needed reassurance. I'd always regarded myself as self-contained and independent, needing no-one. Being married to Lucy was the first time I'd understood that even the most self-reliant of people are made more so simply because they have someone who validates that perception of themselves by rating them above everyone else. I suppose you could call it love. I'm not sure if I came to love Lucy at some stage – certainly it isn't the understanding of love that I have come to since, but as it was, it was sincere and genuine and a bonus for me at the time. Unfortunately, when you regularly have something good at your disposal without question or payment, you take it for granted eventually and then you devalue it yourself. I knew Lucy would eventually raise the idea of starting a family and for a while I fended it off with the usual old arguments – not enough money, need to get settled, wanting to get a better job, we're still young – there's plenty of time – and she patiently accepted them all for a year or so, but after a while her hints became more insistent and her sighs when her monthly came round heavier and more obvious. The writing was rapidly appearing on the wall, and as I had with the wedding, I found myself bending under the pressure, taking the easy route. I don't think women do it intentionally; it is just their inbuilt programming – like a washing machine going into spin cycle. Once you click the controls into the right position, the points on the cycle are inevitable and so is the outcome of the clean but wet washing. For Lucy, the spin cycle started when we got married and the inevitable conclusion was clean but wet nappies, in her view.

We forgot about being careful and watching out for the wrong days of her monthly cycle – they turned instead into the right days of her monthly cycle – the right days to get pregnant. I expected to find the yoke becoming heavier round my neck shortly after that but surprisingly nothing happened. She continued to count off the monthly menstruation cycles and I started to relax a little. In fact it was more sex than less, so what was I complaining about? I knew that by contrast, whereas I breathed a muted sigh of relief each month when she came out of the bathroom with a downcast expression, her mood was becoming lower each time. I did feel guilty as I hid my satisfaction, but hoped that with each new possession we were able to afford because there weren't dozens of nappies to wash and demanding mouths to feed, and after every foreign holiday or lavish night out possible as we had no ties to keep us at home, she would come to accept that this was much better than the drudgery of looking after hordes of snotty kids. She didn't. I saw it coming again, the embarrassed but determined raising of the issue of *why* she wasn't getting pregnant.

'Sometimes it just doesn't happen for some people,' I said.

"We're not just *some people*,' she replied, and her mouth turned down at the corners. I knew she was trying not to cry and my throat tightened. I didn't like seeing her sad like that. It was the one thing I couldn't cope with – it made me feel guilty again – maybe because I acknowledged deep down that I didn't care enough about her and her feelings and so when she was genuinely sad, I had to accept that I wasn't trying all that hard to change it. Conscience; it's responsible for some of the best and worst of things that you do. I wished I'd applied it better with Lucy and maybe we wouldn't have been in this situation. Maybe I would have been honest enough to admit I'd been carried away with the desire to conquer without wanting the responsibility of government too, but I'd laxly taken on marriage and it seemed I was going to saunter further into the mire here because conscience was reminding me I wasn't treating her the way someone who genuinely loved her would. She proposed seeking advice. I grudgingly agreed.

The trip to the GP was probably one of the first truly embarrassing experiences I've ever had. When you have your army medicals, it was simply double-checking that you were still A1. You cough, your balls bounce in the right way and off you go; certified normal. Here it was to find out if that was really so – or worse, why potentially I wasn't performing as a normal man should. It reminded me of the hearing loss and the medical then. Outwardly I looked fine, inside, I was faulty – damaged. Was my very manhood – my ability to reproduce also faulty? Very little happened at that first appointment, just a referral to the fertility clinic at the local hospital, but I already felt judged and found wanting. We trailed along to the next appointment at the hospital; me sheepishly hoping no-one would spot us there, and Lucy barely able to contain her excitement. She was convinced that the answer to our prayers was here. For me it was like walking into an alternative hell. The walls of the waiting room were plastered with posters proclaiming the benefits of Vitamin B and breast feeding, and pictures of modern day Madonna's with their chubby cherubs – all insensitively reinforcing to the waiting clientele that this was what they *hadn't* got.

Our first appointment was two-fold; first a 'chat' with the consultant, in which we had to detail the intricacies of our sex life. I felt like telling him to fuck off when he wanted to know how long we remained 'engaged post-coitus'. It made me feel I was no more than an animal – like the dogs you sometimes see, stuck together, male covering bitch, whilst the bitch is fertilised. I had a mental image of myself and Lucy, half-dog, half-human, in the same position and was revolted. Was making a child – another life, to be reduced to mere mechanics? All the fucking I'd done as a squaddie now took on a different form in my mind too. I viewed the old me with disgust. When I was asked to go and 'perform' into the small plastic container given to me by the nurse, I completed the bestial dog act with another image of me dressed in circus attire, like a prancing dag, complete with tutu and fancy pointed Pierrot's hat. I looked at her uncomprehendingly.

'There are magazines in there if you need them,' she added, gesturing to the half-open door in front of me. I remained where I was, trying to piece together what I was expected to do as Lucy was led off to another curtained space to be 'examined'. The nurse took pity on me. 'Did Mr Hassan not explain to you?'

'He said I needed to produce in the pot?' I left the question in the statement even as it started to dawn on me what I had to produce in the pot. How stupid of me – when we'd been discussing such intimately embarrassing details, I hadn't understood the euphemisms he'd so confusingly switched to when telling me what I had to do. Why be so explicit in one breath and so ambiguous in the next? I followed up the statement-question with a further request for clarification from the pragmatic nurse. 'I have to ...' and made the well-known hand gesture for wanking.

'Yes.' She pursed her lips and ushered me into the room, handing me a sheet of paper as she did so. I wondered how long I had to work up any inclination to do anything, let alone 'produce' as I stood in the small clinical room. In front of me was the pile of magazines she'd referred to, beckoning from the chair, which I suppose was the one concession to comfort in the room. On the wall opposite the door was a washbasin, with a mirror over it. Did they really want me to watch myself wank? Underneath was a bin with the yellow top announcing it was for 'clinical waste only' and next to it an accompanying black lidded one, labelled 'domestic waste'. Which one would my soiled tissue go into when I wiped myself clean I wondered, and shit – how did I get it to go in the pot and not over my hand? Did I take my trousers off? Was that what the chair was for – trousers and Y-fronts? Or did I just drop them round my knees? Either way if the nurse walked in before I'd finished the job in hand it would be humiliating. Standing in front of the mirror, pot clutched in my right hand and instructions in the left, I appreciated the wry humour of 'job in hand' for a brief moment, before straightening my face and actually getting on with the job in hand instead. I settled for dropping my trousers and y-fronts in the end, hoping it wouldn't take long. Having read the instruction sheet – very simple really, *jerk off, fill the pot, put the lid on and give it to the nurse before going back to the waiting room*, I perched the pot on the ledge by the wash basin, lid off, ready, and flicked through one of the magazines. When you're turned on, it's odd how you think nothing at all about getting an erection, or how to get an erection. When you're not, it's like an impossible task. The photo's in the magazine were explicit, some really hard-core – wow, how did they get access to this on the NHS – was there a slush fund somewhere called fertility filth? Who went out and bought it? I imagined the groomed and suave Dr Hassan shiftily palming one of the titles and smuggling it into the clinic under his jacket,

'I've got it Nurse Hardy.'

'Oh, good – is it the one where she's on top after rubbing herself with butter?'

'No, but it's better than that; they are playing with dildo's.'

The whole thing was tasteless. I felt about it like I now felt about all the shags I'd managed to line up for myself during my army days when we got a twenty-four hour pass and were just looking for some fun. It was demeaning. It made me feel dirty. Why did we have to feel dirty and a failure simply to do what every other couple assumed was their right to do – have a child? No wonder it took me nearly an hour to even get hard enough to try manipulating myself. Oddly enough, as my thoughts roamed here and there, trying to find fruitful avenues to encourage desire, it was the musky smell of Will's aftershave at the wedding reception, and that odd intense moment as we stared directly into each other's eyes when I collapsed onto the chair and dragged him with me, that produced the goods. I didn't even try to analyse why. I was just relieved that it happened and I could get out of the stiflingly obscene little room with its grotesque magazines and bare walls that seemed to be waiting for me to splatter semen up them, and yet also taunting me that I wouldn't be man enough to be able to. Lucy was waiting for me outside.

'Did you manage?'

'Yes, thanks.' I pushed her ahead of me back to the waiting room. I wasn't saying any more about this nasty little moment, regardless of her questioning eyes.

The results were conclusive when they finally came back. Apparently Lucy was ovulating, but I wasn't producing normal sperm. Her mucus wasn't acidic – quite hospitable to sperm actually but my sperm were non-motile.

'What does that mean, please?' I asked, but already understanding that the problem lay with me. Dr Hassan was polite but precise.

'It means you produce sperm, but they don't go anywhere. They are lazy. They have to … swoosh … 'He made a little swimming motion with his hands. 'But they don't, they stay basking in the sunshine like this,' and he added a typical sun-worshipper pose to emphasise the already humiliating point. 'They have to be able to swim all the way up your wife's vagina, into her womb and find the little egg that slips down her fallopian tube every month and *boof.'* He made another little action like something exploding. I felt like he was treating me like a child, listening to a simplified version of the facts of life and I resented it. My sperm may not work properly, but that didn't make me mentally defective. The point was clear though; she was ok, but I wasn't.

'Male infertility,' Dr Hassan explained glibly. 'It happens to many couples. You can wait and see – you're both young, maybe we can give you exercises to help them improve, and you can loosen your trousers – he eyed my tight fitting jeans and I felt myself flushing. Or we could put you on our IVF programme if nothing has happened naturally after a couple of years – it is up to you.' He must have seen Lucy's horrified expression at the 'couple of years', and always alive to private patients, added, 'or you could go privately …'

149

Hook, line and sinker. What else could I do? Lucy eyed me and said nothing, but I knew behind the veiled look, she was thinking 'this is your fault.' On our way home was the first time she was sharp with me when I commented sarcastically what a wonderful experience it had been.

'Well, it's not exactly my fault, is it?' She replied pointedly.

Our first private appointment was the next week and we joined the programme the week after. Lucy's face beamed, my heart sank. It cost a fortune, and still made me no less of a failure.

Chapter 7:

Creation, 1982-83

'I need my next injection.' Lucy waved the syringe at me. She wriggled her ass and despite the clinical attack I had to make to deliver the injection, desire raised its head, but I followed the routine as prescribed. I jabbed the needle into the rounded cheek she was offering me and pushed the plunger until the contents of the syringe were all gone. Removing the needle carefully, I slapped her rump where it had been inserted and playfully bent over her to whisper in her ear.

'That was the slap, now how about the tickle.' She straightened up sharply, pushing me back to a standing position as she did so. Her lips were pursed. I knew that look well now, and my temporary good mood sunk back into the doldrums.

'Stop it Tom, you know it's not allowed whilst I'm taking the drugs. What if it interfered with them?'

'Exactly how would it interfere with them?'

She swung round to face me, serious expression pinned firmly in place, repressing my levity.

'Well I might get pre...' she stopped and we regarded each other. I finished the sentence for her.

'Pregnant?'

'Yes. But you know it mustn't happen that way, now – the drugs would have made me over-ovulate – it would be risky. We might end up with a multiple birth.'

'I thought you once said the more the merrier.' I countered, suddenly feeling far from aroused, more like I wanted a fight.

'Tom, please, we've gone all through this before.'

'I know, I know.' I turned away and collected the syringe from where I'd tossed it, carefully ejecting the needle tip into the yellow box labelled 'sharps', as directed by the ever-present instructions sheets. Now we were on the programme we had instructions for everything. Instructions for drug-taking, diet, sleep patterns, timings and most particularly – for sex – or rather abstinence from it – in case it 'interfered'.

Whereas there had been compensations for working the boring shifts in the factory, giving up my freedom to become the steady married man, pandering to the wishes of one person over and above my own, now Lucy was firmly on the baby trail and dragging me along with her, the compensations were all gone. The good sex life, the evenings out, and the indulgent holidays had all disappeared as the cost of the programme became higher and higher both financially and also to our relationship. The once soft-faced sweet voiced Lucy was more often hard-nosed and sharp tongued with me. I was the cause of her having to put up with the injections, indignities and infertility. I wondered at times whether she hated me or merely now tolerated me.

Our routine was governed rigidly by the need to stick with Lucy's timings – she must be injected now, had to have her blood tests to check on hormone levels here, mustn't have sex then – and *then* was actually most of the time. Frustration and irritation were all steadily growing in me. I could control them most of the time to achieve what would make Lucy happy, but increasingly there were times when I wondered how much longer I would put up with it and would it make me happy too? A reply as equally sharp as the needle sprang to mind but rather than voice it and make Lucy cry – a by-product of the massive hormone doses we were injecting into her as part of the IVF programme was a rapidly yo-yoing emotional response, I made a speedy exit instead.

'I'm going down the pub, ok?' I went without waiting for the ok, it didn't matter at the moment if she agreed or not. I was going. On entering the pub, I was immersed in the comforting smell of beer and fags and the maleness of the sports pages and banter about the dogs and the footie. Babies and IVF and female hysteria were all safely left far behind in the unsatisfactory world I now designated 'home'. I was back with the lads here, and that wasn't bad at all. Ironically today, when I could least do with anything more confusing, there it was – at the bar, surrounded by the lads; Susie Evans. An insistent voice in my head said, 'don't' but I was feeling belligerent. *Don't fucking tell me 'don't'*, I thought. I was having far too much of proscriptive 'don'ts from Lucy, let alone having my own head start to say it too. I did. I walked straight up to the bar, slipping in neatly behind her as the other guys made way for me. My army physique still did sufficient talking for me when needed. I poked her unceremoniously in the ribs, knowing as I did so it was completely out of keeping with the behaviour this tall, willowy glamour puss would be expecting from all the guys, but that in itself would single me out, and I wasn't taking any more hits from anyone that day.

She swung round.

'Who did that?'

'Did what?' I smiled smoothly at her as her irritated gaze came to rest on me.

'You – you did it. You poked me!'

'Oh, believe me lady – you'd know if I'd poked you ...' The other guys guffawed appreciatively, and I continued for my audience, 'but I'm happy to oblige if need be ...' She reddened and was about to deliver her put-down – I knew Susie of old – but then recognition took over.

'Tom – Tom Wilson?'

'Susie, gorgeous Susie,' I responded, and added a charming smile for good measure, 'and definitely as gorgeous as ever ...' Luckily for me – or maybe, unluckily, I don't know now – but my hearing was on a good day and everything was crystal clear. It allowed me to banter with her, drawing the attention away from all the rest of her entourage. Let's face it, maybe I had dodgy hearing, and suffered from 'unexplained infertility' but ostensibly the goods on show were pristine – and a head and shoulders above any of the rest of the throng in the pub. I knew the banter would go where I wanted it. I still had the ram radar installed from my army days, and my instincts were sharpened from abstinence. I'd always fancied her, and if she was now receptive to overtures, I was definitely ready to play a concert for her.

'Do you want to go somewhere quieter than here? Relive old school memories?'

'Okay tiger,' and we were away. The little voice that had said *don't*, repeated the exhortation, adding, *what about Lucy?* I didn't want to hear it. Lucy was too wrapped up in her injections and baby-making programme. Where was I in all of that? This was something for ME, and it wouldn't last, anyway. Susie had made it clear, as she was holding court, that she was only passing through, and a cold, hard version of me decided there and then to grab a piece of the action as she passed my way. Lucy need never know – what the eye didn't see, the heart didn't grieve over, did it? I was doing everything else Lucy wanted. This little thing would be forgivable in the grand scheme of things, surely. I forgave myself just in case and Susie and I set off on the journey towards the sins I'd just given myself absolution to commit.

It wasn't particularly romantic, and it didn't even seem that significant an encounter at the time other than in its sexual intensity. I'd always fancied her and she'd always been unattainable for me – exactly why she decided to allow me the satisfaction of the kill that evening, I don't know. Maybe I was a little bit of 'rough' for the night, or the curiosity I felt about her was reciprocated without me knowing it. It was just sex though, as good as it was. We drove out of town, and to the next one for some privacy. I owed Lucy that amount of respect. In the next town there was a passably good 'trattoria' and we slipped into a quiet table at the back of the restaurant. Part of the evening passed companionably in fact. We did relive old school days, and laughed over the awful teachers, the nicknames we'd given them, the dire homework, the boring afternoons glued to the dusty wooden desks as the sun beat tauntingly against the window panes and we remained trapped inside listening to the drone of yet another math's lesson on equilateral triangles or simultaneous equations. We mixed up the names to make it funnier – simultaneous triangles or equilateral equations.

'God they were boring!' She exclaimed. 'And you always sat next to Lucy not me, so I couldn't even flirt.'

'You always made it pretty clear I wasn't *allowed* to sit next to you!'

'Oh, you men – it was a challenge, didn't you get it? Why are you all so dumb?' It reminded me disconcertingly of Will for a moment and I lost focus on Susie whilst Will's almond eyes drew me magnetically into them. There was a little safe house I kept for him my mind. Surveying the street it was placed in, other people came and went in my head, but I noticed that Will appeared to live there permanently. How odd. I allowed my attention to wander as I traced the shape of his eyes, wondering why anyone should have such unusual eyes. Strange – discomforting eyes, yet beautiful too. They made me want to stare.

'Tom?' I realised Susie had asked me a question, and I'd completely missed it; for once not from bad hearing, but from lack of attention.

'Sorry.' I cupped my hand behind my ear to imply I hadn't heard. The hearing issue could work both ways sometimes — and the sympathy card sometimes had immediate and gratifying effect as well as putting people off. On this occasion it was to be my 'get out of jail free' card with Susie as it masked lack of attention, and she played the card for me perfectly.

'Oh poor you, I forgot for a moment; your poor ears. You're so perfect otherwise. Let me make it up to you somehow ...' The invitation was so apparent there was barely anything else I needed to do.

'Somehow?'

'However you'd like.'

Well, I know what I'd like, but do nice girls do that?'

'Who ever said I was a nice girl ...'

'I'll get the bill, not nice naughty girl.' She giggled.

We went up to our room in the lift, barely able to keep our hands off each other, but having to display some decorum as there was a women with her twin daughters, about five years old, I guessed, in it too. I idly wondered if they were naturally conceived or the result of infertility treatment as I observed them through narrowed eyes. Shit — why did I have to think about that now? Bloody IVF and babies — it took over everything, and it made me feel guilty about Lucy too. Damn! I wasn't going to let her affect this. If she wouldn't act like a wife – why shouldn't I look elsewhere? I knew I was wrong but I didn't care. Conscience – amazing how you can shut it off.

The room was standard hotel issue, but that didn't matter. We weren't interested in the surroundings. Susie was long and lean, with an almost perfect tan that must have come from a bottle, because there were no strap marks, no uneven shades and her toes and fingers nails were polished to a high gloss in bright scarlet. An exotic butterfly in the wilds of Wilverton; she was a 'painted lady' compared to Lucy's 'cabbage white'. Even if this hadn't been adultery, she would have had a sense of the forbidden. She peeled her jumper and skirt off without any help from me and draped herself across the double bed, clad only in bra, panties and stockings, rising sensuously from her black knee length stiletto boots.

'Wow, kinky,' I commented admiringly. I was across the room in a couple of strides and she ramped up the playfulness by inviting me to 'ride 'em cowboy!' Sex with someone new to you is usually a bit of a fumbling affair, no matter how much you fancy each other, but with Susie it was a seamless progression from attraction, to intent, to climax. As I approached her she slid onto her side, one arm under her head, the other caressing sinuously up and down the uppermost hip and thigh as if it was me doing it. I wanted it to be me. Her skin had a glossy sheen – almost as if it had been lightly oiled but as soon as I laid a hand on it, I knew that was simply its natural texture, silky and smooth. It invited me to slide further and further and higher and higher. I didn't resist. She rolled flat onto her back, and beckoned to me. I stripped off my clothes, tossing them on the floor, and ending up in just bulging y-fronts.

'Oh get rid of those,' she said laughingly and tugged at the elasticated band. She pushed them over my buttocks and I wriggled free. Then she lay back again, arching her back, which emphasised her breasts. I slipped two hands into the hollow between her back and the bed and unhooked her bra, whisking it off and revelling in the way her breasts bounced free. Two soft mounds topped with a rose bud nipple like a sexual fairy cupcake, inviting me to eat. I took one of the nipples in my mouth and felt it harden rapidly as she moaned and arched against me again. Lying full length on top of her, I slipped into position so I could enter her and started to pull her panties down over her thighs, but she stopped me.

'Oh no, tiger,' she said. 'We have a lot of other things to do first.' She pushed me off of her and I rolled sideways, unresisting but wondering if I'd done something wrong. I wanted to pull her back, but something told me to allow her to lead. She slid gracefully off the bed and stood in front of me as I half sat up to watch her. Gyrating slowly, she swung her hips in a shallow figure of eight, thrusting her cunt towards me and then withdrawing again, as if mimicking the actual act of sex. I made a move as if to rise but she motioned me back and continued her dance. She circled around the bed, making me crane my neck as she moved behind me. Knowing she was there, just out of reach made the hair rise on the back of my neck, promising, promising … Then she moved slowly back into full view, swaying and circling sensuously. I knew my jaw was hanging slackly as I watched; all focus on the one central point of her body – of all bodies. I thought I'd been excited before but this was far better than simply throwing off my clothes and fucking her. I wanted her like I'd wanted no other woman, and the blood throbbed through me, making me feel as if I was pulsating. As she circled back in front of me I looked along the line of my body and she poised in front of me as if her crotch was hovering directly over the tip of my cock. She must have known that it looked from my viewpoint as if I was about to enter her and she remained there grinding away slightly, while I imagined the sensation of sliding in, and her clenching around me.

With one smooth movement she stripped away her panties but put her finger to her lips, then waved it from side to side as if to still caution me against movement. I stretched back a little further on the bed and waited, heart pounding and stomach molten. I could smell her perfume mixing with the heavy scent of her silvery secretions. They glistened at the top of her thighs, like small drops of dew caught in the flush of early morning sun. I could almost taste their sweet salt essence on my tongue as I moistened my dry lips and took in an involuntary gasp of air as I imagined the feel of her around me. Desire made my head spin as the blood rushed away from it. She suddenly knelt in front of me, taking me completely by surprise as she took me in her mouth, flicking her tongue lightly over me in small gossamer strokes, like the painted lady was teasing me. I couldn't stop the moan that escaped as the ecstasy of the moment overwhelmed me, desperate for her to push down, hard onto me. I waited, breath held as the sweet sensation rolled over and around me, 'oh please, please ...' Then her mouth engulfed me completely, hot and wet, making me shudder in an agony of pleasure.

'Oh God, stop that ... Stop that ...' I knew I would come if she didn't and I didn't want it this way – I had waited far too long. She stopped, but then all I wanted was for her to start again, but more than that, I wanted her, wanted to impale her, to pound into her, fill her completely, until the explosion of light and heat and the sensation of pumping, pumping overtook me. I wanted to shout out in the midst of the climax, but the only word that came to me was 'Will'.

I drove home both sated and disgusted with myself. I knew it was likely I'd never see her again, but nor did I want to. It was more than I'd ever experienced physically with Lucy – more than I'd ever experienced with any woman, and somehow I would have liked to have shared how I felt about it, but knew I couldn't. The month came to an end and we completed the IVF cycle. I took Lucy to her appointment for egg retrieval and then brought her home, tender from the surgical intrusion, and groggy from the anaesthetic. She went straight to bed, shutting me out. I turned on the TV, and shut her out. I wanted to block out the uncomfortably intense memories of the last few days too. We waited impatiently for the next day or so for news from the hospital whether any of the eggs had fertilised, and finally the news was good. Lucy spent the rest of the day in thinly disguised excitement until it was time to go back and have the egg replacement completed.

She was full of breathless plans 'if this time works'. I couldn't bring myself to dash the budding hope that I'd seen so many times before. I remained tight-lipped on the drive there and on the way back, but it didn't matter, Lucy had more than enough to say for the both of us.

Then came the worst part of the wait altogether. Fourteen days of waiting and wondering. Waiting to see if any of the eggs had implanted; whether this time when Lucy did the pregnancy test she would come back all smiles, instead of all tears. I buried myself in overtime at the factory. They had a man on long-term sick so I thankfully filled his shifts. We could do with the extra money anyway. This latest programme had dipped beyond our savings and into the normal bank account. At least with the extra shifts, the mortgage and the bills would still get paid this month, even if I did return home dog-tired. Maybe it was good to be dog-tired at the moment – too tired to even think. There were too many things I should think about but none of them had answers I knew I would easily find.

'It's time,' she announced at breakfast on day fourteen.

'Here we go again,' I thought. Aloud I asked the usual question instead.

'Do you want me there? I could take the shift off work.'

'No, it's OK. I can go on my own.' I was always shut out at this point, as if were redundant once fertilisation had taken place.

'Too right,' I thought sarcastically, 'go and earn some more money to pay for the next round.' I simply nodded obediently.

'I'll see you when I get home, then.' I picked up my lunch box and set off for work. I would walk there today so Lucy could take the car to drive to the hospital. I worked my shift and clocked off. I worked on auto now, barely even thinking about what I was doing. It no longer seemed to matter anyway. It was just a means of earning money, paying for another round of treatment to keep Lucy happy and her sharp tongue muted. Again I wondered how I'd wound up here, stuck in the same rut my parents were in; rapidly becoming them but worse. At least nature had taken its course naturally with them – and they were both seemingly engrossed in each other, not two bodies tolerating each other like I and Lucy were now. Where had all the dreams of adventure from boyhood gone? What had happened to the boy who'd nicked apples from old Mother J's just for the sheer hell of it? Such a long time ago and yet it was only ten years. Ten years had taken me into the time warp that was my parents' life all over again, with one or two more difficult twists.

Will had the right idea – he'd escaped altogether to his university life. At the time, I'd pitied him, staying on in Wilverton for another two years whilst I'd swaggered off to the glamour of the army tours, but now it seemed it was he who had escaped to a different life and I'd just done a circular trip, like I lived a self-fulfilling prophesy. The thoughts whirled around in my head as I trudged home. I rarely saw Will, but he was increasingly in my mind these days – sometimes at the oddest times. If I'd shared the experience with Susie with anyone, it would have been him, not Jack, even though a part of me knew he would have had that odd look on his face whilst he listened, and I would feel I was telling him something I knew I shouldn't. Still, despite that sense of difference between us, he'd always felt closer than Jack, and Jack was completely immersed in the army anyway. He was working his way up to Captain – no mean feat for someone who'd started out as a squaddie, but that meant he was always away on another tour and generally hard to reach. He was my best mate as a man, but Will remained the person I'd felt I could share my most vulnerable memories with, even as a child. At the moment the sense of failure I felt in so many diverse ways made me more like a vulnerable child than a hardened man. The vulnerable child sought out the only other vulnerable child he knew. It was like there was a string attached between him and me and every so often he tugged on it. Perhaps, like a puppet-master and his marionette, Will could pull my hand into place or place my foot forward without me even being aware of it. I wondered if he felt the same pull towards me, like we were two parts of a strange push-me-pull-you beast. All I knew was that I would have given a lot to have talked to him right then.

I walked up the garden path and in through the back door with an almost resigned air. I'd done this so many times before now, to find Lucy tight-lipped and sour-faced, or worse, in floods of tears. I wondered which I'd find this time. She beat me to the back door and opened it to me as I reached the step. No sour face, no tears, no down-turned mouth. For a moment I thought I must have got the day wrong. I must have imagined the conversation that morning – was I really so tired?

'Guess what?' Her voice ended shrill and squeaking, like a mouse. She didn't wait for me to answer. 'It worked!' She grabbed my hands and danced me around the kitchen. My empty lunchbox skittered around the floor.

'What?' I couldn't quite bring myself to believe it after all these times. 'Really? Oh my God!' All the confusion of the last couple of weeks fell away and was replaced by a surprised pleasure. I hadn't known I'd wanted it to work quite as much as I did. 'Oh Lucy, that's great!'

I couldn't have known on that happy day that it was one of the last bright moments between us for a long time. Our excitement was rapidly replaced by Lucy starting to feel sick. Morning sickness is good – it means plenty of good hormones racing around, so the midwife claimed. Lucy nodded wanly, looking more grey and gaunt as the weeks passed though, and I started to worry. What about the blossoming mother? I thought women were meant to bloom during pregnancy, not wither. Continuous nausea made her snappy and irritable, and eventually her irritability rubbed off on me. Sex was long since a thing of the past now, and the memory of the exotic evening I'd spent with Susie was shoved into a far recess in my mind, together with the guilty conscience. I'd even stopped thinking that I might one day get caught out and the defence I'd prepared was now dog-eared and musty from lack of practice. Lucy flopped down at the breakfast table, lifeless like a rag doll.

'Coffee?'

'Ugh, you know I can't!'

'Tea then?'

'No!'

'I'm only trying to help.'

'Well you're not. It's alright for you.'

'Lucy, you wanted this.'

'I didn't know it would make me feel so awful though, and you don't help by making stupid remarks like offering me coffee or tea.'

'I'm sorry.'

'You should be. Can't you think of something useful to do? And why's that newspaper there?'

The newspaper was merely laid on the table next to my coffee cup.

'Because I was reading it until you came down.'

'Well it's probably dirty and the news print will go all over my nice clean cloth, then I'll have to wash and iron it again. You are so selfish.'

I picked up the newspaper. There was no pleasing her. She said something but I missed it. My hearing was on a down day today. I got up to go.

'Now where are you going?'

'Well, out – you don't seem to be very happy with me here.'

'Oh you never listen – why are you so dumb sometimes? You just don't understand, do you? Why are you so dumb, so useless? Useless ears and useless di...' She stopped short, just catching herself in time, obviously realising she was about to go too far but I knew what she was going to say. My hearing might be touchy but that comment came across loud and clear. The words I'd said to Will reverberated like a thunderclap around my head as she said it.

'I'm not dumb. I'm just different to you.' Coldly I turned my back on her. I'd worked myself to exhaustion in order to pay for all the IVF treatment she'd wanted, put up with being refused any physical contact with her, accepted the sense of utter failure as a man it had created in me, and now I was being told I was dumb and a failure. Enough was enough. I'd felt guilty about one minor fling? Not anymore. I put the guilt firmly back in the box and nailed the lid on.

'Tom, Tom ...' The whiny voice followed me through the door, but I ignored it and marched on. I didn't know where I was going to, but it was out of that oppressive atmosphere of failure and uselessness. I got in the car and drove for miles out into the local countryside, until the anger that overwhelmed me dissipated enough for me to think beyond the rage and the humiliation and despair. I'd been fighting those feelings for such a long time now, but always managed to stuff them down beneath the surface again. Rage at being treated like a useless piece of rubbish as she'd criticised and denounced me in the kitchen before I walked out. Humiliation with being nothing more than a factory hand, working shift after shift – and all for what – a whining wife, and shortly no doubt, an equally whining kid. Despair – was there going to be nothing more than this in my life? I sat for a long time just looking unseeing into the far hills, shrouded in a low-lying mist but rising up ethereally out of it like they belonged to another land. A fairy tale land I'd somehow missed out on when I grew up.

I didn't go home until dark, when remorse that Lucy would be worried about me had nagged enough to sway me. I was prepared to be apologetic and conciliatory again. There wasn't a lot left for it, really, was there? As my mother would have said, I'd made my bed and now I would have to lie on it. I prepared my expression as I turned up our narrow drive. What greeted me was a vicious harpy, screaming in my face as soon as I walked through the door.

'I know.'

'You know?' For a moment I was completely lost, then the far recess of my mind gave up the secret I'd stuffed into the 'forget it' box, and so did I. 'How?' I added, just to make sure, 'I'm assuming you mean Susie?'

'Is that the sluts' name? It doesn't really matter, whatever it is.' Her storm was replaced just as suddenly by calm and that unnerved me more than the sound and fury. Her voice was flat and final, so unlike Lucy's that it was barely recognisable, but then Lucy had been becoming steadily less like Lucy ever since I'd married her, so maybe I'd never really known who Lucy was at all. Her expression was implacable.

'How did you find out?'

'I was worried about you. Huh!' She spat it out. 'I rung round some of your Rose and Crown drinking buddies and one of them didn't realise he was talking to me. He thought he was talking to your slut.'

'Can't we talk about it?'

'You are a useless bastard. You can't hear and you can't even make a baby like most men. You could at least have kept it in your pants, even if it doesn't work properly.' I reeled from the venom. She continued, 'once you've set up the maintenance payments, I never even want to see you again. '

I didn't know what to say back, probably because there was very little other than, 'the feeling is mutual'. Eventually I said the most facile thing that came into my head, but also the most comforting.

'I'll go and stay with Will.'

Chapter 8:

Billie's beast, 1980 to 1982

It seems so ironic that although I didn't know it at the time, Will was having as hard a time as me. When I turned up on his door step, he was obviously surprised but almost immediately the blank amazement turned to an expression of delight and he flung the door wide. It was as if the invisible string had tugged us both at the same time and both ends of the push-me-pull-you beast had pinged together to impact together on the doorstep. There was no hearty back slapping or veiled antagonism, just a sense of coming home to an old friend. I knew I'd done the right thing.

Will's beast was obviously rampaging far and wide at the time though, clear enough now from his diary entries, if not apparent to the observer then – or maybe I was too engrossed in my own confusion to notice his? Now I can't believe I missed any of it. Of course it became apparent after a while but I'd never known what it had been like in his mind until now.

***

April 28th 1980

Ok, so now I know I'm not gay. The revulsion I felt last night is still making me feel sick today, but I'm trying to put aside the physical response and just look at the issue intellectually now. It's a problem. Who am I? What am I? Now I've no idea. Katie left me cold, and Freddie left me disgusted. The only person I've felt any physical response to is Tom – and yet I know I'm not gay. I can't decide what to do, and I'm dreading seeing Freddie because it is going to be so awkward. I know I have to face him but I'm being a coward and leaving it as long as possible. In fact I'm going to leave the whole thing as long as possible and just live day to day until I know what to do.

The woman from the shop on the day of the fire slipped back into my mind today just before I wrote this. I wondered what she felt when she looked at herself, how she'd made that huge transition from one person to another. I wished I had asked her now. When she told me her story I'd listened to the facts, the details, amazed at how the life history of one person could be so garish – so outlandishly different as to change their physical body to reflect their inner self. One sex to another; it was an enormous step to take and although I'd fantasised about it in my dreams – the half-man, half-woman morph, it had never been more than a strange story I'd become part of for a short while.

I tried to think myself into her head. Suzanne. The Leonard Cohen song of the same name accompanied her face into my mind and snaked insidiously around it. I found myself humming the tune and half mouthing the words. It had always created elusively beautiful images and sensations for me, without actually fully understanding its meaning. Now I understood it like someone had flicked a switch and I was illuminated with light. When something inspires you, no matter how crazy or unreal it may be, you will follow it to the end of its trail – like a water droplet flowing in the torrent of a river. That is the nature of faith and belief, you don't know where it will lead you but you know you want to end up in that place. When you have a belief you see beyond the dank and despairing to the beauty within; beyond the everyday reality to the dream that inspires. Womanhood was my Suzanne's dream, and that led me to another question. What was mine? I had no idea now, but the question has taken root in my mind like a seed burrowing into fertile ground.

November 12th 1980

I haven't written in here in months. Now I've opened it up again, I feel guilty. All the thoughts I've had since that night in April have passed through my head and got lost in the slipstream of indecision, lack of conclusion, confusion. It's like a train has gone from one destination to another and left the passengers behind, but the passengers continued to have a conversation in the station waiting room. As the train draws back into the station to collect them again, the snippets of their continuing conversation float into the air through the open door as it arrives. The guard leans out of the train to whistle and wave his flag to tell the engine driver they have arrived, apply the brakes, to slow down. The passengers board; their conversation continues as it had been all this time, but with the explanatory chunk in the middle missing. Here is mine. Where the conversation re-starts: I'm not gay, I'm not straight. I'm somewhere in between and Suzanne has metaphorically taken my hand as determinedly as in the song.

I avoided Freddie for a good week after that evening. It wasn't easy because everywhere I went he seemed to be there too. Habit took me into the Kings Road shop, but there was Freddie, rifling through some Beatles paraphernalia that is all the rage. I walked in the door and straight back out as if I'd become entangled in the revolving door at the Ritz and the doorman on reception had thrown me straight back into its return revolution, so I landed up on the streets again, where I belonged. I walked down the road to the café on the corner where Suzanne and I had the conversation after the fire, settling into a table in the furthest recess and ordering black coffee to clear my head. The door banged as my coffee arrived and over the waitresses shoulder, there was Freddie, large as life and booming out his 'dear boy' as camp as Danny La Rue in full costume. One of the TV's who frequented the Kings Road boutique knew Danny and had taken a group of us back stage to meet him after one of his shows. I stood as far back as I could in the little group, dazzled by the conglomeration of sequins and ostrich feathers, hanging in dense swathes from the coat rails which lined the walls. I could almost sink into one of rails and disappear altogether. Maybe that would be best? Engulfed in feather and frills; lost without a trace. The sensation of opulent luxury mixed with tawdry glamour lingered long after we'd left, together with the scent of powder and pan stick make-up, cloying and sickly. I found it unbelievably enticing – almost erotic to be so close to all those different textures, and yet also disturbingly strange. I felt a familiarity with them, and yet they were alien too – like a distantly remembered dream. I sensed, rather than remembered it. Freddie's presence raised the tentatively submerged emotions of revulsion, but mixed with the lure of that glamour. I didn't want to feel either at the moment, and I certainly didn't want to run into Freddie so close to the last encounter so I downed my espresso, cringing at its bitterness, left a stack of coins on the table for the waitress to find and slipped back out the door just in time to avoid Freddie as he swept towards an empty table in the centre of the café, effusive 'dear boys' being scattered liberally in his wake.

Back outside, I breathed freely again, feeling as if the cold air made me cleaner. An irritating sense of confusion still niggled at me even though I'd walked away from one of the perpetrators of it so I set off smartly down the road, leaving it, and him, as far behind me as possible. I needed to get away from this area, this place In my life. I needed clarity, not strange longings and insidious desires. I was due some time off from work at the local library where I'd found myself a job after university, and I thought I would take it and go away. Away completely from London and find some lucidity for myself. It wasn't that the job caused the confusion – far from it. My more colourful university friends couldn't understand how I could cope with what they termed such a dull and dreary routine in a provincial library, but its' very ordinariness was a relief from the lurid posturing and exotic lifestyles I spent the rest of my personal time teetering on the edge of. The first thing cup of tea – so English – and polite 'good mornings' made me feel as if there was something secure, solid, in what, the rest of the time felt like a life spent on shifting sands; one minute wondering if this emotion was right and the next finding the understanding of it had slipped away into a murky morass of misapprehension and had been replaced by another notion, all revolving round the central *am I gay, am I straight, what am I* issue. Routinely filing away papers, replacing books on the shelves in the right alphabetical order, straightening the borrowers library tickets, neatly containing the relevant book reference card into date order and flattening them into a standard run, not a card out of place, gave my addled mind temporary relief, like I could file all the confusions away for a while and only have to deal with the steady humdrum of the day. The tedium comforted my feverish brain, and when I'd spent a day just filing and sorting, stacking and piling, ironically my head felt clear, not fatigued. I gladly let the whole odd issue just fester until contact with that other world of feathers and frenetic glitz threw my hat back into the ring and there I was tiptoeing through the mire again, sinking here and struggling onto what seemed to be solid ground again there, until that caved in too.

I agreed a weeks' leave, packed up my boneshaker of a car and left. My week of Quaker-like simplicity, away from Freddie and his kind beckoned. I didn't know where I was going. It didn't really matter. I just wanted peace and space to put confused thoughts out in the open where there were no other influences and decide how I felt about the three questions that revolved around my head. Each felt like it had a number of other side issues attached to it and my intellectual brain kicked in even as I drove out of London and joined the M3.

I imagined the three questions as part of a spider diagram, with long legs trailing off from the juicy body, containing the crux of the problem in the centre. The body hid fangs within its corpulent exterior – sharp and venomous so each time I approached the core issue, I found myself bitten and injured. Was I gay? Maybe; I didn't have sexual feelings generally for girls, it was true. One leg was completed, examined and linked to the core of the body. Ok, then that suggested I was gay. Was I gay? I examined that leg, travelling its spindly length from the initial question to the core. At the pustulent core was the experience with Freddie. I reeled back as the fangs struck. No! I wasn't gay. That was foul, disgusting. The feeling of having been used, simply as a receptacle for Freddie's physical need, flowed through me like poison. I winced and recoiled. I pulled over onto the hard shoulder and shuffled awkwardly over to the passenger seat so I could hang out of the window and retch as the memory of the disgust and the pain rolled over me again. No, I was not gay. I let the burst of cold air circulate the car to freshen its atmosphere and then wound up the window.

I must be straight then? Katie. How had Katie made me feel? That had led me to nothingness; simple physical release, no more. Ok, but no emotion – and all I'd wanted to do was get away, escape her. Maybe I was straight; maybe, but not with her. No not with her. The sharp points of the fangs caressed me, making my skin shiver but not wince. Numb, that's all it made me feel, numb. So, what didn't make me feel numb? Now, my skin shivered in uncomfortable embarrassment and the numbness of apathy seared away in a white heat of remembered desire. Tom. The memory of his strong brown arms, lightly covered with hair, like the soft fur of an animal pelt, stirred an unmistakable longing in me. Christ, Tom, why did I feel this way about Tom? The fangs sunk in deep and I let the poison flow. I leaned back against the passenger head rest, head aching and thoughts swarming like angry bees against the outer edges of my skull.

Other memories followed the swarm as it stung and battled for freedom. My sisters dress skimming my hips and the sensuous feel of the blue sheath as I smoothed my hands over its fabric. Looking at myself in the mirror, I'd mimicked that under-the-eyelashes look that the girls had coquettishly aimed so cleverly as a weapon at the boys in my teens. The girl that could have been Will had looked back at me from the mirror, disturbingly real. The woman in the back room of the Kings Road shop stood behind me in the shadows. Suzanne: half-woman, half-man in her dainty lace bra, and grotesque bulge in her panties. I examined her in my imagination – every part of her; from her finely coiffed hair and neat features with slightly too square jaw, down the smooth neck and onto the sharply defined shoulders. The soft swell of her breasts led in a smooth sweep to the gentle curve of her belly, then the downy line from navel to crotch. I ignored her crotch and followed the line of her legs as the thighs narrowed to neat knees and shapely calves, and finally to well-shaped, slightly broad feet, with pretty coral pink painted toe nails. I hadn't realised my cursory glance over her in the changing room had taken in so much fine detail. The one detail I'd missed out was the fly in the ointment. What made her more man than woman, despite the feminine form; her cock. I flipped back up to her face again, and recoiled. The face I'd superimposed over hers was mine.

My eyes jerked open but the woman with the cock was still right in front of me. She was me. I reached up and pulled down the sun visor above the windscreen and peered as best I could at my face in the mirror attached to it. I was on the woman's side of the car. They only put a mirror on the passenger-side sun visor because generally the passenger there is a woman. That's what someone once told me. The dream where I was trying to see myself in a small fragment of broken mirror came back in waves and I felt as if I was drowning. I couldn't see much else but my eyes in the mirror because it was so small, but they were the eyes of a woman; it was unmistakable, now I looked in close confines. I manoeuvred so I could survey other parts of my face in the minute mirror. My mouth – full and soft, curving slightly at the corners, and a bruised raspberry pink; my cheeks, slightly hollowed with a sleek, almost Slavic look to them. My eyebrows; delicately arched over the deep brown almond eyes. All the features – all of them, they were women's features. The only thing that masculinised me was having shorter hair.

I imagined myself as a woman instead of a man. What would I feel like wearing those pretty frilled laced nothings the man-woman had been wearing in the changing room? I allowed my imagination to recreate the texture of the bra, satin topped, with small lace frill over the cups. I could feel the tautness of the straps as they pulled over my shoulder, near the clavicle, and the heaviness of my breasts as they dropped gently into the cups. I wanted to run my hands tenderly over them, caressing them and relishing the swell of them under my palms, from the soft curve of plumped flesh to the dimpled skin around the areola and the hard jutting bud of the nipple. Now I could see what Tom had seen in breasts when he'd talked so greedily about them as a teenager. My hands slid down both sides of my body to the vulnerable ticklish part on my stomach, just above my thighs. Imagine you have no cock, nothing at all. It's not there. You have a cunt, a little girl's hole, a fanny, a pussy, tight and sweet. Oh my God, I wanted to feel something inside me right now. The sensation burned fiercely as I imagined Toms firm arm next to mine, imagined it brushing against me, touching me, encircling me. I could feel the blood heat suffusing my face with colour. Christ if I'm not gay, then what are these feelings? But I knew. All of a sudden I knew there was only the smallest difference between me and the woman in the changing room at the Kings Road shop. She already knew what she was, and I'd only just started to realise for myself.

Where did I go from there? She'd told me her story, and I knew what she was going to have done – the surgery, which sounded excruciatingly painful to me, and yet ... I wished I'd written down her full name. I remembered the scrap of serviette she'd written her number on and cursed myself for having left it in my jeans pocket to become simply a mangled piece of garbage after I'd washed them. At the time I'd merely been stunned and confused by this mythical person, this oddity who rang so many alarm bells for me that all I wanted to do was push her to the back of my mind. Damn. Irritation suffused me. Why was it that you so carelessly discard the things that turn out to be so important to you later?

It was no good trying to find her, and I didn't want to ask around in the Kings Road shop where it would spark off unwanted curiosity, and then maybe prompt questions. I needed to answer my own questions before I attempted to answer anyone else's. Anyway, I'd promised to keep her story secret and I kept promises. What else could I do? The first stop, maybe, ironically, was the library, because it was at least a knowledge store, even if it was the place I associated the most with order and the least with chaos, and this idea was certainly the start of chaos for me.

'Cry havoc and let slip the dogs of war.'[1] I knew it was a quote from a piece of literature I'd studied, but my befuddled brain couldn't place it any more than I could place myself within the world any more. I was disturbed from the crazy quest to place the literary quote by a rap on the car window.

'Hey, mister, you know you're on the hard shoulder. Have you broken down?' I hurriedly wound down the window, incredibly glad he hadn't appeared there a few minutes earlier when I'd been mentally masturbating.

'Oh, it's ok officer, I just felt a bit queasy and thought it would be safer if I stopped for a moment. I'll get back on the road now.'

'Ok.' He sounded vaguely unsure, as if he wanted to detain me, but had no real reason to. Maybe he *had* seen me stroking myself down – or had that all been in my imagination? I slipped back over into the driver's seat and turned the key in the ignition before he had time to think of an excuse to keep me from leaving. He stepped back and allowed me to go, replacing his helmet as I moved away and straddling his heavy 1000cc bike. He followed me part of the rest of the way on the M3, until I deliberately turned off, not really caring where I ended up for the moment. Anywhere would work for thinking time. He didn't follow me and I felt less under threat. I followed the B road until I hit a small town, and then continued into the town centre. I was undecided whether to stay there or go home. What decided me in the end was seeing a sign saying 'Public Library'. At least I could research here without anyone identifying me. I pulled into the next car park I spotted and made my way back to the library. It was only just after two so I had until five to find out some basic information.

It was quite a large library, which was another bonus. I lost myself in the rows of medical tomes, unsure where to start, but gender seemed a good possibility. By the time five o'clock arrived, I'd learned the basics of how the human embryo establishes gender via chromosomes XX and XY. Which was I? Maybe XXY, if there was such a thing? I'd also learned that I wasn't the only man to feel this way – as the man-woman had already proved.

London was possibly one of the best places to be in the UK with this particular issue. There was little more that I could gain from this library. It was too small and provincial, as was the one where I worked. I no longer needed to get out of London, I needed to get back there, and into the largest medical library I could find.

The rest of my week was spent in detailed research. By the end of it I knew the facts. It wasn't a new phenomenon, just not much publicised. As far back as 1886, a German doctor had been studying gender divergence among the homosexual population. Just after the turn of the century, he described something he called, "metamorphosis sexualis paranoia", where a homosexual truly believed themself to be the opposite sex, but he attributed this to mental illness. Then followed Dr Magnus Hirschfeld; a gay physician who was the first to coin two of the most popular terms to describe transgenderism: transvestism and transsexualism. He founded the world's first sexological institute in Berlin and some nine or so years later he delivered the first scientific lecture on transsexualism. The first incomplete sex-reassignment surgeries – sex-change operations as they became known, in female-to-male patients were performed in Berlin in 1912 and in 1921, when a private surgeon called Gohrbandt began to practice it in its' most basic form. The first complete male-to-female sexual reassignment surgery was reported in 1931. The patient lived and worked in Hirschfeld's institute for more than ten years as a housemaid.

In 1930, Lili Elbe – formerly the Dutch painter, Einar Wegener, also had sex change surgery under Dr Gohrbandt. She died from complications the following year, but not before being trumpeted as the world's first *transsexual*. Dutch newspapers began reporting the news at the end of 1930, and her posthumous autobiography, 'Man into Woman', was published two years after she died. I made a mental note to find it and read it. In the late 1940s and early 1950s, transsexualism moved forward when the first American had sex-reassignment surgery. The December 1952 headline in the New York Daily News was 'Ex-GI Becomes Blonde Beauty!' I wondered what the reception from the reading public had been, and my mind strayed to Tom and his tales of beasting, physical hardship and outright homophobia. How on earth had this blonde beauty survived all of that?

Following America's lead, other countries started to accept gender reassignment treatment – or SRS as it became renamed. In 1967, British law allowed Charing Cross Hospital to begin performing SRS, in 1969, Germany decriminalised it and in 1971, the first sex reassignment operation was performed in Paris. Transsexualism had become international.

183

A series of international symposia on gender identity followed and in the years between then and just recently, there had been changes varying from outright support and the dampening down of treatment options. Finally this year had seen transsexualism listed as an official disorder by the American Psychiatric Association. How had this passed me by until now?

At least its history and acknowledgement had a base, and attitudes were more open now than if I had found myself facing this issue twenty years before. I read on, more intent on the trials I had to face if I were to make the transition myself now it had a name and a reality for me. I had to be sure, really sure, that under this skin that said *man*, I really was a woman. That would mean trying to live as one until I not only convinced myself, but also a whole panel of doctors and psychiatrists too. What troubled me about that was not just the fact that now I had to tell the world what was innermost in my soul – and therefore make myself completely vulnerable, but that I didn't know how any of it would make me feel. I could put all the facts I liked together, but I couldn't even begin to plumb the emotions they would produce. I read the most heartfelt of cries – a letter from a transgender that I found in my searches with both empathy and fear.

'...That ignorance and prejudice costs lives is no new discovery, it is the bane of every age whether it shows up in war or in civil violence or in silent hatred and misunderstanding. In this case though it was my own life that has been bled away year by year in my efforts to correspond to

what body may have indicated but my soul knew to be an alien fabric out of which I could never hope to weave a complete or a happy life. The only comfort I have for those lost days and years during which I was a stranger to myself frantically seeking to garb my soul in the personalities and expectations of others, is that I might be the last generation to know such pointless suffering. That is why I am writing today to spare others lost years, lost hopes, lost lives.

No other birth defect or developmental disability is treated with the snide and brutal complacency of transsexualism. People would be ashamed at the thoughtless cruelty seen so often in talk shows when brave people have attempted to tell of their pain and to grope towards a solution both for themselves and for others. We are in many ways a barbaric society in spite of all our technology. It is time that such treatment cease and that compassion that is so rare in society find a home in the families of the oppressed.

I cannot tell you now to try and understand what is in its very nature an incomprehensible condition, nor can I tell you what specific measures to take to ease your child through the transition to her true life. Your own love, courage, and imagination must be your guides along this path. I can tell you this, that no act of love will be a cause of regret, that no one profits when lives burn on in futility and frustration simply to sustain society's bland comfort in illusion...'[2]

The *alien fabric* echoed my dreams. Suzanne had indeed led me to a river. I wondered if it would drown me.

Chapter 9:

Tom – in suspension, 1983

I moved into the spare room that night, thinking maybe Lucy's anger would dissipate by the morning. Life had to go on for the moment anyway. I woke as usual at 5am the next day, disorientated because of being in a strange room. The bed was single and my back ached from having to sleep cramped up to fit in it. There was no reason to linger under the covers. No warm body to curl around and absorb their dreaming softness – not that Lucy had been very welcoming for some while now, but the very presence of another person is comforting in the cold grey hours of dawn. They say the early hours of the morning are the ones when we are most vulnerable. Indeed they are the ones that most people leave this life; when biorhythms are at the lowest ebb. That may be so, but the hours just before dawn are the loneliest – the time when you know you have to face the difficult parts of the forthcoming day but there is no way of halting the dawn. I didn't wait to face it, I rose with it, and dressed quickly and silently, exiting the house equally swiftly so I placed the longest spell of time between the moment I'd stared into Lucy's cold eyes last night, and when I would have to face them again that evening.

I hoped something would happen to soften them during the day, although heaven knew what that would be.

My lunch box contained little apart from a couple of slices of bread and some scraps of meat from tea the night before – a tea we'd eaten in separate rooms. She'd sat in the lounge, picking at hers like a bird, and then pushing the plate aside. I'd sat at the kitchen table, spying on her through the open door. Her back remained firmly against me, no matter what the sounds emanating from the kitchen. I probably could have hung myself from a rope and swung from the centre of the room, choking and gurgling, until all life left me, without her twitching a muscle or even casting a glance in my direction. She treated me as if I didn't even exist, simply waiting impatiently for me to complete my own self-annihilation. I filled the hole in the lunch box with one of the apples from the bowl, completely forgetting to pick the one without the bruise in it. When I bit into it at lunchtime, the mouthful I got was soft and rotten – sour. I spat it out and cast it into the nearest rubbish bin in disgust.

Returning home that evening, the frosty reception remained in place. There was no meal for me at all. When I attempted conversation, there was only minimal reply.

'I thought you said you'd go and stay with Will?'

'I haven't asked him yet. Couldn't we talk?' She looked at me – a cold hard look, forgiving nothing and condemning everything.

'No.' I waited for her to elaborate but she didn't. The subject was closed. Had the subject ever been open?

'What about my job? I can't work at Gleason's, and stay at Wills'. Will lives in London.'

'Get another job.'

'And the maintenance you want?'

She sighed. Her tone was patronising.

'That's your problem. Just make sure it gets paid.' Then as if she'd only just thought it, 'or you could sign the whole house over to me, and forget the maintenance.' It wasn't a suggestion, more like a way out. It didn't sound like a spur of the moment suggestion. I scrutinised her suspiciously but she looked back blank-eyed at me, playing dumb. The iciness that had greeted me, combined with the feeling that I had simply been used all this time – to be the husband, to provide the home, to pay the bills, to create the child – and now to take all the blame, reminded me of the way Will's mother had talked about his father whenever she'd stopped by to have a cuppa with my mam, or when they'd gossiped in the street on market days. They never bothered that I could hear, hanging onto my mothers' hand as the bustle of the shoppers and traders carried on around us.

'And I told him he was a lazy so-and so, and there'd be none of that tonight.'

'Quite right, Mary. He should think himself lucky to have someone like you.'

'I was one of the Murrays, you know, before I married him.'

'You've told me before, Mary.'

'My father always behaved like the gentleman. Does your Jim always leave his dirty clothes on the floor like my George does?'

My mother shifted her weight onto her other leg. I fidgeted, wanting the litany of George's faults to be finished so we could examine the stalls, and maybe I could persuade Mam to buy a bag of liquorice from the sweet stall that was always at the outermost tip of the market. It was the prize for having made it past the fruit and veg, the rolls of gingham fabric to make table cloths and the stands full of tat and 'antiques'. In my mother's defence, even though she listened to Mary Robinsons' regular denouncement of the male species, I knew from the perpetually long face when my father was away that she didn't like turning a critical eye on him and Mary's comments made her uncomfortable. She tactfully let Mary continue instead.

'Why are they so lazy? What about the toilet lid, and the toothpaste cap? He never puts them back, either. And after you know what, well, it's not nice, is it ... Thank goodness I don't have him under my feet during the day so the house stays tidy.' Mam's fidgeting would increase with her embarrassment.

'It must be nice to have him around in the evenings and weekends though.' Mam's voice was timid – wanting to contribute, but not sure how to. Will's mum pursed her lips and looked doubtful.

'Sometimes. But not when he's had a bit too much – if you know what I mean.' I didn't, but Mam obviously did. She nodded sympathetically, and whilst she cast around for another similarity to share, the other woman filled the gap again. 'Oh they just want to be waited on hand and foot. The only thing they're good for is paying the bills.' Suddenly my mam surprised me with her enthusiasm.

'I know – and then they have to be reminded, don't they? Jim's home for such short spells, it's a good job I know what he's doing all the time he's home except when he goes to the pub, and I can make sure it all gets done. But he's a good husband – never strayed or played me up.'

Oddly, Will's mother would always seem to lose interest in the conversation at that point. She would gather up her shopping bags to depart.

'Well, I must be getting along Maureen, can't stay chatting to you all day.'

Of course at the time most of it was like Morse code to me. I knew the two women were tapping out signals about their marriages to each other, but not what they were. Now I know from the small comments that slipped through Wills' reticence about home life since that his mother regularly got a beating on a Saturday night, and he and his sister had loathed their father. What his mother had felt towards his father, I didn't know, but she put up with the beatings for another twelve years until George Robinson finally swung his fist for the last time and broke his neck, having toppled down the stairs in his own home, blind drunk. The funeral was a subdued little affair. My father had helped carry the coffin and seen Mary home, slightly tipsy, at the end of the wake. Will and his sister

Fran had stayed on with my mam, and helped clear up the little back room at the Rose and Crown where the wake had been held. My father had returned a couple of hours later, flush-faced, causing Mam to fuss around him in case he was ill.

'Leave me alone, woman,' he'd said testily as he waved her away from him. 'It was a long walk on a hot day.' Fran thanked him for taking care of their mother, but Will studiously ignored him. I'd always thought that uncharacteristically rude of Will, but maybe we all behave differently in extremes of emotion. He never commented on it.

Mary Robinson had good reason to be critical of men, but the impression of men being no better than the bill-payers and the sperm providers had lingered with me from those remembered diatribes. Here was Lucy taking exactly the same attitude with me. One minor indiscretion – far less than George Robinsons regular pounding of his wife – and Lucy was damning and disposing of me. On reflection, I couldn't imagine ever wanting to talk this over with her now. I turned on my heel, returning to Gleason's to hand in my notice, steadfastly refusing to answer their surprised questioning, and returned home to pack.

The journey to Wills' was crowded and uncomfortable as I'd unwisely chosen first thing in the morning to travel on the train, so I had to cram in with all the commuters going to London for a day's work. I didn't even stop to think whether Will would be home, and of course he wasn't. Ringing the doorbell and hearing it echo emptily inside the flat, I remembered that he'd told me he was applying for jobs in

191

libraries the last time I'd seen him after Fran's wedding. It was only eleven-thirty now so I guessed he wouldn't be home until after five; nothing for it but to kill time. I made my way to Waterloo station and left my bag at the left luggage office and then walked out onto the muggy streets of the capital. Straight ahead were the arches of the bridges that supported the lines coming into Waterloo. I didn't like London much and they symbolised what it meant to me, soot-blackened, old and ugly; grime, squalor, and jaded pomp. The city felt dirty to me, but I had no choice at the moment other than to be here. I made for the only place that appealed – the river. Although it wasn't like being in the fresh air of the countryside around Wilverton walking along the South Bank at least made me feel able to breath, compared to the claustrophobically crowding buildings of the city itself. I paced its banks, looking across to Big Ben and the Houses of Parliament in the distance, past the huge Tate gallery building – not my scene, but definitely Wills, I thought ruefully. OK, there was sense of history here – of solidity, but I already felt as grimy as it. It added to my feeling of being jaded and discarded. I wondered if I would ever feel as alive and happy as I had those times when Will and I had legged it through our little village's streets, jumpers full of stolen apples, laughing at our crime, but inherently innocent nevertheless, in the way only children can be. The act was mischief at best and yet it was done without malice – just for the hell of it.

I hung over the edge of the railings and watched the river flow past, steely grey. How deep was it? Deep enough to drown in? My mood was a dull and miserable as the water. The thought crossed my mind that jumping in it would solve all my problems. I hung there, railings digging into my armpits, slumped over the arched tops, mesmerized by the water. The days and months of the past years flowed with them, as if my life was flowing away from me. I realised that it had done. I'd allowed Lucy to lead me no differently to the way Susie had done in the hotel room. I'd allowed other people to pull me along by the nose all my life in fact. My parents had treated me merely as a body they were responsible for educating and maturing enough to be able to push into the world at large. I'd followed my father into the army because it was the only thing I could imagine doing. They'd done nothing to show me any other possibilities. The army had manipulated me to its needs and then spat me out the other end, defective. Lucy had picked me up from there and manipulated me into a husband and reproductive machine, before again finding me faulty and spitting me out too. Here I was, with no idea how to be anything other than ordered around and found wanting. It was pointless. I might as well jump. The bag was at left luggage, Will didn't even know I was coming and Lucy could simply take over the house and keep going. The child wasn't even mine. In a last spiteful dig at me, she'd told me how they'd used donor sperm this time because mine were so useless. My humiliation was complete. More water flowed past and I got lost in the rush of it and the faintly smoky air. I remembered Gary, and how he hadn't had the choice I was wondering whether to make now. I hesitated.

'Hey mate.' My indecision over whether to jump or not was decided by a prod in my back and an overpoweringly foul smell. I turned slowly, arms dragging back over the railings. A tramp was standing behind me, hand possessively on a dirty red check pull-along shopping trolley. He smelt of over-ripe cheese and rotting fish. I wanting to get away from the stench but he was directly in front of me so the only way was backwards. I flattened against the railings, and tried to stop myself grimacing.

'What?'

He cupped has hand behind his ear and shifted painfully from side by side as if his whole body ached, but his voice came out loud and clear from behind the grizzled beard.

'I been watching you. If you're gonna jump, can I 'ave yer gear?'

The sheer incongruity of my thoughts and his made me laugh out loud. No, this wasn't the way out at all. If this pathetic old man could still maintain such a tight grasp on life when he was shrivelled and disgusting and had nothing, I wasn't about to give in when I had vigour and youth. I just needed hope.

'Sorry mate.' I gave him a fiver. He deserved that for saving my life.

I walked back along the river bank until I reached the bridge again and made my way to Waterloo where I picked up my bag. I ignored the stuffiness of the tube on the way to Wills. I looked past the blank grey faces of the other passengers. I shut out the hooting taxi's and rush of the traffic as I walked along the road from the tube station. My hearing was acute for once, as were all my senses suddenly. Was it the fact that Will had never judged me, never rated me defective? Was it the recognition of how close I'd come to giving up something as precious as life? Was it the prospect of a fresh start that made sound and sense and sight all sharper? I rang the doorbell again and this time the echoing jangle was followed by the sound of footsteps.

Chapter 10:

Hair and make up, darling 1982

January 1982

Another awkward Christmas has gone past with its gaudy trappings and pretence of goodwill. I had to spend part of it back home with Mother. She's so depressed since Tom's dad died. Of course I know why, but can never say – not even to Fran. It was a tedious few days back at Wilverton, with her fussing about the turkey being too dry, Mrs Evans snubbing her in the supermarket and the interminable knitting. Knitting a pair of bootees, then a tiny cardigan, then a bonnet, then back to another pair of bootees, creating a neat stack of woollen offerings for Fran and the baby due in just a few weeks' time. Fran lumbered over on Christmas Day with Joe, belly popping out in front of her. Joe's belly had swollen too since I'd last seen him, apparently in sympathy, but his was filled with beer not baby. I wanted to ask Fran if she was still happy – as happy as she'd been on her wedding day. Despite her excited chatter about the imminent birth, something in her eyes seemed empty. I didn't dare ask. The very emptiness scared me. If she couldn't be happy when everything she'd wanted seemed to be coming her way, how could I? I didn't want to hear that and damn myself to the expectation of eternal unhappiness. And what could I do to help her if the answer was no? It was easier to concentrate on my own dissatisfaction than compound hers by making her voice it.

Joe tried to talk football to me a couple of times but thankfully soon gave up with a look of disgust. You look at me with disgust, Joe? I look at your puffy, pale skin and globular stomach, listen to your nasal Liverpudlian twang and heavy breathing as you mount the stairs and try not to think of you mounting my sister, who deserves much more than you. I'm so relieved to be back in London now, although the hug I gave Fran when I left was warm between us. Even the childishness of the Kings Road TV's chatter brings more rewards than familial closeness, and mine never was close anyway. Their conversation is of interest to me too, whereas babies, bootees and beer are so far out of my orbit as to be laughable.

'Hair and make-up, darling. That's what matters most.' Christine balanced a heavily lacquered hand on her hip and allowed the hip to bounce with attitude.

'*Dahhhling,* no!' Millie took up the cudgels. 'Clothes are the thing.'

'Clothes? Oh *sweetie,* where have you been?' Jasmine joined in the fight and I wondered if I should duck out from the battling cat claws as if ducking out of the bottom of a rugby scrum, and slip away with the ball. Yet, I wanted to hear what they had to say too. It was an education for me that I was so far sadly lacking in, but desperately in need of. It didn't mean I was going to follow their advice but what did I know of make-up or hairstyles? Jasmine was still talking, holding forth with gusto.

'Undergarments, girls, that's what makes the difference.' She cupped her falsies with an exaggerated gesture and wiggled them. The other TV's howled with laughter and I had to concede a smile to the comic appeal of the action. She tipped her head back in a Miss Piggy style flick and pouted. 'Gorgeous' she added, rolling the word luxuriously round her mouth before sliding it out.

'Ooh, show!' squealed Christine.

'Now, now,' she cautioned. 'Patience is a virtue, waiting is a sin.' The 'girls' howled raucously and Jasmine waggled her 'tits' again. I wondered what I was going to learn from them after all. It was descending merely into a TV love-in, whereas I was after hard facts. I decided to move it along a little and added my comments – more in the form of an innocent question.

'How would you know what to choose, you all look so glamorous. I wouldn't know where to start, if I were you.' I knew I'd appealed to their ego's and the lesson began in earnest.

'Marksies is best for undies – they expect you to be buying for your wife so they even help you choose. You just have to remember to double up the size when you buy the bra though, otherwise it won't fit round your chest.'

'But not the cup size or you'll end up with massive titties!' Whooped Millie and they all started to cackle again. I waited for them to calm down. Christine was in full flow now in between the crude additions and she went on helpfully to describe her last knicker-buying trip.

'Such a darling little lady. She helped me choose all the matching sets. When she asked me my wife's preference I nearly said 'gay darling', but I managed to change it to gay colours!' The laughter kicked off again, and I tired of their over-exuberance. I started to move away, leaving them to their crude stories and flippant insults, directed teasingly at each other. They sounded like utter bitches but the regular bursts of hearty laughter that engulfed them spoke in reality of mutual appreciation and friendship. They were an enclave, a gang, and I wasn't one of them, despite my interest in dressing like them. I decided I might be better of just window-shopping and making my own observations. At least I'd gleaned one useful bit of information to start me off. 'Marksies' was good for knickers. I set off down the Kings Road, diverting into South Ken tube station.

The tube was an interesting place to start my recce. During the day, when the tube isn't so crowded, you can comfortably sit on one of the banks of seats and innocently scrutinise your opposite number. Under the cover of the ennuie that affects all tube users, your gaze can fall on the person opposite, and while you appear to be far away in thought, with eyes just resting wherever they have landed, you are in truth cataloguing and describing the exact essence of that person in your head. The way they hold their head just so, the curl of a stray strand of hair, the tufts of baby hair at their hairline, the dimple in one cheek only. They shift in their seat and you gain a sense of their weight, their posture, their smell even. Is it heavy and dense, as if laden with sweat or soft and light? As if filled with the sweet perfume of wild flowers drifting in the fields? Men and women have a very different presence, even sitting perfectly still. A man is squat and secure. You feel that they will move with a solidity and determination that is the very heart of their masculinity. Men are hard and fixed, strong and invasive. Women on the other hand – even the ugliest and oldest of them – have softness in their very structure. I think I would know, even with my eyes blindfolded and no sound made, that a woman was approaching me rather than a man. I would sense that grace, that lightness that makes up the essence of femininity. As I sat on the tube, closely and secretly observing its female cargo, I realised that to be a woman, I first had to master that air. No amount of fancy clothes, make-up or undies would turn the male Will into the female alternative otherwise.

We arrived at Oxford Circus and the throng piled off the tube.

'Mind the gap, mind the gap' echoed around the stale air and we shuffled through the heat and doldrums of the tunnels that took us from burrowers to borrowers on the streets of Oxford Street. I stayed relentlessly behind my chosen group of subjects and noted the way they swung their hips, the smaller steps, the dainty placing of feet, the slightly reticent stance they all took. It seemed to be a common feature of women to stand back, let the male of the species go first. To be authentic, I somehow had to adopt that style too. That was going to be difficult because having been nurtured a male from birth, it was my natural inclination to expect to go first, be asked first, to take first. Even with the limited experience I'd had of sex, I'd noticed that distinction between the sex with Katie — she'd accepted and I'd taken, whereas with Freddie — he being in the male role, had taken from me. They obligingly led me to 'Marksies' anyway, so I had no need to detour or lose their input. I lost myself in the rows of bras and knickers; the bra's hanging from hangers like mini breastplates or suits of lady-armour. I listened to their chatter.

'I don't like the underwire; it pokes in me.' Underwire? What was that? I listened avidly.

'Oh I do, it makes them look bigger.'

'My Fred likes them like that. He says they look like they're going to pop.' Their laughter sounded disconcertingly like that of the TV's and I wondered if I'd got it wrong, but it diluted much quicker into desultory comments about lace trims and padding, size and cup shapes. After processing most of what they'd discussed, I summarised for myself that 'underwire' was a wire threaded through the supporting structure of the cup to provide extra bolstering for the heavier breast, you needed to measure around your chest for the size and then select the 'cup' size to accommodate the size of the breast itself. I added for myself that a tea cup was probably a good size, a mug size probably wasn't, but the cup sizes weren't in thimble, egg cup, tea cup and mug, they were A, B, C and D. Oh well, reasonably straight forward, at least — presumably devised by a man, ironically, given the logic. I rounded the day off with checking the sizes of the knickers. This was rather more confusing as my tour guides had moved on without considering the knickers. The sizes here oddly delineated in numbers instead of alpha-numero. Sizes ranged from 8 to 18 in alternate numbers, but were accompanied by some additional information in inches. *Ah, they were the same as dress sizes.* I had already mastered those in the Kings Road boutique. I'd developed an eye for matching a size to a body there, but had never – obviously – applied it to myself. I made a mental note of the inches ranges that applied to a couple of centrally – placed dress sizes and bought a tape measure from a haberdashers department in one of the big stores. I wasn't going to rush this. I would use today to observe and collate information. I went home with the tape measure and carefully recorded my hip, chest and waist sizes. I stood awkwardly up against the wall and balanced a book on my head, wedging it tightly against the wall, and twisting away from underneath it to mark my height. I was 5 foot 7 inches. That made me tallish for a woman, but short for a man. Either way, the median range worked for me in either sex. Finally I stood in front of the mirror in the bathroom and made a critical examination of myself. If I wanted to make even a passable attempt at appearing feminine, I had to be embarrassingly honest with myself.

My assessment: Height could be acceptable – I would just need to target a tall man. Tom was easily six feet. *Stop it.* Face – well I'd already remarked the feminine slant to my features when I'd peered in the car mirror. Make-up was next but for that I might have to simply experiment in private. Body: wider shouldered than a woman, but slight overall. I knew from the research I'd done so far that men transforming to women were given hormone treatment which changed their body shape and skin texture, so I decided to set aside the fear that my shape was inherently wrong and the tendency to the inverted triangle would give the game away. If I got as far as taking the transformation to its ultimate conclusion, the drugs would take care of that. My skin; I'd never made much of shaving. The boys at school when I was a teenager had religiously shaved their chins until they were sore. Often wet-shaving until their faces were red, the downy fleece that covered their upper lip and cheeks had become harsher and darker proportionate to the redness and soreness, and their self-satisfaction matched both. I had never wanted the harsh stubble – it was a nuisance, apart from – in my eyes, being unattractive. I preferred the down – that sometimes could be left for days – even weeks on end, without any attention. Consequently, I didn't have red and sore skin, and luckily I'd never been afflicted with the pulsating hard-lumped acne that some had suffered either, leaving their faces pitted and cratered like a planet surface. I peered at it closely in the mirror. It was passable as a woman's even without any treatment. I'd certainly seen women with worse skin than I had, and I had no appreciable Adam's apple either. Finally; hands and feet. I'd already noticed that women's hands were appreciably smaller than men's but again, because of my small stature, my feet were no more than a size six and my hands were small for a man. It was not going to be easy, but I could try it without looking like one of the TV's or CD's who made me cringe with embarrassment at their gaudy displays. Tomorrow, I would shop.

I'd rather dreaded the shopping to be honest, because I knew once I'd bought everything, I would have to try it all on, and then what if I DID look like one of the TV's or the CD's? Where would I go then? It was best to not think about that. Keep on to where I had been originally headed. I did my shopping over the next three days so by the time I got to Friday I had a complete women's wardrobe. I spread it out over the bed and gloated over it. It was winter so I had chosen winter clothes – good because they were much kinder on my female shortcomings than flimsy summer things would have been. I delayed the moment of actually trying them on as if teasing myself. It was like how you piled all the things you most liked to eat onto one side of your plate as a child and waited to eat them, altogether; savouring the mouth-watering tastes and forgetting that once you had eaten all the nice things there would be the nasty things to suffer too. My nasty things were facing what the future meant after that initial trying on session. That was extremely unpalatable – and yet it would have to be done if I wanted to transform from the indecisive state of unhappiness mixed with isolation that I currently hovered in. Not that the isolation would improve. I knew one of the other unpleasant side effects would be to isolate me more, ostracise me even. I wondered what my job would be, where I would live, who would deign to talk to me once the transition started – but all those nasty tastes could wait until I tested out the sensation of the nice one.

On the bed were first, as if building the layers that re-shaped the man to the woman, the bra, knickers and stockings

I had selected on my first shopping trip. I had decided my style would be ultra-feminine and dainty as I thought ultimately I would be able to carry that off. I wouldn't be one of those women that looked like a man. I would be a woman who *was* a woman. The bra was pink and frilly, like the one had been on the transsexual in the changing room. It was like that was my foundation for the whole venture so it was fitting it should mimic hers. Size 40B, so quite large, but that was because of my broader back size. It was otherwise so feminine I could hardly bear to put it on to start with. I stripped off, naked and stood in front of the full-length mirror that had been my last purchase the day before. Smooth limbed, and long chested, my body flowed away in a fluid arc from my shoulders which sloped elegantly from a long neck, down to a flat belly, covered in down. I liked my body generally. I would have been described as an attractive *sensitive* man, no doubt. I ran my hands lightly down the length of my body, thrilling to the touch, pleased with the smoothness of my skin. Now was the time to start.

I put my arms through the straps of the bra and tried to reach round to the back to slip the hooks into the eyes on the elasticated ends. I couldn't reach. I swiped at the eyes with the hooks, waiting for one to catch, like you manoeuvre a picture string over a nail in the wall. They didn't. Each time, the sides of the bra catapulted back to my sides. Dammit – how did women do this? It can't be this difficult. A small memory from childhood flashed through my mind. The only time I had seen my mother's breasts after she stopped suckling me. I'd run upstairs excitedly after school, keen to get her confirmation that I could go on the school trip that had been announced that day. It was to a local zoo and I'd never been to a zoo before. I must have rushed straight past Uncle Jim's kit bag in the hall, without even noticing it.

Clattering up the uncarpeted stairs, I'd raised the alarm for them, luckily, with just enough time for them to disentangle, and Uncle Jim to slide under the sheet, covering his hard naked body with it, but leaving a growing opaque patch of damp over the mound where his crotch was. Mum was struggling into her knickers, back to me so her ass cheeks wobbled as her left foot caught in the leg hole and she lost her balance momentarily, before untangling her toes and thrusting them quickly through and yanking the knickers up over the unhealthily white flesh. She swung round, as I reached the door with my call to action.

'Mam, Mam ...' Her breasts swung with her, elongated and drooping, with dark, dark areolas and pouting nipples rising from them like cow teats.

'Will!' she exclaimed, her face a picture of outrage. I was confused. I looked beyond her to the bed, not understanding. What was Tom's dad doing there?

'Why's Uncle Jim here?'

'Go downstairs at once – haven't I told you to never barge in on anyone without knocking on the door?'

'But the door is open already ...' In the background, the radio was playing – downstairs, it must have been. The country twang of the vocalist was familiar, but at that age I didn't know their names, only the tunes. I watched her frantically fasten her bra back to front, the bra fastening dangling over her striated stomach and the cups of the bra pointing out of her back as if she was dromedary. Then with one smooth action she whisked it round so the back was the front and the front the back and encased her dangling breasts like armour. My world stayed back to front as I tried to place Uncle Jim in both the front – Tom's home, and the back – mine. She didn't explain, and now of course, I didn't need her to, but I did also know how to fasten a bra too.

The knickers followed, and then the stockings, rolling them over my toes and then up past my knees, careful not to snag them with rough fingernails or chewed quick's. It occurred to me then that my hands were not those of a woman yet and would need more work than a cursory application of hand cream. The stockings melted into place nevertheless, and I snapped the suspender fastening. I rolled two socks into balls and moulded them into breasts within the bra cups. What had Jasmine said? *Undergarments, girls, that's what makes the difference.*

The first layer was complete. I stopped to admire it, and the sensation that flowed through me was intense and exciting. There was the disparity of overall shape, but looking beyond that, and disregarding the loathsome bulge in the centre of the panties, I was no longer Will. I was that someone else. A strange creature – a creation partly from the world of my dreams – who I wanted to be, and partly based in the real world – the man standing in front of a mirror in a dingy backroom maisonette in Raynes Park, dreaming a dream of another life. It made me afraid but tingling with anticipation too, as if not only my image but also my whole world was about to change dramatically around me. If I completed the picture, would it change almost involuntarily? If I put on the rest of the clothes, would my life change whatever I did, whoever I was? I hesitated, but only for a moment, and Will became – who?

A new song was playing on the radio in my kitchen, and its jaunty strains were persistent. Country and western; I didn't like the style much but it fitted snugly into the memory of my mother and Uncle Jim. Maybe it was even the same song? Maybe the sounds and smells of the moment mix with the sight and sensations to complete it and fix a memory forever in place. My memory associated the sight of myself with that country and western song as I heard its strains float away into the distance. I listened carefully for the name of the singer as it faded into the DJ's link; Billie Jo Spears. Oh yes, I'd heard that name before, in my childhood. Billie Jo. Billie. How crazily ridiculous that she had the female version of my name: Billie. I don't believe in signs or symbols – things either are, or they are not. That name was – me. And I was me – not male any more, but a woman.

I looked at the transformed creature in the mirror. I knew I was still partially mythical, like the woman I'd seen in the changing room. I knew I was merely the chrysalis in the cocoon, but one day that cocoon would split apart and the final version would emerge. I had no doubts at all now. That indefinable person I'd dreamt of had taken shape and I no longer wondered who I was, or what I was. I knew. I was Billie.

***

I put the diary down. The background music in the café invaded again and my mind was a buzzing confusion of images I didn't want to look at, sounds I didn't want to hear and people I didn't want to remember. 'Sweet little lies' obligingly jangled on the radio and I snorted at the irony of the aptness. The first image I wanted to avoid had to be my fathers. Even against the disturbing backdrop of Billie's own description of the man-woman morph she described Suzanne to be, and she now was becoming herself, hers wasn't as disturbing as the image of my father. His was an image I'd naively never placed in the stage setting that was our lives back in Wilverton all those years ago, other than as a leader; head of the household, above reproach. A farcical stage setting: a play about disloyalty and betrayal. My God, it ran in our family, but the sins of the father were well and truly turned on me now, weren't they?

Against my will I conjured up my father's face, smiling blandly, slightly florid. He must have had high blood pressure even then, when I was still a child. A time bomb ticking away; but thick brown hair without any grey, solid muscular frame and a rich baritone voice gave him the impression of rampant masculinity and supreme health. I saw now it also probably made him an attractive local lothario; a substitute superstar for the local women who fluttered over the likes of Tom Jones, or the current romantic heart throb of the upper working class women of the day. In fact the physical similarity was marked. I trawled my childhood view of him. Could I remember any signs of his intimacy with Will's mother? She simpered at him when they met, but then she'd done that with every man. I remembered that quite clearly about her. Perhaps that simpering had fanned the flames of jealousy in her bully of a husband? The artfully coy expression and sickly sweet smile reserved for men, the hawkish critical tone she took with women. Mam had called her 'catty' in an unguarded moment once. As a child the comment had made me smile impishly. I'd superimposed a cat face over Mary Robinsons'. It fitted well – the exaggeratedly high cheekbones that in Will gave a mysteriously eastern European look made her look hard and calculating. The eyes were almond shaped like Will's but the cheekbones emphasised the sense of calculating predator. She had a sneering smile. I imagined her baring sharp feline incisors instead of eye teeth, and hissing instead of smiling. Yes, Mrs Robinson definitely looked catty to me too, but I couldn't say that to Will then. What on earth had Dad seen in her compared to Mam?

Alongside the cat I placed my mother, the faithful dog. Yes, if I were allocating analogous animals to them she was without doubt the faithful homely mongrel, indeterminate colouring, soft face, deep soulful brown eyes, always eager to please. That meant Dad was the rutting stag, careless of where he shared his physical favours, sowing where he pleased. Almost bestial in how little he'd cared about the fragility of my childhood friendships or my mother's feelings. The image of him pulling the sheet over his hard post-sex body turned him into a stranger to me, one I now hated. I felt angry with Will for showing me this world I'd been blithely unaware of – and then the anger turned inwards as I chided myself for my blindness. Why had I never seen these people for who they were when they were alive? Deaf with my ears and blind with my mind: stupid.

A surge of grief for my mother and the betrayal my father had regularly subjected her to made me weak with pain. My throat hardened into a solid lump. In this soulless café I wanted to cry aloud for my mother as I'd never cried when she died. As I'd never grieved when I'd watched her plain wooden coffin being placed alongside my father's in the freshly dug grave just after my prison sentence had started. The musty smell of the loam we'd thrown in a moist brown clod was fresh in my nostrils, the feel of it as it crumbled away and landed in a pitter-patter like rain on the coffin lid, muddy confetti disfiguring the name plate vied with the sounds and smells of the cafe. The family had stood apart from me, dressed in my shabby black suit – the one allocated for use by inmates attending relative's funerals, and to be returned at the prison entrance. Even my clothing for a funeral had been the states to determine, but it didn't matter by then. What had I left anyway? Dignity meant little when I'd already lost self-respect long ago. It was the day I'd said goodbye to Billie too. Two losses in one day. Too much to dwell on normally.

I wished I could have grieved for her then, but I'd only felt anger at her for dragging me back to witness Lucy's deception when the baby was due. She'd thought she was trying to recreate the happy family that I'd destroyed, but I knew only sour betrayal and resented her interference. She'd been trying to make for me what she thought she'd had, a home and a marriage. Now I knew hers had been as illusory as my 'happy' home. I hoped she hadn't known about Dad and Mary Robinson. My heart ached for her. I knew she'd done everything for me out of love, but love makes a mockery of us. It makes us vulnerable and thrown into the force of the battle without the armour to survive.

The sins of the father had visited down the line – and to my shame I'd followed in his footsteps with my indiscretion with Susie, but my sin had rebounded on me a hundred fold. The grief subsided and gave way to guilt. If I hadn't had the fling with Susie, would Lucy and I been struggling on now as my mother and father had done, papering over the cracks, living a lie, but both of us here, surviving, and prison one of those stories I'd never known, like my father's indiscretions with Will's mother? Would Billie be living the life she'd envisaged for herself now? Would the guilt, the blame, the prejudice, the pain be numbed – or even non-existent?

As if to answer me with no answer at all, Maclean's 'Empty Chairs' lilted through the café, cutting through the clanging of the door as another customer arrived and one left. The cappuccino machine hissed and the low rumble of the outside traffic echoed inside. It was too emotionally haunting to attract the attention of anyone but me, and the waitress who watched me suspiciously from time to time. For me, it was the epitome of my life. All the people in my life who had gone, all of them, had left me here – and the best and the worst of them was you, Billie.

Chapter 11:

Beginnings and endings, 1982-1983

I let the diary rest back I on the table and the memories settled round me like a dark cloak. The noise of the café bubbled around me as the waitresses watchful eyes checked on me from time to time as she weaved amongst the tables, taking and distributing orders. For the moment I was undisturbed in my back seat, deep in the belly of the belching café. Steam spewed from the boiling hot water urn in great welts of heat and I idly imagined myself in the gated factory setting of one of the old paper or linen mills that had once dominated my father's Midland's childhood home. The crackle of the chip pan churning out its next batch of greasy fries dragged me unceremoniously back to the present I was trying to avoid. Dull grey customers and dull grey lives. I counted myself amongst them. The unhealthy pallor of prison life must have long since taken the freshness from my once rosy boyhood cheeks, just as I'd thought death had stolen it from yours, Billie. Maybe worst was the wrong word to use about you; how we ended made me feel the worst.

The Will I thought I knew was already a different Will to the one I imagined. There were some elements of the tale I already knew. He'd told me parts, in summarised form in some of those late night confessionals we'd had later, but the words had been measured, almost impersonal – like he didn't want to let me too far into his thoughts until he'd completed them for himself. Reading the intimacy of the diary was like being in another world, one I'd lived in without any idea of the pain or bewilderment it contained for him. It was hard to read on, knowing I'd contributed to some of that pain, especially in a place where my thoughts might be reflected on my face for all the other bums and time wasters to see, but it was necessary now. Blindness had to be replaced by sight if I was to be able to move on from here.

I shifted on the hard plastic chair, deflecting the waitress's intrusive look with a hard stare and then shielding my face by cupping my forehead and top of my head in my hand and propping my elbow on the table top. The rickety table wobbled with the movement and the dregs of coffee in the cup in front of me shivered, disturbing the thick slimy skin the congealing milk had formed on it. It ripped in two, like a tea leaf reading, foretelling separation – couldn't have been more apt. I smoothed the diary open, flattening the spine where the densely packed pages made it crowd in on itself. The café slipped a million miles away as I immersed myself in it again.

***

February 1982

I've not been encouraged much by the doctor I'd seen. He'd looked me up and down as if I was psychotic and asked exactly why such a normal and good looking young man would want to disfigure a perfectly good God-given body. His Scottish accent rolled the questions briskly off his tongue in a way that applied more censure than the words alone did, and the raised eyebrows and wrinkled brow over the small framed glasses that hung on the end of his nose wedged there merely by the flare of his nostrils completed the picture of distaste. A clock ticked bleakly in the coldness of his consulting room and the room smelt as musty as the attitude of the man pronouncing judgement over me. But he was my doctor, so he had to offer treatment of a sort. He meted it out like a sentence. At least a year as living fully as a woman and accepted as such before anyone at Charing Cross Hospital would even see me – and there would have to be the psych evaluation beforehand. He implied that if I even got as far as the psych evaluation, its' very results would damn me. I supposed they would – either way; damned as a failure, or damned as an abomination, in his eyes. I nodded, depressed at the length of time before anything could change. Yet I also knew, as I walked away, that having undertaken to start the process – the change was already underway; had been underway from the very moment I looked at myself in the car mirror and defined myself as female not male. Tracking my progress required me to report in at regular intervals with the doctor and suffer the raised eyebrows each time, and the interrogation about what I was doing to prove I was more woman than man. He rolled the 'more woman' over his tongue with disdain, looking me up and down again, as he did so.

I started by walking the evening streets, working on the basis that the half-light would mask the inconsistencies I had still to iron out. After a while I'd lured wolf-whistles from the brickies on the construction site at the end of the road. I knew they'd whistle at anything in a skirt, but simply being the something in the skirt had reinforced my view of myself as a woman and given me sufficient confidence to approach the doctor to tentatively ask what else could be done. My research had established what gender change entailed and the whole picture was a gruesome one, with numerous operations, and prejudice to overcome, and yet, having now stood in Billies' place as well as Wills', I knew there was nowhere to go but forward. The walks out at twilight, the regular practicing of the more feminine posture, the mannerisms – even the way women spoke and flirted whether they were merely talking to a tradesman or they were targeting an interest – they were all part of the regime I now had to follow if I was to make that move forward.

April 1982

The most difficult change has been at work. How do you explain to a group of middle-class, middle-aged conformist women that you want to reject your normal male status and become one of them? It was the most difficult conversation I'd ever had, and my stomach churned over and over like the cement mixer on the brickie's site before it happened, and the foundations were laid to move forward. We were all gathered in a staff meeting at the end of the day. It was Wednesday. The mid-week 'wag', Sheila called it. Sheila was a bit of a wag in her own way. I liked Sheila. She looked after all of us. 'Wag' was short for chinwag, and our staff meetings were more chin-wag than strategy. The usual round of gossip completed, we moved onto more important things.

'I like your shoes, Dot.'

'Oh, thank you. I got them last weekend; bit frivolous for work, but sometimes you have to, don't you?'

'I know, that's what I thought about this.' Joan rummaged in her shopping bag and produced a blouse, still with its sales tags swinging off it. Dot considered it with pursed lips. She obviously wasn't sure but didn't like to comment. I was invited into the party as I sat back down next to them with a fresh coffee.

'Will, you have a good eye, do you like this?' Dot was handing me the hot coal and I knew it. I decided I would hand the hot coal back to all of them right then. Everyone was sitting round the table, comfortably tête-à-tête. The invitation to make the decision over the blouse was the signal that my acceptance was at the highest level I could hope to achieve. I took a deep breath as my stomach gurgled awkwardly and I felt like I wanted to vomit it out, not explain it.

'I have something difficult to tell you all.' The hum of their chatter hushed immediately and five pairs of eyes swivelled towards me. I put the blouse carefully back in Joan's bag and met their onslaught.

'I've made a difficult decision recently because I've not been happy the way I am.' I felt too hot as if their eyes were spotlights and I was star of the show. It was now or never. I continued, feeling the sweat trickling down my back and gathering in a round patch under my arms. 'I want to be a woman, and in order to do so, I have to live like one for a year before the doctor will refer me for any treatment.' It came out in a rush, and I wondered after I said it if I'd made sense at all. Their eyes remained fixed on me as if I'd spoken in an alien tongue. I thought they must be able to hear my heart pounding in the silence, but no-one acknowledged it. My stomach gurgled ridiculously and it broke the stifling silence. Dot was the first to speak.

'You're a man. You can't be a woman.' There was bewilderment in her voice. Joan frowned at me and shook her head as if I'd said something bad in her class. She took the afternoon mother and toddler story times so there was more than a little of the schoolmarm in her.

'What on earth are you talking about, Will?' That brought a clamour of similar questions. It was Sheila to whom I will remain eternally grateful; Sheila with her chinwags and motherly homilies. Sheila; the grandmother who knitted tea cosies and wore sensible shoes, but had a mischievous twinkle in her eyes maybe only I noticed. No-nonsense and solid as a rock, she took over for me.

'Oh for goodness sake, he can't be much clearer, can he? He wants to be a woman. He's a man, but he wants to be a woman. What would you prefer dear?' She addressed this last to me. 'Are you a transvestite or do you want to actually *be* a woman?' I could barely believe what I was hearing. The words from Sheila's mouth were just too incongruous and I wanted to laugh hysterically. This was like a scene from a Cambridge footlights sketch.

'Actually be one,' was all I could stutter. Sheila carried on comfortably for me, winding a new colour strand of wool onto her needles and starting another row.

'It's not that uncommon,' she began, and went on to give the rest of the team a concise summary of how some people felt that their gender was confused and in reality they were the opposite sex to the one they were born as. It was a scholarly and precise lecture delivered matter of fact as I listened in amazement, and the rest of the team gave her their rapt attention. She ended it with 'am I right?' to me. I didn't reply straightaway. My mouth was wide open like a fish in mid swallow and my tongue was stuck to the roof. It was just too surreal. Then I registered her question was aimed at me.

'Yes.' My reply was strangled, completely astonished by her familiarity with the subject. There was silence as the women round the table eyed each other and me.

'Are you like that?' Dot asked incredulously.

'Yes.' It was barely audible, but they all heard me. The suffocating hush in the room settled around us again apart from that one question and answer. I felt doomed. It was a far cry from the normal comfortably gossip laden wag and I wished I hadn't spoiled it for them. My resignation letter was already in my pocket. I reached to draw the slightly crumpled envelope out and put it on the table in front of me.

'What's that?' asked Dot.

'My resignation letter.'

'Why?' asked Joan.

'Because I didn't think you'd want to work with me now.' My guts rolled over as a batch of vomit churned to completion in my cement mixer stomach. A wave of nausea passed through me, making me prickle with heat and light headedness. The moment that presaged the start of my new life had come and gone and now it was done. I shifted in my seat in readiness to leave before the nausea made me disgrace myself too.

'I think you'd make a lovely woman.' It was said very quietly and came from June, the shyest and most retiring of the whole team, sitting nondescriptly at the far end of the table. Everyone's gaze swivelled immediately to June. June hardly ever said anything. She blushed deeply. 'I do,' she added, defiantly. There was another silence, and all the eyes swivelled back to me.

'Actually, so do I,' agreed Dot. The eyes travelled to her.

'Of course he would.' No-nonsense Sheila sealed the deal. The murmurings of agreement round the table left me confused.

'You don't mind?' I was nonplussed.

'Why would we, dear? What you want to be is up to you.' Sheila again. 'That's what I tell my grandchildren. Why are you any different?' Sheila's lead encouraged followers. The murmurings were more definite. Joan added merrily,

'You'll have to change your shoes.'

'And your hairstyle,' from Joan.

'You need more colour.'

'What about make-up?'

All of a sudden the silence had turned to a buzz of excitement, leaving me punch drunk. Over the weeks and months that followed I couldn't help feeling that I became their plaything, and they returned to girlhood, but with the benefit of a walking-talking-living-doll body to dress and fashion. I didn't care. In the depths of suburbia, our little local library became a hot bed of subterfuge and liberalist gender anarchy as I outwardly transformed from Will to Billie, with the help of my team. Sometimes they were as arch and exuberantly raucous as the TV's in the Kings Road shop had been. Without them I wouldn't have been at the point I was when Tom rang my doorbell, and disaster walked in with him.

'How did you know?' I asked Sheila.

'I read all the books you did, when I was reviewing the withdrawals,' she replied. 'And it was obvious as soon as you walked through the door anyway,' she added enigmatically, and walked away. I didn't bother to ask her to explain. I was too stupidly happy.

May 1982

Prejudice is odd. My middle class female co-workers set it completely aside and embraced me as one of their own; the last ones I could have expected to do that, whereas the doctor I consulted was the complete opposite. The monthly check-in was excruciatingly awkward. I would come home wanting to cry, feeling dirty, warped, worse than the worse serial killer or child molester. He delighted in asking the most debasingly embarrassing questions, but I had to answer otherwise I wasn't working co-operatively with him.

'Do you wank often?'

'Pardon?'

'Wank; masturbate – you know what I mean, you're a man.' He emphasised the last word, and looked over his glasses meaningfully at me. I swallowed my anger for the countless time and replied with as much dignity as the answer gave me.

'No.'

'Are you odd?' He looked at me in mock surprise. I guessed he relished the opportunity to call me odd that my reply to the question had given him.

'No, I just don't.'

'Abnormal sexual response.' He read aloud as he made the note.

'I don't have an abnormal sexual response, I just don't want to have a sexual response that way – it's like affirming masculinity whereas I don't feel masculine at all, that's why I'm here talking to you.'

'But you're a man at the moment.'

'I know, but I don't want to be.' I tried hard not to sound sarcastic. I knew he was looking for just one reason – any reason – to be able to refuse to see me again. We faced each other out. I remained silent. You will not find that reason, I thought over and over again like a mantra. The frustration with him dissipated. He breathed out heavily.

'Next appointment, one month's time.'

'How long will this go on for?'

'Why, don't think you can hack it over a long time?'

'No, I'm fine with it, just want to know.'

'Ah, well I'll see you at least eleven times more.'

That will be over a year then,'

'Will it?'

'Yes, can something start to happen then?'

'Only when I think it's appropriate.' He smiled at me, cruelly polite. He knew he had all the power. I got up to leave.

'Like the skirt,' he called sarcastically after me as I walked out. He kept me hanging on a further two months after that one year appointment, but guidelines are guidelines , and I'd read up on them. He had no choice but to refer me for the psych appointment when I'd completed the year. My team at the library made it possible, fussing around me like mother hens seeing their daughter off to her first prom, but of course it was only the beginning.

June 1982

So here I am, in front of the mirror, wondering whether I have the guts to go out again this morning. A night's sleep and sanctuary in my home has done nothing to dispel the sense of ridicule I felt when I walked home yesterday evening. I suppose I'd become blasé. The women at work have all been so supportive and I realise now they must have hushed or deflected the embarrassing questions the library customers have asked. I've been living in a cocoon, thinking this was so easy, that the only difficult encounter I had was the monthly visit to the GP, but yesterday I met prejudice head on.

The usual wolf-whistles rained down on me from the building site down the road. I walked jauntily past it, complacent that I was really starting to look feminine. One of the whistles was followed by a comment.

'Hey darlin', like the way your ass wiggles.' I smirked to myself.

'And yer tits.' Whoops and more wolf-whistles followed. 'Yeah, get yer tits out for us love.' The voice was crude but like music to me. Ironic that most women would shiver with disgust at the obscenities that followed, but to me they were like endorsement of my better self. A bubble of joy inflated inside my chest, and the pavement sprung under my feet like a mattress bouncing me home. The high was better than dope and I sashayed along the road, giving an extra twist to my ass wiggle and hoping my tits were swaying for them. My performance encouraged the audience and one of them scrambled down the ladder from the upper level of scaffolding to get a better look. He stopped, mid step and then continued to the bottom level. He wolf-whistled again and I turned, so puffed out with pride I didn't see where this was going.

'Get yer tits out love,' he repeated clearly, and then waited for my response. I didn't see the calculation in it until it was too late. I stuck my hip out, hand on it and faced him, feeling every inch the sassy female. He roared with laughter.

'Hey, Skanky,' he called over his shoulder to the figure leaning precariously over the edge of the scaffolding two levels higher. 'You owe me a fiver. I'm right, she's not a bird. She's a bloke in drag. A queen.' He bent double with the laughter, and then came up again, pointing at me. 'You got an ass, *lady,* but not for wiggling, for fucking!' The quip brought a chorus of obscenities and crude laughter from the other workmen now gathered on the top level, pointing and making fun. I froze, not sure how to respond. In all these months I'd never experienced being made fun of or insulted. It had made me assume I never would – that all the claims that prejudice was rife were exaggerated to try to put you off. How stupid could I have been? Of course I was going to experience hostility. My cheeks flamed and the tears pricked my eyes. I'd failed. Then suddenly the anger at being deliberately ridiculed took over and flamed white hot. Dropping all semblance of femininity, I shouted back at them.

'You fucking assholes, you're all no brainers with dicks for mouths!' I stood defiantly for a few seconds as the insult sunk in, until the first piece of debris hit the pavement about three feet away. It was a small piece of broken brick, jagged on one edge. It bounced and rolled a short distance along the pavement, leaving a trail of red brick dust like blood in its wake. I looked up and the youth who'd thrown it down on me, held his arm aloft, making a fist. I was shocked and stood indecisively for a second or two, more insults and outrage rolling around my head. The second stone hit within inches of my feet and the third narrowly missed my head. I turned and ran, tripping awkwardly over the bumps in the cracked pavement and twisting my ankle over in the high heels, stumbling inelegantly to one side as I struggled to escape the steady rain of stones and shingle they were now flinging. A small piece of gravel stung as it whipped past my cheek, cutting it. I put my hand up instinctively to shield it and another piece scratched the knuckles as it hurtled past. The insults followed the stones until I rounded the corner of the road and my garden gate was in sight.

'Weirdo.'

'Bum fucker.'

'Perv.'

I slowed after I turned the corner, trying to catch the breath that was coming in ragged gasps, ankles and calves burning from trying to run in heels, and heart pounding with a mixture of fear and anger. My face stung where the gravel had cut and my hand was sore. I held it as if protecting it would make the pain go away, but the pain was as much inside as from the outer wound. Shaken, I fumbled with the key in the lock. It slipped as usual and my clumsiness was doubled by frustration and trembling. The key twisted reluctantly and I flung the door back, and slammed it behind me. The only other time I'd felt as shaken and afraid as this was when Old Mother J's son had caught Tom when we'd been stealing apples as teenagers and had beaten him up. The sight of his split nose and blood streaming down his face had compounded in me the fear of violence I'd had from childhood, always aware that my mother took the beatings from my father to spare Fran and me. I wanted to save her but couldn't face the thought of feeling the pain myself. Shame made the pain and the fear worse.

I kicked off the now twisted and mud splattered shoe, one heel sticking out at an oblique angle from the sole where it had split and given way as I twisted over in it. I climbed the stairs slowly to the bathroom and steeled myself to look in the mirror. The cut on my cheek and the grazed knuckles were superficial, but I couldn't stop the shaking. It was like an inner part of me had lost its core intensity and I shook from the inside out. Still in front of the bathroom mirror I tried to wipe the cut with wet cotton wool, but my fingers felt leaden and out of control. In the end I went back downstairs and just sat at the grey table in the kitchen and waited for the trembling to stop. It took a long while and then I felt icy cold. I went from the kitchen to the bedroom and climbed into bed without even taking off my clothes; curling into the small foetal ball I'd last curled myself into after the night with Freddie. The world went from full of excitement and hope to mean and frightening. I felt so alone, but couldn't even find the tears to cry. When I woke in the morning, the first thing I thought of was how I would face the route to work, and I knew I couldn't.

My semi-judgemental attitude towards the TV's changed to admiration for their fortitude in parading their peacock of colours despite the derogatory comments that were made to them. Comments I'd heard so many times but ignored – or worse still laughed along with in the past. How had I not equated myself with them before now? How was I different? Oh I could fool myself by saying I'd a feminine look, and my hair was long and lush now; I have great eyes, and good clothes style, but what am I really? They may have been designed to hurt, but those insults flung at me were all true. Looking long and hard at my reflection in the mirror I am a pathetic parody of a woman. I had no hips other than what I produced by careful clothes choice – the right cut and colour. The swell of my breasts were socks stuffed in a bra, not living flesh that would tense and respond to a caress. I was a fraud. I wanted to talk to someone but who was there to talk to? I stayed in bed the next day, huddled around a pillow. It felt as if I was holding on tight to someone, but there was no-one there. Unexpectedly, I wanted to be holding onto my mother or Fran. I fell asleep and woke later and the sky was dark. It was night and all I could delineate for myself was day and night. Everything else felt numb – future, past, present. All lost in a cocoon of misery. The insults from the building site gang played over and over in my mind. The stones and rocks aimed at me had shaken my belief in humanity as dramatically as if I had been part of a volcanic eruption and the lava of hate had spewed up and flowed around me. Now it felt as if it had set around me like a prison. How could I go out into public if that was how they looked on me? How could I live out a life with these people who wanted to maim and ridicule me? How could I live a life so alone? I felt as if I was spiralling further down into a bottomless black pit and each minute and second took me further into it. I didn't want to move.

I heard a noise at my front door and tensed – was it one of them, come to taunt me again? Come to beat me? I listened, stock still in my foetal curl, heart pounding unsteadily. The noise went away. After half an hour, curiosity drove me to the top of the stairs. Looking down a plain envelope lay face down on the mat. The post usually arrived earlier. I stood at the top of the stairs, tempted to go down and retrieve the envelope, but afraid of someone still being at the door. I peered at the glass in the front door trying to make out a shape. There didn't seem to be one, just the occasional blurred flash of a car as it passed, so I walked gingerly down the stairs and edged towards the door, sliding cautiously along the wall. I grabbed the envelope and ran back upstairs, fear catching at my heels and making my heart skip beats as I slipped back into bed and pulled the covers round me as if that would make me safer. The writing on the envelope was all in capitals and it had no stamp so it must have been hand-delivered. I slit the envelope open and pulled out the single sheet inside.

'WE KNOW WHAT YOU ARE – PERVERT. STAY AWAY FROM OUR KIDS OR YOU WON'T NEED SURRGERY TO BE LIKE A WOMEN.'

From the misspellings, they were plainly uneducated. It didn't say anything else but it didn't need to. The threat from the building site had passed on like wildfire to the neighbourhood. The sheet fused to my hand like a death sentence proclaimed by the court of humanity. What was the point? I couldn't think of anything else to do but pull my knees up and hug them, resting my forehead on them to sob. There was no-one to turn to. Maybe it was time to tell Fran and my mother now?

I stayed in bed until the following evening when hunger pangs eventually forced me out, but I couldn't bring myself to go to work for the rest of the week. My self-enforced exile was broken by Sheila, of all people, and chicken soup. The knocking at the door made me think that the letter writer had come back and was maybe considering continuing with what they'd suggested they would do. I cowered in the lounge, behind the door, hoping they'd think I'd gone out. The knocking continued and I felt as if I my heart was thundering in my chest as I wondered how I could get out without anyone seeing me.

'Billie?' The voice took me further off-balance, nearly wetting myself. I couldn't place the voice. Who was it? Which one of my neighbours had come to torture and cut me? I felt sick and my stomach clenched painfully in terror. 'Billie, its Sheila – come to see how you are. Are you there? I can see lights on.' The relief at hearing her name and realising that I did know the voice, it was just fear that had wiped her from my mind made me run to open the door. The soup pot came through the door before she did. She took in the dishevelled look, the grazed cheek, which by now had developed a large grey blue bruise as well, and the scratched fingers. My eyes must have still had the kind of look that rabbits have when caught in the headlights of a car. That was how I imagined I must have looked – wide-eyed and frozen-faced.

'Sticks and stones,' was all she said as she pushed the door open enough for her to follow the soup pot. She didn't ask what had happened and I didn't tell her. She talked about what had been going on at the library all week, related the domestic disasters of the rest of the team and made life seem just normal and mundane again. By the time she got up to leave, having watched me eat all of the soup in the pot, I felt as if my life might have a routine again; one of ordinary people and ordinary things that I was part of. Not an oddity or a pervert, as the labourers had called me, just different. The next day was Saturday and it wasn't my turn to work so I had time to reinforce the sense of returning to some kind of normality. I didn't think the building site was active at the weekend and I decided to brave walking past it as part of my rehabilitation. Why should I not live out my life how I wanted to? What harm was I doing to anyone? The fear was as great as when I watched old Mother J's son beat Tom black and blue. I nearly turned back at the corner but Sheila's voice came back to me.

'Sticks and stones.'

Wasn't that also what the literature I'd read had implied? It wouldn't be easy, and there would be enormous prejudice and rejection. I'd merely taken some while to encounter it. With trepidation but heartfelt relief I saw the site was completely deserted as I neared it. I hurried down into the depths of the tube station, very aware of any glance in my direction. The young woman on the seat opposite me on the tube looked me over once and then ignored me, nose buried in her paperback. I looked surreptitiously either side of me but the Rasta to the left was in his own world and the couple entwined on the seats the other side were too engrossed in sucking face to notice anything else but each other. I felt thankfully invisible on the short trip to the Kings Road and disappeared into the shop as if it was the same kind of sanctuary as my home. Christine and one of the other TV's were browsing through the 'for sale' rail and greeted me noisily as I came in. One glance and one word told me I needn't worry that I could be mistaken for a TV, but I also knew that I had a long way to go until my transition was complete.

Sticks and stones. No, they wouldn't break me.

July 1982

After that incident I decided it was time to brave telling Mother and Fran. I couldn't rely on Sheila being my moral support all the time, and the feeling of needing my mother around had made me feel oddly like a vulnerable child again. There were some more letters of the same ilk but no further stone-throwing from the workmen, just regular loud and disgusting abuse, concentrating on my ass and what they could do with it.

'Got anything up there today, Queenie?'

'Yer tights are ripped Queenie – oh no, it's just brown stuff dribbling down yer legs.'

'Close yer legs Queenie, yer breath smells like fart.'

After the first round of abuse, I laid aside my non-confrontational stance and stuck one finger up at them as I passed when the volley of insults started. It produced raucous laughter and some more insults but no stones. I walked on, seething, but head held high, muttering 'sticks and stones, sticks and stones,' under my breath. It wasn't until I rounded the corner and got to the tube entrance that I let out my breath fully, expecting one of them to run up behind me and swing me round into a fist heading straight for my face or worse, but it didn't happen. A week later I went to see Mother and Fran in Wilverton. I went dressed as Will, with my new life as Billie contained in a bag to change into once I'd explained to them. I knew it would raise a storm but I was in fighting mood. Fran answered the door to me, the baby stuck on her hip, chubbily waving happy fists at me and cooing. She didn't care if I was male, female or morph. I was simply another human. Fran would though.

'Hello there,' she leaned towards me for the mandatory kiss. She smelled of talcum powder and baby sick. She was chubbier than the last time I'd seen her, even despite the loss of the baby bump. I kissed the cheek she held out to me.

'How are you?' I asked as the baby's small clenched fist thumped ineffectually against my head and she announced 'da!'

'No that's not your da,' Fran laughed. 'This is Will, your uncle.' The baby waved her fist again and repeated the 'da-da' insistently as if disagreeing with Fran.

'She's grown.' I commented.

'Well of course she has, she's nearly six months old now – not that you would know, stranger.' Her playful punch was a little harder than the babies and I suspected there was more than a little intent behind it. The strange link that had appeared from nowhere the night before her wedding re-established itself with the punch and she tipped her head on one side and followed up with 'is everything ok?'

'Why?'

'Because you're visiting when normally you try like hell to avoid us – not that I blame you sometimes.' She tossed her head meaningfully towards the door at the end of the hall; the door to the front room. Mother would be sitting primly in there on the edge of the sofa, waiting for me – like a visit from royalty was being allowed, anxious to show me that all was perfect here. The best china would be set out on the tea tray in the kitchen and Mother would pour the milk politely from the small crystal milk jug that was really only moulded glass that she kept for these occasions. I hated it, her pretence that she was alright – that in my childhood days, she was fine, not hurting or afraid or anxious. I'd always just wanted a happy family like the other kids seemed to have. It seemed I'd never had one and never would. 'She's got a lot worse recently. The doctor said it might be something called senile dementia. She thought Joe was Dad the other day, and I had to explain some of it to him, which was embarrassing.'

'Some of what?' I feigned ignorance because I was surprised at Fran mentioning being aware of anything even vaguely inappropriate within our family. I hadn't been sure if she'd known about the beatings. She looked at me as if I was mad. I stayed silent, not wanting to put my foot in it before I even got to my news. 'Well how they used to...' she stopped and pursed her lips at me how Mother did and I glimpsed Fran at sixty. It chilled me. 'Oh Will, didn't you know?' I still said nothing. This was turning out to be revelatory for me as well as for her. 'The other man and the arguments.'

'What other man and arguments?' Now I was nonplussed. Fran looked amazed. Didn't you know about Tom's father and Mum? Oh Will, I'm sorry I've put my foot in it.' She looked concerned, forehead wrinkling in the same way Mothers did when she was vexed. She bit her lip. Now that Mother didn't do, and I was relieved to see a Fran characteristic that wasn't Mothers. Genes could do a lot but innate personality would win through. I wanted an ally in my family at all costs.

'Well there was one day I came home early and Mum was getting dressed and Tom's father was here. I only remembered it the other day. I think I'd buried it. But I thought that must have been a one-off – not that it makes it any better.' Fran shook her head.

'I was always home early on Wednesdays, remember? Mrs Grigson used to have to go home to Mr Grigson at 2 o'clock when I was in primary because the nurse couldn't visit him then and someone had to change his bag or he would have gone toxic.' Her eyes wandered wistfully off my face for a second as she went into herself and recalled her childhood memories. 'Frankie Roberts liked me then. I wonder whatever became of him? And I always wondered what going toxic was like.' She came back to the present day with what seemed a wrench and looked me full in the face again. 'We were meant to stay and do our homework but on the quiet we all used to slip home early. The first time was like you and they were just getting dressed. I didn't understand but after that I caught them out several times and Irene Atkins had just had a little brother born and she'd caught her parents at it so she told me what she thought they were doing. Dad already knew anyway. That's what they used to argue about and that's why he hit her. He was jealous.' In those few words my whole view of my father and mother and childhood whirled and turned on its head.

'Frailty, thy name is woman.'₃

'Pardon?' Fran frowned at me.

'It's a quote about betrayal.' It was automatic, not really a comment on my mother. I hadn't even started to get my head round that. Realising she'd been unfaithful once was shocking enough. Now knowing it was a serial offence and that my sister, her friend and probably most of the school – even the village – knew, given Irene Atkins blabbing mouth, was something quite different. We stood looking at each other in the hallway, uncertain where to go from here. Life had taken on yet another hue, darker than ever before. I wondered if Tom knew what his father and my mother did when no-one else was home. I couldn't imagine telling him. He'd worshipped his father.

'You didn't know she had a long term affair with him?' Fran asked again tentatively.

'No.'

'Oh.'

'Did you know about the beatings?'

'Yes.'

'Then I've been protecting you all these years, and you knew more than I did.' Now I felt betrayed, and stupid.

'She hurt him too. It was that kind of a relationship – mutually abusive.' She grimaced. Not a nice thing to have to acknowledge about your parents, but maybe it showed that Fran would be tolerant of my situation. Perhaps even Mother might too. I took a deep breath and launched my offensive.

'I've got something to tell you that you don't know then.'

'What. You're not ill are you?'

'No, I'm fine.'

'You've lost weight.' She looked me over critically.

'Really, I'm not ill, but I am,' I hesitated, trying to find a word that might introduce the topic without telling all straight away. A gentle lead in, 'troubled, 'I ended with eventually.

'Tom?'

'No, not Tom – why do you always make a beeline for Tom?'

'Because you do, Will, you've always hero-worshipped him. But he's not your sort, you know. There's talk around town that he's trouble. Don't get drawn into it with him, whatever it is if you're in touch. You've always kept your nose clean and led a respectable life.' I snorted at that.

'Respectable. Well that's where you're wrong about me.'

'So there is something wrong – are you in debt, lost your job, got a girl in trouble?' The questions came out like gun fire. I shook my head vigorously at them and laughed wildly at the irony of the last suggestion.

'Fran, stop. Please listen to me, before I have to tell Mum. I'm a transsexual.' Fran stared at me uncomprehendingly. The door at the end of the hall opened at precisely the same moment. Fran's mouth opened and shut like she was miming words in a silent movie but Mothers voice cut across the hall before they could develop into sound. I could see the light slowly dawning as Mother intervened.

'There you are Will. What are you doing out here? I've been waiting for you to come into the front room ever since the doorbell went. Come on, I have the tea all ready.' She looked at Fran's open mouth and shocked expression and then back at me. The timing of my bombshell couldn't have been worse. I'd wanted to explain a bit before the issue was aired in front of Mother but Fran's response detonated then, like the delay between throwing the grenade and it exploding.

'Oh my God, you're one of those cross-thingies like the murderer in that 'Dressed to Kill' film Joe brought home the other day.' The pronouncement was to the hall at large, but 'that's disgusting!' felt like it was aimed at me specifically. Her face screwed up as if a bad smell had wafted into the cramped hallway. 'It's perverted to have men dressing up like women. What do you think you are doing, what do you think you are doing?' Her voice edged up a tone until the last 'what do you think you are doing' was almost a screech. I was surprised by the intensity of her response. I'd expected her to be surprised, but not horrified. 'Get away, get away from Jenny! You're sick!' She clasped the baby tightly to her as if to protect her from me, pinioning the baby's head against her chest. The baby wailed in protest and suddenly where the hall had been hushed, it was full of sound and fury. I stepped forward to remonstrate with her. She stepped back from me as if I was diseased and she might catch my infection.

'Fran, please, I'm not perverted or sick.' She shook her head and backed away further. Like an emotional recoil.

'Oh my God, I've put up with a mother who shags her friend's husband, a father who beats his wife and a husband who drinks too much. People called me *that poor girl,* and now it's *that poor woman.* They've done that since we were children but at least you were ok, Will. Now they'll whisper *wierdos* behind my back too. When you led me down the aisle to get married, I was so proud of you. All the teasing I used to do about Tom, it was only jealousy to wind you up because you were more interested in him than me. You were the clever one, the one who went to London, went to university, was going to make something of yourself, was going to escape this shit hole; this bloody awful life of abuse and artificiality. But this is what you've made of yourself – a pervert!' She spat the last word at me and a fleck of spittle landed on my cheek. 'How could you let me down? How could you be like them?' Mother's voice floated up the hallway, querulous.

'The tea is getting cold. What is all this arguing about? Fran, go and tell your Dad that the tea is ready.'

Neither of us answered her. Fran stood belligerently in front of me, chin jutting angrily, lips pursed, but strangely she was trembling too. I waited for her to calm down.

'Fran I'm not like them, I'm me. But me isn't straightforward.' Her face softened but the fire in her eyes still burned. The heat of her anger scarred me and my mouth tasted of the ash of my own charred life as I continued quietly, still hoping the underlying affection we'd discovered as we'd stood looking up at the stars the night before her wedding would heal the rift the dereliction of our family had caused. 'I came to talk to you and Mother about it so you would understand.'

'Oh my God, you *are* one of them, oh my God.' Just as suddenly as she'd rounded angrily on me, now her face crumpled and she cried, tears dripping down her face and raining onto her light blue jumper, staining it with dark splotches. The baby copied and started to howl too. 'You're my brother. You should be normal. I just want something normal in my life.' The combined wailing of woman and child was like the eerie howl of a storm tearing around the house. I cringed at the pain I was causing. If I'd known she'd react so badly, I would have said nothing, but how could I have known? How could I have known there was so much beneath her surface I hadn't been aware of? It was like expecting her to know what had been under mine, and even I hadn't figured that out until now. I hadn't realised on that pre-wedding night I'd become her symbol of the single decent thing in her childhood – something she'd set apart from the sins and abuses of our parents, and now I'd proclaimed myself as flawed as they.

There was a noise behind Fran and Mother shook her shoulder. Not the gently confused mother of a few moments ago, the stern dictatorial mother of my childhood.

'What on earth is going on?' Her tongue could whip to shreds in minutes. It was getting ready to lash at both of us now. A moment ago she had been soft, compliant. Was she schizophrenic? I looked from Fran to her in puzzlement. The whole scene was surreal, not least my contribution to it. Then I remembered what Fran had said about senile dementia. Mothers face changed again as I looked at her, softening to a supplicatory plea, moon faced, despite the angular cheek bones that were her trademark and had once made her a beauty. Her cheeks sunk in cavernously now, eyes hollowed, lips creased where the pursing had created permanent indentations over the years. The harridan disappeared and was replaced by a doddering old woman. 'Ah there's a love. Come with Nanny.' She held her arms out to the baby and made chich-chiching sounds at her. The baby clung firmly to Fran. She stopped the noises on seeing me and looked bewildered.

'Who is this person?' She snapped at Fran. Fran took in a shuddering breath and recovered some of her earlier bonhomie.

'It's Will, Mum – remember he was coming to visit you? That's why we got the tea tray ready.'

'Visit me? What about. He never comes to see me unless he has to.' She pointed her angular face at me. 'What are you here for? Speak up. Tell him to speak up.' Fran ignored her.

'Will.' Fran's voice died away into nothingness. She looked completely defeated, smaller somehow than when she'd first opened the door to me. 'She's having a bad day. Don't say anything please. She won't understand.' Even the baby seemed to sense the intensity of the plea. There wasn't a sound between us, like a vacuum had grown for one of us to be sucked into; a black hole. I knew from Fran's face it would be me.

'I've brought all my things to show you what I'm really like. I want you to understand.' She cut across the end of my explanation.

'Will, she won't understand and I don't want to. I can't. I can't take this in. I don't want to know. I want you to be what you were. The only way that can be is if I don't know any more. Please go away now, and don't come back.' The finality of her words stunned me. The black hole sucked at me, until I reached its edge.

'*Never* come back?'

'No, never. I won't have a brother anymore.' I succumbed to the dark depths. Her heart was closed to me. The only door left open was the entrance to hell and the front door of my childhood home. She turned and handed the fretful baby to Mother who took her absent-mindedly. Then Fran propelled me to the door and pushed me firmly through it, face frozen like a death mask. As the door clicked shut on me, I heard Mother demand querulously, 'who was that person, Fran?'

'No-one, Mum. No-one. Let's have that tea shall we?'

I stood facing the closed door, mind blank, stunned by the completeness of the rejection. She'd not allowed me even a word of explanation. The closeness of the night before her wedding – where had that gone? I felt as if I had been cleaved in two. One half still existed, the other was lost. Lost: like a childhood never lived, parents never known, and a sibling who never existed. Where had my life gone? I didn't cry. I walked back to my car and climbed in, empty of anything but the need to get away from there and hide myself away from everyone. In the rear view mirror my eyes looked back dully at me. The black hole had consumed me, pulled me into its vacuum of no place, no identity. This dream of womanhood was taking everything from me – dignity, belonging, Joy. Was it worth it, and even if I achieved it, what would my life have left in it by then?

I didn't cry when I got home. I threw the bag with my woman's body in it onto the floor and lay on the bed. I didn't have the energy to get in. Loneliness and desolation washed over me. The light faded and as I lay in the dark, the tiny speck of hope that had flown out of Pandora's Box glimmered and faded away. I didn't cry when I slept. I didn't even cry when I awoke and the sound of the silence and the vast expanse of nothing and no-one around me made my head spin. I felt so empty I couldn't imagine ever having life and laughter and love to fill me up again. And then I knew. There was no point in it, in the fight, the pain, in the disappointment. No point to enduring the loneliness, turning my cheek to the insults and surviving the sting as they hit home. No point to putting on a brave face or convincing myself I would get through it. Without any kind of love, I didn't want to try anymore.

I cried finally when I emptied the aspirin bottle contents into a cup and swilled it down with gin. I cried for the sharp acid taste, for a life unlived, a dream unfulfilled and the sister I briefly found and then lost. I cried for loneliness and for the pointlessness of it all. The crying exhausted me and the aspirin started to work at the same time. I lay back on the bed, feeling the heavy warmth in my limbs and a leaden taste in my mouth, like I was being welded down, fused to despair. I felt drowsy but sick too. The mucous and catarrh the crying had produced lay uneasily in my stomach, rebelling against the aspirin, but sleep won the fight. I thought I dreamed of children playing; small girls, with twirling skirts and dainty faces. I was dancing with them, one of them; plaits flying out around my head like ribbons from a maypole as I whirled around dizzily in the reel we were performing. The girls danced away and I was left alone, sad I was alone again. I walked on my own until I saw a house ahead of me. Tudor beams criss-crossed the front. It stood on a corner, wrapping itself around the street as if hugging it. On its top, like a shock of unruly hair on a schoolboy's head, sprawled an untidy thatched roof.

It was late afternoon and the sun was just starting to drop on the horizon as autumn knocked on the door of the building. The air smelled crisp – a slight chill to it; fresh and clean. By comparison as I pushed the door open, but stayed rooted to the threshold, the inside was dark and musty smelling. Why was I there? I was not sure what happened here, just as I wasn't sure why I was invited. Was I invited, or did I choose to come here?

I pushed the door again as it had swung shut when I'd hesitated the first time. The door was heavy and dark, with a large knocker in the shape of a lion's head. The hinges creaked slightly as it swung open again at my pressure. I stepped gingerly over the doorstep and onto a dusty wooden floor. The late afternoon sun streamed through the diamond panes, lighting the floating dust particles into specks of gold. The room descended into shadows in the corner, deep and cavernous. The sun pooled on the floor in the middle of the room and I took in the heavy cream walls squatting around the edge of the room.

I felt anxious. There was a sense of foreboding in the quiet sunlit room – not simply because I didn't know why I was there, but because I sensed the voices and movements of people long passed on, and that despite their passing, they were still near. The floor and window ledges were thick with dust, greasy to the touch. The dank smell of desertion surrounded me and wrapped me up like an old wet wool blanket. I didn't want the feeling. I wanted the whirling girls back and feeling joy, joy to be alive.

I took the paper out of my pocket to read the instructions. Where did that come from? Did I write it or did someone give it to me?

'Come in, close the door. I will be there and you will know by instinct where I am – follow that instinct, and you will find me.'

My instinct told me to run, but my feet took me forward nevertheless, through the door opposite me and into a corridor. I could almost feel eyes on my back as I walked slowly down it, on tiptoe, trying to stop my heels clicking on the floor boards. Ahead of me was another door. I pushed this door open too and there they were, in front of me, settled in a large oak chair – the writer of the letter.

'Ah, there you are.' A hand was held out to me in welcome. 'Now let me show you why you're here.' They stood up but remained indistinct, like I was straining to look through a veil. The hand raised in welcome took one of mine and half-led, half-pulled me towards the wall on the left hand side of the room. Suddenly I was moving through the wall into another space altogether. It was brightly coloured, like a kaleidoscope. The whirling colours and patterns – diamonds, squares, circles, crescent moons silhouetted on the walls – meeting, dispersing, colliding; making my eyes ache and my head spin. I gasped. I was shocked, confused, afraid – smothered by the continual movement. I stuttered. The patterns changed again and I had to look down at the floor to stop myself shaking and feeling nauseous. The floor, by contrast, was deep, thick black; the black of despair. I looked up. The ceiling was the same.

Apart from the shifting, wheeling patterns on the walls, the room was empty and it seemed at once so huge my head spun, and yet claustrophobic because it was so crammed full of colour and light. As my eyes adjusted to the visual impact the patterns made, I realised that there was a continuous clicking and whirring accompanying the pattern shifts. Once I'd noticed it, it became almost deafening. I had the strongest sensation of wanting to reach out and touch one of the jewelled shapes in the patterns, to see if it felt solid or if my hand would pass through it.

Having entered the room – if I can call it that – it seemed seamless, almost as if it was the spherical , but I was sure I had entered through a straight wall , so was it not a cube ? I stood as close to the wall that I had entered through as I could, back almost touching it. I was too overwhelmed to move from that spot. 'I must be going mad,' I thought. Mother would have said I was on drugs no doubt, but I'd have loved to have heard her reaction if she'd been me – 'oh my!' I could imagine …

I started as my hand was touched gently and I realised that I'd let go of my guide after we'd emerged from the wall.

'Is it familiar to you?' Now I could see the person clearly as if the veil had been pulled aside. The face looking back at me intently was my own.

'I don't think so,' I stammered.

'Ah well, it will be after eternity,' I replied.

'But I don't want to stay here. I want to be out there!' I flung my arm out to encompass whatever was outside the room.

'But you can't be if you are dead ...' I smiled gently at myself. I felt a sudden pull on my chest and somehow we had shifted places.

'Wait, what's happening? Instead of looking at me coming in, I was looking at me going out. What's happened to me?' I shouted.

'We have swapped,' he/I said calmly with a small smile, 'and now it's time for me to go.' With that he / I took a step backwards and was partially engulfed by the wall. I grabbed at my alter ego's hand before it disappeared fully, terrified I would be left alone. The hand was attached to Tom; Tom, pulling me out from the place in my soul that was empty apart from the continuous pattern shifts and the deafening clicks and whirrs as the shapes spun around me. I rose up high in the air and my heart felt like it was bursting with joy at escaping that deadly place, and it was Tom, Tom who had saved me. I was expanding, spreading across the sky until the bursting feeling spread to my stomach and then became a dagger stabbing through my guts. The voice I'd first thought of as Tom's still called me, but it had changed into another voice I knew but didn't recognise. The pain grew and grew and the bursting feeling exploded in a kaleidoscope of shapes and sound, like the ones in the odd room.

'Will, Will, Will, Will ...' I swatted the annoying wasp away and realised that the wasp wasn't a wasp, it was a noise, calling my name. It sounded like my name anyway, and my guts hurt like someone had poured acid on me and it had seeped through and burned a hole from stomach to back bone. I rolled over and the acid poured out of me like vomit.

'That's better,' the voice said soothingly. It was Fran's voice. I knew it now. I opened my eyes briefly to the blank white walls of the austere room, the ticking of the institutionalised clock against the vague sounds of industriousness in the hospital, and my sister's anxious face, relaxing into a smile of welcome. 'Don't do that again, will you?'

'What?' I didn't understand what was happening. She brushed the hair off my forehead.

'I was angry and confused but you didn't have to take all those pills. I'll still be here when you wake up.' The great well of misery that had dammed up in me as I stood at the closed front door broke through and I cried helplessly through the vomit and the acid burned stomach. They were tears of gratefulness that I hadn't remained in the kaleidoscopic room of death, and that my sister was here, caressing my face. She told me later as she'd watched me drive away the emotions had caught up with her in a terrifying rush. Looking at Mother gazing vacantly at her, and the photograph of her and Joe's wedding with his face already flushed from too much booze, and plainly leaning heavily on her for support, she'd numbered the things in her life in their order of importance.

Jenny and I were the only two she could think of. She'd sat mindlessly drinking tea with Mother for another hour, debating what to do. Logic and respectability told her to stay put, that pre-wedding hug had urged her to follow me.

She'd had to get someone to break the door down and it had taken them several hours to pump all the contents of my stomach out, but luckily I'd already puked some of the aspirin up because of the amount of mucous I'd generated from the earlier frenzied crying. I was lucky. I didn't feel like it then, but I knew she was right.

'What do you call yourself now?' She asked on the afternoon before I was discharged a few days later.

'Billie.'

'Billie. Does this mean I have a brother or a sister now?'

'A sister, I hope one day. I'm still working towards it though.'

'Make sure you get there, then,' she hesitated and then added, 'Billie.'

'I will now.'

September 1982

I saw Freddie today for the first time in a long time. I'd started spending more time at the Kings Road shop since the building site incident and eventually gave in to the TV's invitations to some of the clubs they frequent. My life as a woman had become restricted to work and the travel between it and home; home and shopping for food. It contained the essentials for life but without really living. It had become humdrum to the extreme and yet with the recent bad experiences, I had only wanted security and routine. As routine built confidence again, I found I wanted more. The first time I accompanied the TV's I was pop-eyed with wonder. Their night life world was full of all kinds of people – bohemia was the watchword. Suddenly there were no holds barred and everything was accepted. It was both a revelation, and a liberation. I stayed on the periphery of the action, observing and marvelling. It was a vibrant world of colour and spectacle, but also duplicity and abuse. Rife in it was the seamy underside of Soho life, sex for cash, and whatever you wanted if you were prepared to pay. I felt vulnerable yet exhilarated by the laissez-faire attitude. The TV's dressed to the extreme, inch long eyelashes, pantomime dame make-up, super-coiffed hair and skin-tight outfits peacocking to the world. The other more non-definitive clientele were a mix of gays and straights who liked gays. I merged into the background and observed before engaging the enemy. Just as its growing familiarity bred a sense of total relaxation in me too, there was Freddie.

It was the 'dear boy' that reached me first. I couldn't locate where the voice was coming from but I could only think of Freddie. The mellifluent strains of Freddie-style greetings rolled up behind me again later on in the evening and this time when I scanned the crowded bar I saw him a little further along and near a group of gays I knew sometimes worked the streets. His style was unchanged but now he looked grey and strained, whereas he'd looked tanned and in control when I'd known him. The familiar shiver went through me as I remembered the night of the party. The same booming bonhomie preceded him as he held court but his pallor made me recoil. I made my way surreptitiously to Christine, who was busy running down a john to Millie and nudged her arm. I didn't normally spend too much time with the TV's, even though they had introduced me to the bar and the life here. There was a kind of social strata here that dictated who you socialised with depending on your status and orientation. There was a general cross-mix, like there was a general cross-dress, but the subtleties were learned and had to be observed. However, of all the people there, the TV's always seemed to know the gossip and pass it on. If anyone knew about Freddie, Christine or her cronies would. I nodded in the direction of Freddie.

'Oh I wouldn't dahling,' commented Christine after she'd followed the direction of my nod. Her face was too close to mine as she spoke; hot breath on my cheek, smelling of stale ash, whisky and the cloying cosmetic perfume of heavy pan stick make-up. I tried to shift backwards but there was no room behind me. To get the information I wanted I had to put up with it.

'Why?'

'He's got it, dahling. You can tell it a mile off. '

'What?' I knew I should know by the conspiratorial way Christine spoke, and there was something registering at the back of my mind but I couldn't place it. Christine looked at me as if I was a stupid child. Then she made a face which implied renewed understanding.

'Ah, you aren't into the guys are you? He's a queen. He says he hasn't got it, but he's HIV I reckon and you really don't want to get into that, sweetie. You can tell from the skin colour and the sag – too bony and no life; like he's already the walking dead.' I looked at Freddie and shivered, not from the memory of the party night this time but from the prospect of his future. I remembered the items on the news last year about HIV and AIDs. I hadn't paid much attention to them other than to register that it was another reason to avoid gay sex and the likes of Freddie. I hadn't thought about them in relation to me at the time. It was just an illness starting to be prevalent amongst gays. Now another thought made me shiver as well as the memory of Freddie's grasping hands and the thrusting pain.

'How do you get it?' It wasn't something that was talked about much but all the things I'd heard were coming back to me now. As if to mock me, an old Commodore's hit came on as the chance to dance intimately pumped through the dance floor and the dancers snaked together to its mournful rhythm. The cheesy lyrics warbled through the sound system. I didn't feel like three times a lady now. I felt soiled and vulnerable.

'Gay sex, dahling.' Christine stated, then as if I might need more elaboration – still the stupid child, 'up the bum. Don't do it myself. Men are dirty bastards; should wash or douche but they don't. I'll do oral, but not up the ass or fisting.' Inwardly I cringed. I knew what she meant but until now that night had been a bad memory I had been able to box away in a small recess of my mind, only revisited and the lid lifted when I was unable to stop it. Now it took on a different importance. I had only experienced gay sex once and knew it was not for me, but because of who it was with, maybe there was a lasting legacy – AIDs.

'How do you find out if you have it?' Christine gave me a curious look.

'Why?' I could tell from her sharp look that she suspected there was gossip to be had from me. I thought fast and responded nonchalantly.

'Oh just don't know much about it, that's all, and I think I remember that guy from uni. It was big news last year but there's been nothing much said about it this year until you did just now. '

'Really?' Christine's interest was still awakened, despite my attempt to divert her down a dead end. She ignored the generalities and went in for the specifics, obviously hoping for scandal worth trading. 'Has he always been like that? They say he's pretty well off, but of course with that shit going on, no-one is going to get too close just in case.' She waited for an answer and I was about to mutter something about not knowing him well and hope he didn't recognise me when Millie settled in beside me and the group Freddie was with moved in our direction too. My stomach turned over as I realised they were heading straight for us. I hoped Christine wouldn't spill the beans and that I'd be able to sidle away.

Freddie and his entourage completely took over the area of the bar we were standing in. Mimi was no longer perched on his shoulder, but the impact was the same. He wore a rich burgundy colour smoking jacket over a heavy tapestry waistcoat. He gave off the impression of elegant debauchery. The drinks flowed as lavishly as of old. I could hear his voice cutting through the beat of the music, almost overcoming the low bass notes with his deeper tone. His audience deferred to him and he played to them. Same old Freddie, but he didn't cast more than a glance in my direction. He wasn't interested in women – and that's what you are, remember? I relaxed and settled as far into the recesses of one of the alcoves near the bar as I could, planning my escape. Christine became distracted by a hefty sailor who had strayed into the bar on his own. Millie spotted him at about the same time and they both headed in his direction, obviously with but one thought in mind. His bewildered expression told me he had no idea what he was letting himself in for and I wondered if I should pitch in and warn him, but then loyalty to Christine and Millie overcame my sympathy for his naivety. What sailor was really that naïve? Anyway, they weren't ruthless like Cara and her type. He would be ok, if a bit surprised later. If he had too much to drink I imagined he wouldn't even notice, just feel heartily glad for the excellent blow job no doubt one of them would deliver for the right return. I wondered what would happen if there was a cat fight over him between Christine and Millie, but traded off the curiosity to see what would happen against the desire to make an escape before Freddie noticed me. I stepped out of the alcove just as he turned around and faced me. Even though the music pounded louder and the bar was stifling from sweating bodies and aroused passion, I felt as if I was standing in a spotlight made of ice cold white light. My stomach tightened in a spasm of fear.

'Pretty girl,' he commented and then continued his half turn, dismissing me so he could concentrate on a pretty boy standing hopefully at his elbow. The lights dimmed and the strobe came on making everything fracture into jagged snapshots of bodies silhouetted in positions expressing the dance. I took the opportunity to escape, moving across the dance floor as swiftly as I could as I slithered between the dancers. It felt like I was moving in slow-motion even though I pushed hastily through them as the strobe fix-framed them for a second. I moved purposefully through the cartoon-stills until I reached the door and left, leaving behind me the heavy atmosphere of cigarette and dope smoke, strobe effect and noise like I'd dropped a thick dark cloak behind me.

The next monthly visit to the doctor was more uncomfortable than ever as I had to raise the spectre of the AIDs fear I now had. I could tell he enjoyed making me squirm as he asked for every minute detail of the lead up and the actual encounter.

'And so anal intercourse actually took place?' He asked the question in a flat tone, but the inflection on the words *anal intercourse* left me in no doubt of my much reduced position of respectability.

'Yes.'

'Pardon? Could you speak a little louder? I need to record your goings on so the psychologist can make a full evaluation of your suitability for any further consideration.'

'Surely this doesn't make any difference?'

'You told me you weren't homosexual. Now you've told me you've been active sexually with men. That rather changes things doesn't it?'

'Not active sexually with *men*. It was *once* with *one* man and it was a huge mistake and I regretted it immediately afterwards. That rather *doesn't* change things, does it?' I couldn't keep the sarcasm out of my voice.

'So you think this is something for you to be proud of? That you might have been so irresponsible, you now have AIDs?'

'No, I'm not proud of it and I hope I haven't got AIDs. I just wanted to find out. That is being responsible, isn't it?' I consciously bit back the other angry words I wanted to say to him; the words that denounced him as sick and cruel and twisted. I had seen the sly enjoyment of the description he'd forced from me of the actual act, the fleck of spittle that had formed on the inner corner of his mouth as he'd licked his lips and sat forward too avidly in his chair, coaxing the whole painful and disgusting memory from me. He smiled slowly. *I know you.* I thought. *I know what you are now.*

'We'll have to see. We'll review the situation next month. In the meantime, don't have sex with anyone, will you.' His offhand wave of the hand dismissed me and his lip curled with wry humour. I couldn't believe it. I didn't move. He looked up.

'And?'

'I want an AIDs test.'

'You told me you don't have it so why do you need one?' He smiled spitefully at me.

'I told you I wanted to check if I had it or not. Not that I don't have it. I want the test.' His expression was smug. I wanted to beat my fist into his face and smash it. I'd never wanted to be violent ever before but now I wanted to pulverise this evil bastard, see him whimpering and begging for mercy. 'Or I tell everyone you told me to go out and try to spread it and refused me the test.' His smile faded. We eyed each other. So this was war? He had something I wanted – passport to the psychologist, the next stage on my journey to womanhood. I had something he wanted. 'But if you give me the test, I'll report that one homosexual incident every time I come to see you – in fine detail.' The fleck of spittle foamed. I could see him weighing up the offer. He pulled a blue sheet out of the rack of forms in front of him and rapidly completed the details. He thrust it at me.

'Here, you'll have to make an appointment at the hospital and the results will take about a month. They may be here when you come back for your usual appointment. I'll be able to tell you them at the end of it.' The contract was signed. The base metal was turned to gold. With that I knew, as long as I didn't have AIDs, I would get the referral to the psychologist. He couldn't afford not to now.

December 1982

It took three months to wring the results out of the doctor in the end. Three months; three appointments, in which I had to describe that night in fine detail over and over again, watching the greedy workings of his mouth and the glittering of his mean eyes. He disgusted me. It was like I was reliving the humiliation and the pain in real life. I never felt like a pervert in any other thing I did but in retelling that tale, I did. The fear that the results might be positive gnawed at me. I tried to reason that the doctor would tell me rather than risk me potentially spreading it further if I was sexually active, yet I knew inside him prejudice was the bitter canker that ate him away, and far from seeking life and health for patients like me, he actually didn't care at all. I watched for signs of my skin greying or the plumpness dropping away from my bones like it had from Freddie, who I never saw in Jimmies club again after that one visit. It didn't. My skin remained healthy and pink, my figure stayed unchanged, plumped out more, if anything. The icy cold fear was a wasteland in my core that I tried never to access in case it froze me over completely. He played on my fear to squeeze out as much perverted pleasure as possible but at the beginning of the third subsequent visit I refused to follow the routine of reporting the details of my homosexual encounter until the results were spread out on his old mahogany desk for me to see.

The icy wasteland crept up my gullet, until its furthest icicle point stuck sharply in my throat as the paper was unfolded. I saw angrily it had been filed in my notes since October. The only word that could melt the fear – *negative* – was printed clearly in the result. I had spent the last three months in unnecessary abject terror of a painful death. I hated him with a savage bitterness then and knew that one day, if ever the chance came my way, I wanted him to feel that same exquisitely paralysing fear I'd lived with. I said nothing, just folded the paper back up and tucked it into the notes again. I told him the story as required, but denying him the details I knew he craved. Then I left. I would wait out the remaining appointments and demand my rite of passage. I didn't have AIDs. The contract was complete.

July 1983

More than a year of waiting and enduring Dr Johnson's crude and cutting abuses has gone by and finally he's had to refer me on. I feel like celebrating, but what comes next is far harder. If I'd thought the doctor's questions and treatment were embarrassing, the psychiatrists were invasive, challenging, demanding, and problematic. Not rude or judgemental, but they forced me to look so far inwards, other motivations and memories insisted on making their way out. I remembered my mother and Tom's father in the bedroom, and although instinctively I knew what they'd been doing, suddenly it fell into place. I'd known; of course I'd known when I was older – that was why I'd so angrily ignored him at my father's funeral. It had seemed obscene for him to be there and then walking my mother home, knowing they would probably have scrabbled under the sheets as soon as they could, even on the day she consigned my father's body to eternity.

Had it affected my sexuality, the desire to be a woman? Had it engendered disgust that this man was using my mother in such a way – and why was he? His wife – Tom's mother – was besotted with him, even in middle age. Surely he got enough sex from her to keep him contented without moving on to what was, to him no more than another piece of meat? I realised that even thinking of my mother as a piece of meat raised issues about how I felt about her and about men in general. What did I think? Why if I thought that about my mother, did I want to be a woman? Surely womanhood was debased by what I thought of my mother? *But you're better than that, and you're better than the man who just used her body for sex.* The thought remained in my mind. Why did I think I was better than that – which woman made me think I was better than that? The image of the woman from the Kings Road shop sprang into my mind. Tall, commanding, with a dignity she retained, even as she stood half-naked and exposed to ridicule in front of me when the fire bell rang and I saw what she was trying to hide; the betrayal of her real sexuality underneath the façade of the pretty underwear. She was better than my mother. She was better because she'd made a conscious decision against prejudice and tradition and convention. She was better because she had courage and self-respect. I would have that too.

I had to face my feelings about Tom as part of the introspection. The psychologist delved ruthlessly into them and I plumbed their depths unwillingly but knowing if I didn't, he may refuse me the right of passage from man to woman for that very denial. The feelings stretched back to childhood. Hero-worship to start with, and fear. Yes I'd been afraid of Tom on some level. Afraid of his masculinity because I didn't understand it or feel it in myself, afraid of the lust to experience violence that his inclination to challenge old Mother J's son might have led me into as well. Most importantly though, fear that I would respond openly to him in a way he would reject; ironically, fear of love.

September 1983

I'd reached and had spent the next months trying to accommodate that point when the doorbell rang: and fear of love. Shit. The timing was undoubtedly impeccable and yet also unspeakably awful. The doorbell rang, and there was Tom. Just Tom, almost the way I remembered him as a swaggering teenager, but with a look of weary hesitation too. The years dropped away and I was looking at the friend I'd listened to talking about the best and worst decisions he'd made or was about to make, the anxieties he had about his manhood – although how anyone as alpha male as Tom could have such doubts had always amused me – and the hidden moments of insecurity and weakness only I knew about. The man, Tom, was still the boy to me as he stood there, shoulders dropping with fatigue and face spread with an embarrassed grin.

I hadn't long changed out of my daytime female persona that evening, having removed the make-up and was now relaxing in sweats. I loved the woman I was becoming in the day, but I still hadn't quite made the transition into keeping it up when no-one else was watching. Men's shapes aren't made for women's clothes and I still had to start that real transformation that would make the clothes comfortable whether I was on show or not. For nearly two years now I'd been Billie by day, and neither Will nor Billie by night – a strange amorphous mass, not quite sure what to be in the quiet privacy of home. Waiting for someone else to force the decision, I suppose.

Chapter 12:

Dawns a new day, 1984

I didn't know what I expected to happen when Will opened the door, but within moments I felt I'd come home. That's an odd feeling when you've never even walked in a place before, but then that feeling of settling, being secure is really nothing to do with a place is it? It's all to do with the people. Ironic too, that I didn't actually really know this man well any more. We had started out in childhood, but here we were grown men – each with our own secret store of life experience, good and bad, and thus we were different people from those two schoolboys who'd shinned up trees, endured the dull routine of school and looked curiously at each other as each new nuance of our teenage character had peeped round the side of the infant-boy-man facades we'd lived our lives behind until then.

My first sight of him in the doorway was standing in front of a huge painting of apples, covering the whole of the wall behind him. My senses were immediately full of the remembered tastes and smells of childhood. The apples on it were of all shapes and sizes – small and pinched, like crab apples, juicy and inviting – like large coxes, gnarled and bruised. The fallers at the end of the harvest, battered by life, were left forgotten and rejected on the grassy carpet encroaching the trees. How like us – a conglomeration of rejects and prizes, beauties and beasts, perfect and damaged – and Will standing in the vortex of the apple storm, calm – serene even, if you could use that word for a man.

'Christ, that's a lot of them!' His expression was bemused, as if he didn't register who I was for a moment.

'What?' He turned and followed my gaze to the painting behind him. 'Oh, I couldn't resist it really,' he laughed. 'It must have all the ones we ever stole in it, mustn't it?' He swung round and a happy smile had replaced the bewilderment. 'Tom!'

I dropped my bag and the embrace was like relief flooding through me.

I'd not really noticed the man he'd become, despite the times we'd seen each other in adulthood – times when I'd been home on leave and he home from university, Fran's wedding and then my own. He'd grown up to be dramatically handsome – the boyhood promise of the fringed almond eyes and symmetrical features translating into impossibly good looks, but still slight and enigmatic – like a puff of wind might take him away, a fluttering leaf atop one of those russet apples. His hair had grown long since I'd last seen him, swinging almost to his shoulders. It was the fashion now, but army ways and my father's rules had long since planted a different attitude in me. My hair remained only just slightly longer than I would have had it if I'd still been cannon fodder.

Will was like one of the crisp, green apples with a rosy blush on the outer sheen of the skin. If you bit into that apple it would be sharp but sweet, crunching under the pressure of teeth and yielding just the right amount of juice to savour the texture of the hard flesh. Clean-cut, neat, fantastically yet unusually fine-featured for a man; the unpalatably fibrous inner core and pips well concealed within his outer perfection. He dispatched the rest of his dingy surroundings to oblivion, he and the vibrant apples behind him. Even his voice was attractive – low and well-modulated, despite the harsher note surprise slipped in there. Damn, why wasn't I as perfect as he was?

'Sorry, I should have called but I didn't know your number. I only knew your address from the old wedding invitation stuff we'd kept.'

'No problem, no problem at all.' He hovered in the doorway a moment longer before exclaiming again and stepping back to allow me to enter. He was dressed in jogging pants and a tee shirt, barefoot and relaxed. There was the slightest sense of hesitancy from him, quickly masked by the wide smile, but I knew he was taking in my bag as well as me I stepped over the threshold.

'I'd better explain,' I tipped my head towards the bag.

'Well, I was wondering.' His expression was quizzical, and I thought he said something else but as usual my hearing played up precisely when I needed it clear but it didn't seem to matter. The smile remained. It was the old Will smile I'd seen so many times as a boy when Will hadn't the faintest idea what I was thinking and vice versa, but it hadn't mattered at all then either. I was home.

We spent the rest of the evening catching up on what had been happening since seventeen – the last time we'd really talked. After the awkward explanation of how things had collapsed with Lucy, Will didn't even mention her again and it was a relief to be both away from the oppression of the situation and the sense of my own failure. Here in this grey suburban maisonette, I was in another world – one in which the colour was in the people not the surrounding. I'd felt the opposite when in the comfortably furnished home I'd shared with Lucy. It was a small place, but with the bonus of two bedrooms. Will described it as a luxury since he could contain his mess in the tiny spare room whilst keeping the rest more or less tidy. My arrival meant the tiny spare room had to rapidly be cleared up but for that night, it didn't matter that I slept with piles of books around me. I didn't even so much as open my bag when I went to bed, just dropped onto the lumpy mattress like a stone into mud, sinking gracelessly but completely into its welcome. I don't remember much of what we talked about that first night, other than my cursory explanation of the Lucy situation then followed by hour upon hour of childhood memories, as if simply to find a foothold to start our ascent from. In the morning I awoke as the dawn was breaking, muzzy headed from two bottles of wine, and a mouth tasting like the bottom of a parrots cage but at peace for the first time in months.

I idly looked around the room as I lay in bed, wide awake regardless of the few hours sleep I'd had in reality, but too lazy to get up yet. It really was a tiny room, just big enough to fit in a single bed, a bedside cupboard, an old wheel back chair and a built in cupboard. Both the bedside cupboard and the chair were piled high with books, and the doors to the built-in cupboard were similarly barricaded. Donne, Webster, Marlowe, Johnson were some of the names on the spines of the books, decorated with depictions of Jacobean ladies and gentleman, in resplendent costumes and in full flow as thespians. I remembered now that Will had studied English at university. This must have been his favourite era then. Curiosity to find out what Will had been so taken with reading, when I had simply skimmed through the Sun most of the time, got the better of laziness. I slipped out of bed, just in boxers, and crouching down, started to leaf through the topmost book. It was by a playwright called Webster. The language was courtly and difficult for me, but I persevered, starting to get a sense of what was going on amidst the complex sentence structures. Ferdinand – a Duke – fancied his own sister, basically. Kinky. I hadn't thought English literature was about incest. Good old-fashioned porn then?

I took the book back to bed, nestling under the blankets, ignoring their scratchiness as they raked over my bare legs. The bed hadn't been made up and although Will had fussed about finding a full set of bed linen, I'd pooh-poohed the idea the night before and just crashed.

'I'm pissed, man – no need for sheeshs, jush shleep.'

'If you're sure,' he'd lingered awkwardly and then seeing me sit heavily on the side of the bed and then crash backwards like a tree falling in the forest, he grinned and left me to it. This would be the third time he'd seen me drunk to bed. It was definitely becoming a habit.

I made quite an inroad into the play, which was called 'The Duchess of Malfi', before losing interest in having to concentrate so hard to decipher the meaning behind the language. Was this what he read all the time? It was heavy going. I knew Will had a good intellect, but surely he must read something else for light relief. I scanned the rest of the room, taking in the detail of it that I'd missed in the alcoholic haze the night before. Early morning sunlight was starting to filter through the thin curtains. They did little more than cover the modesty of the naked window. Fitting where they touched, a central gap where they didn't quite meet displayed the guts of the day. It was going to be a nice one. The light from them lay in bands across the mauve toned floor, highlighting the floral pattern and making parts of it seem brighter and less leeched of colour than others. The walls mirrored the floral pattern of the carpet, but in a muted pink. The paintwork was violent purple. The place looked tired, yet gaudy – like an old Kings Cross prostitute. The room smelt vaguely musty – shut in. I supposed Will didn't use it much if it was the spare room. That would account for the downtrodden feel. Good job I hadn't noticed the mismatch last night otherwise my drunkenness might have developed into nausea at the lurid colours.

Suddenly inactivity irritated me and I jumped out of bed again, wanting to see more of what Wills home was like, and needing a pee. I padded to the bathroom, which I remembered was the second door off the corridor. The colour scheme in here was green and red.

'Bloody hell.' I couldn't help saying it aloud, I was so surprised by the garish colour scheme that seemed to loom so suddenly out of what was otherwise a grim grey background. The only stylish thing I'd seen here so far — apart from Will — was the apple picture.

'You ok?' It was Will appearing at the open bathroom door, with a worried look on his face.

'Oh yeah. I was just admiring your colour scheme.' There was a momentary pause before Will replied. I shook the drips off and turned to see his reaction to my wry comment. He was in the doorway, barefoot in the tracksuit bottoms again but with a pink shirt this time. His face was flushed as I grinned at him.

'Colour scheme?' He seemed bewildered and I thought it was unlike Will to miss a joke. Even as a teenager he had always been quick and last night he'd demonstrated as much wit as then, having me roaring with laughter despite my shitty situation. His eyes remained fixed on my face whilst he assimilated the comment.

'It's foul … Oh, I see what you mean. Yeah.' He broke into a grin. I flushed the toilet — a black plastic toggle hanging off a discoloured chain, attached to an archaic metal arm that worked on a pulley basis. It faltered and sputtered before gushing reluctantly into life and then leaving the pipes clanking as they refilled with water.

'Jesus, Will – how out of the ark is this place?' I was surprised he hadn't chosen a classier place to live – after all he'd been working for several years now so surely he had sufficient income to live a more stylish life?

'I know.' He looked rueful.

'I thought you were working.'

'I am.' He seemed surprised.

'So why aren't you living in a decent place, I mean, I don't want to be rude but...' I didn't need to illustrate the point but I did with a sweep of my arm around the bathroom. It took in the grimy obscured window with its peeling paintwork, the antique bath, with claw feet and loose plug, the squared red lino flooring, curling slightly as it met the skirting, and the grass green paintwork of the skirting.

'I know.' He said again, eyes still fixed on my face. We stayed looking at each other for a while, me waiting for more information, him withholding it. 'There are reasons,' he added eventually. 'D'you want some coffee?'

'Yeah, please.' I followed him into the kitchen. This room was at least only black and white, or maybe more accurately, off-white. He dumped the kettle on the hob and leaned against one of the sets of cupboard ranges. I sensed I was about to get some explanation so I remained silent and waited. Funny how you can slip so quickly and easily into being in tune with some people, even when you haven't spent time with them for years. Yet others, you never find a common bond with. I consigned Lucy to the latter, and found I was glad I was never likely to have to try to find that bond with her now.

'I'm saving.' He said eventually, as if that explained everything. At the time, my simple mind took it at face value. Years of respectable suburban attitudes ingrained in me by my parents and then Lucy made that an entirely acceptable answer. Saving – for a house, a car, a holiday – yes all acceptable, so I accepted his answer and we moved on.

'You'll need somewhere to leave your stuff,' he ventured.

'Would it be ok if?'

'You want to stay here?'

'If that would be ok?'

'Yeah, of course.'

'I'll go job-hunting today.' It was Friday today. I'd not even noticed until now that I'd left Lucy on a Thursday. *Thursday's child is full of woe.* I wondered if the child Lucy was carrying would be born on a Thursday.

'It's OK,' he smiled. 'I know you'll find a job and will pay our way.'

I felt relieved. This new dawn was so much more positive than the new dawn of two days ago.

'I'll clear out the cupboard in your room while you're out.' I almost missed the 'your', but it warmed me.

'I can help you.'

'No, it's fine, really. I'll do it.' He sounded a little defensive, rebuffing my help almost too quickly and I felt awkward for a moment, before he smiled again and the awkwardness was dispelled. The kettle whistled and he whipped it quickly off the hob.

'How do you take it?' It almost sounded like a woman asking her new date how he liked his coffee. I smiled. Christ we were like a couple already.

By the time I got back later that day, with a job at a factory in Putney under my belt, 'my' room had been completely transformed. The bed had been made up, the piles of books removed and my clothes hung neatly in the wardrobe.

'I didn't do all of it, just the things that would crease.'

'Bloody hell, you're not my maid, you know Will.' He looked affronted for a moment and then laughed aloud.

'No, you'd never be able to afford me.' He paused and then added almost coquettishly, 'but don't you think I'd make a good one?' I was nonplussed and not quite sure how to reply. There was something almost flirtatious about the comment, but this was a bloke to a bloke. Will didn't seem to find his remark strange at all, and moved away easily to the kitchen. I shrugged my shoulders and assumed I'd misunderstood.

Life quickly took on a steady routine between us. We agreed our bathroom rota almost without talking about it. I always went first as I took less time. Will went second as he lingered in there like a woman. He cooked – he was a good cook, I washed up. He teased me once he would get me a flowery pinny and rubber gloves, and I retorted that was more his style, waited for that old sensitivity he'd shown as a teenager to anything that suggested he was effeminate, noticed obliquely that it didn't come, and relaxed completely.

That strange sense of being about to be treated to a confidence passed between us, like it had when he'd said he was saving, but the comment passed on with a chuckle and was forgotten again. We went out once for a drink together, but thereafter we went out alone. Will seemed to already have his own plans a lot of the time, which he didn't elaborate on so I didn't seek to interfere. I made a few mates at the factory and developed a regular routine of watching the match on a Saturday afternoon with them and then going for a drink afterwards. I invited Will but he reminded me that football left him cold and I wondered again at how two such disparate personalities as we could be such good friends, and then dismissed it. I no longer felt like a failure. I felt like Tom again. Tom: an OK person, because his mates thought so too.

We rolled on into spring, our routine solid and our friendship secure without either of us seeming to need to discuss our separate lives outside of joint domesticity. I once or twice wondered who Will went out with in the evenings when I went out with my factory buddies, but the question never came up and he never commented so it dwindled to little importance. Our routine was comfortable and comforting. He was my best mate. It was good. I counted off the months and knew that Lucy was due to deliver soon, but avoided thinking about that. I occasionally got recriminatory letters from my mother, which I ignored, and pompous demand letters from Lucy's solicitor, which I paid. I was going to be a father but it meant nothing to me now. It wasn't mine, this manufactured child. According to Lucy, anyway, although she was careful to never admit that in writing. I remained trapped by the mechanics that had made it though, and would have continued that way if out of the blue there hadn't been a panicky phone call from my mother, saying Lucy had been rushed into hospital with complications and that I should come quickly.

Arriving back in Wilverton, the old sense of failure and oppression overwhelmed me, but I knew I had to grit my teeth and carry out my responsibilities whilst there. I walked the twenty minutes to the hospital, even though it was raining, arriving soaked through and irritable. The officiousness of the NHS took over where the rain left off and I had to answer to what felt like two of the highest ranking officers of the Spanish Inquisition before I was accepted as being who I said I was and allowed access to Lucy. She was in a side room in the delivery suite, propped up against a pile of pillows and swathed in a large white hospital gown. She looked very small, lying on the bed in the centre of the room, surrounded only by equipment and monitors, a tray of instruments laid out on the top of a blue sheet draped over a hospital trolley.

'Tom. What are you doing here?'

'Mam called me and told me things weren't so good.'

'They're fine thanks. WE'RE fine thanks – much that you care.'

'I do care, but Lucy, you didn't want me around so I did as you asked – I've always done as you've asked.'

'I asked you to be faithful in the marriage service and you weren't.' It was spat at me like venom and I nearly turned on my heel and walked out, complications or not, but I was stopped in my tracks by the midwife coming into the room.

'Your husband's here,' she announced jovially, and a mousy haired man with a droopy moustache and round wire-rimmed Lennon glasses followed her into the room. There was a hiss from Lucy as she drew in her breath. For a moment I thought I'd misheard, that my ears had chosen this precise moment to parade my failure in my face again, but no – now the cats spitting venom was turning back on itself. The mousy haired moustache mumbled and the midwife stared from one of us to the other in confusion.

'Who are you?'

'I'm her husband.' I replied clearly.

'And who are you, then?' She swung round to Mousy Moustache. Lucy broke in. 'He's the father.'

'Who's the father?' The midwife and I chorused at the same time.

'I'm the father,' Moustache confirmed humbly. Lucy glared defiantly at the midwife and me. I shook my head uncomprehendingly.

'Really?'

'Yes, really,' she said, turning to me now with contempt. 'How many times did we try IVF and it never worked? I worked OK, but you never did. It was never going to happen that way, so I found a better one.' I looked at Moustache.

'Him? You mean he's the sperm donor?' I couldn't keep the disbelief out of my voice.

'What's wrong with him?' I shook my head. Moustache moved over to her side. They clasped hands defensively.

'Sperm donor?' Moustache asked hesitantly.

'It's what I told him in case the hair colour was wrong.' Lucy explained. I stared at her open-mouthed, stunned by her duplicity.

'So not test-tube donor sperm either I assume.' She glared back, neither denying nor confirming. I didn't really need her answer though. 'All those times you said not to because...?' Another thought occurred to me, 'if you were having it away with him, what about all the money to pay for the IVF cycles?'

'Oh I did both, just to make sure.'

'Jesus! Why?'

'I wanted a child.' I felt my jaw set with anger. Moustache clutched her hand protectively, but shuffled away from me as I felt my fists clench involuntarily. So intent on the one thing she wanted, she'd betrayed me more than I'd ever failed her.

'And me, did I ever matter?'

'You never *didn't* matter but a child mattered more in the end.' She paused and then said in a quieter voice, 'sorry.' The blood rushed through my ears and I couldn't be sure if it was disability or rage that deafened me at that precise moment.

'Are there complications?' I asked the midwife. She looked completely confused by the unexpected melodrama in the delivery room. Most dramas revolved around the delivery of the child, this was all about the creation of it.

'Oh a bit of blood pressure, but she should be alright.'

'Then I'm not needed here?' It was a question, but I wasn't interested in the answer, so it was more of a statement. The midwife shook her head bemusedly. I consciously uncurled my fists. I wasn't going to make a spectacle of myself over this little tramp. I looked squarely at Lucy. 'You and I are quits, agreed?' She didn't answer but her expression implied it. 'Then you also agree you have no more demands on me financially or commitment-wise?'

'I have Jeff.'

'Then I'm gone. Goodbye,' to Lucy. 'Good luck,' to Moustache, and 'thanks,' to the midwife. They silently watched me leave. I waited until I had exited the building before I allowed myself to feel anything. What did I feel? An odd mix of betrayal, anger, disappointment and relief, but the only thing I really wanted to do was get back to London, and to tell Will. I knew I'd feel better about it then than I did now, however I ultimately ended up feeling. The train journey back was tediously slow, with delays from a suicide on the line, and missed connections along the way. I quick-marched the last part of the walk back from the tube station to the flat and slipped in the front door, hardly stopping before barging straight in to Wills bedroom to tell him what kind of complications the day had really been about. I knew he'd been to a friend's funeral, but he'd referred to it only obliquely so I'd assumed it wasn't of major importance to him – more a duty.

'Complications, my arse, she'd…' The rest of the words stuck in my throat. Will wheeled around in surprise, his far away expression rapidly changing to one of shock.

'Tom.'

'Fucking hell!' He was dressed completely as a woman. Short cerise dress, high court heels, hair curled artfully round one ear in a kiss curl effect, face skilfully made-up with long black lashes and deep coral pink lips. I could have been looking at a woman but for the slight mismanagement of shape with not quite full enough hips and slightly too prominent shoulders. He was Will, but not Will. 'Complications, my arse.' I said again.

Chapter 13:

Endings and beginnings, September 1983

I put the diary down. I remembered that whole episode well – too well now. Was it such a surprise that first sight of Will in woman's clothing? I wonder if it was now or did I play the part of the outraged horrified male too well because I feared what not doing so might say about me? Surely there had been clues in those months leading up to it? Yes, of course I could see them now in hindsight. The effeminate posture he relaxed into when unaware of my quiet observation, the fastidiousness of his hygiene routines. My wry comment, 'blimey you're worse than a woman,' when I was waiting outside the bathroom door was closer to the truth than I'd openly admitted. His nails were immaculate manicured; mine were rough-edged and occasionally grime-ridged too. I overheard him from a distance once and only realised latterly it was him. I'd assumed the husky- voiced contralto was a woman on the TV.

In my preconceptions that he was no different to me, underneath – because I never looked beyond the surface until I was forced to, I took the perfection of his appearance as a gift and was secretly envious of his good looks. But under the smooth skin of the apple – the unblemished outer and the solid mass of its flesh, the pips and core of Will were made of quite different matter to me. I just didn't want to acknowledge the potential for yet another upheaval in my already shaky world. Will, my childhood mate was a safe bet. Will the unknown adult person I instinctively avoided, despite being drawn to, was quite something else. It was mid-September 1983. The trees were just turning as I hurried back from the fiasco at the hospital. The odd tawny-gold leaf floated down as I strode on, a pre-cursor to the imminent autumn deluge. My mood was like the leaves, turning from one state to another, like the season turning. It felt natural to leave Lucy behind in the haze of the late summer heat – the heat of betrayal and passion and foolhardiness, and move into a season of bounty and harvest. This was hardly the harvest I expected though.

'Fucking hell, what are you playing at?'

'I'm not playing. This is something I was going to have to tell you about.'

'Something you were going to have to tell me about? What, that you dress up like a, like a ... Christ, Will! What are you?'

'I'm me; that's who I am.' He didn't flinch at my expression but I knew my lip was curling in disgust.

'Me.' I said it sourly. As mean as I could. 'And is me male or female?'

'Female, I think.' He said it very quietly – barely audible, especially as my hearing started to dip in and out, like it always did when I was under pressure. I carried on anyway, determinedly deaf to anything he might say.

'Female? Really?' My eyes swept up and down his body as if I was appraising a woman, stopping finally on his face. I'd done that so many times, to so many women, in my army days. Some of them prostitutes, some of them just eager to open their legs because they'd been on their own and lonely too long. Some simply liked a hardworking soldier boy between their thighs. It had been all the same to me then, but they had really been women. He was passably feminine under the façade; the height, the substance, impression. I could almost accept the illusion, but when I reached his face was when the likeness disappeared. He was Will – for Christ sake – *Will*!

Until then as I appraised the legs – not bad, the undulation of the hips into the waist and then up to the bulge of the breasts, it could almost have been a woman's body. It was the shock of finding my eyes looking down into Will's eyes, rimmed with make-up that made me recoil in disgust. This was no weirdo, no gay, not a tranny. It was my mate Will, who I'd been to school with, who I'd relied on when I was on my uppers, who I'd trusted. Now he was obscenely disfigured in pretence of womanhood. The bloke I'd stood naked in front of, peed in front of, slumped on my bed in front of with my dick shrivelled and my body slack when I'd been blind drunk and he'd undressed me ... Christ, when he'd undressed me and put me to bed! My skin crawled and the next words came out harsher than I intended, scared at what the answer might imply about me and when he'd helped me to bed, naked and ineffectual.

283

"Are you a tranny?' My face felt wooden, shock only just starting to give way to the other insidiously foul fears.

His expression didn't give anything away, but he trembled almost involuntarily. The prejudice in my voice was apparent. He didn't answer and in the pause, the other insidious ideas started to get the better of me. For a moment I thought I remembered a lingering touch on my bare arm, or a moment when he stood too close to me and I'd felt his breath on my neck as I sat at the little kitchen table poring over the newspaper for jobs. He'd looked over my shoulder, ostensibly helping my search, but was that really all it had been? Christ, I felt dirty. I wanted to hurt him with my next words – to make it clear that if he'd done any of that I hadn't enjoyed it, hadn't been encouraging it and even if he was perverted, I wasn't. So I said it as cruelly as I could. *Let's make my revulsion quite clear.* 'We had one of those little arses when I was in. He used to let all comers get up his bum too. God knows what they caught off him. Jesus!' I stared at Will, consciously making my face a study in horror. 'Are you a bum-fucker too?'

He recoiled. I barely hid my smile of satisfaction. *That moved you.* His stillness transformed into an expression of disbelief.

'No!' He almost shouted his reply. It was followed by a silence between us as leaden as the after-sound of gunshot. The strain on my muscles made me realise my fists were clenched and at the same time I noticed his were too. We faced each other like two boxers about to beat the shit out of each other but I knew Will would never hit me – never hit

284

anyone. Coward, I thought; fucking coward. I tensed my fist, ready to translate anger into action but I couldn't bring myself too. *This was Will, who hated violence.* He shifted his weight and so did I, challenging him to take one step – even just one inch step closer to me – *fucking weirdo*. The words hung in my head, making me unsteady with rage until another small but insistent little voice challenged them. *But this is Will. Will isn't a weirdo. He's Will.* Yeah, Will? No, this wasn't Will; this was someone I didn't know.

He seemed almost to relax as I studied him, warring voices making me unsure how to react next. I'd taken my stance, but now I almost wished I hadn't. There was a quiet dignity to him that made me feel embarrassed at my outburst. His eyes followed the movement of my fists as one balled into the other. Was he anticipating me hitting him? Just when I thought we'd be stuck there like that for hours, neither saying any more to defuse the situation he spoke.

'I'm not sick or a homo, if that's what you mean. Nor am I a tranny.' His voice was firm and steady. He waited for my reply. I hadn't got anything to say. I was starting to feel cruel for having been so offensive to him, so I remained silent, but I felt sick, like I wanted to walk out of the room and then come back in again and find him just in jeans and tee shirt, looking like the Will I knew. The day had already been too unkind. Of all the emotions I could have felt, I couldn't identify a single one – just a kind of confused emptiness. I just wanted it to all make sense for a solitary moment. Exhaustion battled with unreality. I closed my eyes, looking through the lids as if that would create a different view of the world. The glow of the late afternoon sunshine through them made them seem golden brown, the colour of deep oak. *Open them*, I instructed myself. *Open them and it'll all be back to what it should be. You can tell him what a bitch Lucy has been and how she'd been doing it with that wet faced little prat all the time she was stinging you for the IVF. How betrayed you feel, how alone, how stupid; what a complete failure. He'll listen and give you some of that philosophical good Will-advice he can dredge up whatever the crappy situation.*

I opened my eyes and the oak-gold faded to Will again. The reality was what it was. Will looking like a woman; in drag, but terrifyingly convincing if I forgot he was Will. My stomach churned and as it completed a full turn, I had to lurch to the bathroom to be sick. It was only a passing spasm – a momentary reaction to the surprise, but I knew how it must have looked for Will. It gave my own hurt cruel validation for him to see my revulsion so clearly. *See, I'm a man, not a fucking weirdo, and don't you forget it matey.*

When the heaving and shuddering had finished, I splashed cold water on my face, dried it on the greyed towel that had been washed too many times, and knew I couldn't postpone making the decision about him and me any longer. As I returned to where he was still standing in front of the full length mirror, I felt pain for him despite the lingering sense of distaste as sour as my mouth was. He hadn't moved at either my words or my puking. He stood in exactly the position I'd left him, shoulders back and chin up, like he was awaiting

286

sentencing. I was surprised. If that had been me, I would have felt cowed, wanted to hide away, ashamed. He surveyed me as if I was the one in drag, looking ridiculous, not he. Actually he didn't look ridiculous, that was what made me so angry. Secretly I was impressed by both his bearing and his resolution, and Christ, did he look convincing! Bastard, how could he mess with my head so much? Anger took over again.

'Then what the fuck are you, then? Dressed in women's stuff and mincing in front of a mirror?' I flicked viciously at the edge of his dress, feeling mean but unable to stop the petty gesture. He still didn't move.

'I'm a pre-op transsexual.' He replied quietly.

'A pre-op trans-sexual.' I mimicked the phrase in a derogatory voice. 'What the fuck is that?' But I didn't need to ask, I knew. I'd heard the phrase before now. Not much gets past you in the army – and I'd been abroad enough and in enough different places to have met lady boys and trannys and even know of all the positions and tricks they would turn for you if that was your bag. He did me the courtesy of explaining, politely and fully. He even used the correct terminology where I would have referred to fannys and fags and less pleasant versions of the explanations of confused sexuality, transsexual identity and prosthetic or artificial genitalia. His dignity wasn't put on. Inside I knew he had never interfered or been inappropriate with me in any way, but I still felt betrayed and angry. The days' events overwhelmed me and I wanted to hurt, to maim, so he was as disfigured and humiliated as I felt. I'd been cut enough times today. I wanted payback. Will was just too vulnerable and I couldn't help myself.

'You're a warped fucker who wants to chop his dick off in the mistaken belief that if he sucks it up inside himself, he'll become a bird.' He did wince at that, and momentarily I felt satisfied. I knew I'd offended, really offended, but something inside me hurt as well – something deeper and more intense than anger and I didn't understand it – didn't want to understand it. It made me run all the faster, head-on into battle. I forced myself to look him straight in the eye, past the eye liner and mascara, past the mask of a woman he'd overlaid on his features and try to see what was behind it all. There was pain and I hated him for it. I turned away angrily to avoid seeing it. I didn't want to see the person beneath the make-up, the one I'd known all my life. I wanted to stay angry, with him, with Lucy, with the army, with my loss of hearing, with my father sleeping with Wills mother, with being a stupid sad loser, with this, whatever this was. Another turn of the key in an already locked door. I kicked out again.

'I'm out of here before you do anything to me. Dress up all you like, but don't come anywhere near me. You're just a sad, sick fuck.' He moved towards me but I slammed his outstretched hand away and flung out of the room and down the stairs. I didn't know where I was going. A haze of rage, misery and hurt propelled me on, slamming the door as hard as I could behind me. *Now you're sorry*. If I'd been a child I would have hidden in a corner and cried. The tears pricked at my eyes. *Stupid fucking shit.* I didn't know if that was me or him, but I knew I was going to do what I always did when I didn't know what to do, and I hated him for causing that too. I would fill my head with booze until I drowned out that face in front of my eyes – half Will, half woman. *Yeah, and Lucy – you can fuck off too!*

The first bar I went into was relatively empty. It was too early for the office workers to have congregated there after close of business. I downed a double brandy. Not my normal poison, but I wanted to get ratted as quickly as possible. I slumped over the bar, ignoring everyone and everything. There wasn't much to see anyway. The optics ranged along the bar, reflecting brightly back in its mirrored background, like the colours on a fairground ride. I could see what was going on behind me in the mirror anyway. My own face was reflected in there, surly and defensive. The bar fell away into gloom behind me, with the stale smell of smoked cigarettes from lunchtime and yesterday's customers lingering like old news. The curling wrapper of a crisp packet was abandoned on the table in the mirrors reflection. The empty glasses of its previous occupants were still uncleared by the lazy bar staff. It made me depressed – like they represented me and my life. Emptied, eaten away, consumed and discarded. The first shot of brandy did nothing for my mood so I ordered another one.

'Bad day, bud?' The barman's transatlantic twang irritated me too. *Bloody yanks, always bigger and better than we were, or so they thought.*

'None of yours,' I retorted and slung the price of the drink on the bar. One of the coins rolled towards the edge of it and the barman caught it expertly before it plummeted off the end. He probably mixed cocktails in the evening.

'No problem,' he replied jovially and tipped a salute at me before moving away to chat to a more amenable prospect further along. I drank the second double more slowly – about four swallows, pacing myself. The thoughts swilling around my head started to settle with the brandy. If I could have categorised them, they were all versions of rage; rage with everyone and everything. What did I do with all of that? I didn't want to think about Will or Lucy or what to do next. I didn't even want to be here. The third brandy took a little longer to arrive. I'd obviously pissed off the barman despite his casual jocularity. By contrast the alcohol was starting to soften me instead so I tossed a 'cheers' to him as he pushed the glass across the bar to me.

'It won't take too many of those to get you pissed, Bud,' he suggested in return. I was going to tell him to mind his own business again, but the softening from the brandy caused me to hold back. The expression on his face was sympathetic.

'Yeah, right, I know.'

'Sounds like that's what you want?'

'Yeah, I guess.' I propped my chin on my hands and my elbows on the bar. The barman lingered. For some reason he wanted to talk.

'I won't be able to serve you if you look like you're getting too drunk, Bud.' He shrugged his shoulders apologetically, 'it's rules.'

'Ok.'

'Nothin' ain't that bad, really, you know.' He gave me a grimace of a smile. I laughed harshly.

'Wanna bet?'

'Well, I know it can seem bad at the time, but give it a bit and there's usually a solution. Live and let live, hey?' I made a glum face at him, and he mirrored it sympathetically. 'The office lot will be in soon, and then I'll be under pressure – and so will you. Here,' he pushed another brandy in front of me. 'On the house, but then maybe go walk it off a bit before you have anymore, eh, Bud?' I was surprised by the sympathy. He reached across the bar and clapped me on the shoulder, then moved back towards another waiting customer. He was right. The office lot were starting to drift in. A small cluster was already forming at the far end of the bar, young men in brash suits and girls in mini-skirts and heels, too much red lipstick staining their wine glass as soon as they took the first sip. They looked like tarts to me. Tart. I'd wanted to use that word on Will, but that was a word you used about a woman. He wasn't a woman. The woman's figure as I'd looked up and down his body plagued me. No, he wasn't a woman and this was just sick. I shut him out of my thoughts and dwelt on Lucy instead. She, I could call a tart and mean it. I still couldn't believe she'd betrayed me the way she had. She'd never seemed the type to betray, not like Susie Evans might have. Susie I could believe it of but not Lucy. Not the Lucy who'd once been so shy, so sweet, so kind. The girl I'd felt I had to behave for otherwise I would be too coarse, too demanding, too selfish. I pictured the weak moustached face of Jeff. Was that what she really wanted? I'd always thought of myself as attractive, strong — the preferred option, but she'd rejected me like a faulty batch. I was a faulty batch. Mentally I returned to the river and wondered why I hadn't jumped then.

The gloom of the bar was becoming filled with the colour of new customers and I started to feel claustrophobic. I downed the remaining brandy, the taste now sticking to my tongue like a coating. My mouth already felt thick, like it didn't want to open properly.

'Tanks,' I called to the barman. He lifted an arm in acknowledgement before turning to another waiting drinker. In the bleakness, his lifted arm and the on-the-house drink were a moment of kindness that made me feel unsteady with emotion — or maybe it was the brandy that was causing the unsteadiness. I slid off the bar stool quickly before any of the self-pitying tears welling up could escape and stumbled from the dark of the bar into the gloom of the falling evening. The brandies were definitely more in control than I was and I wished I'd had a pee before I'd left the bar. The easiest thing was to make for another one but my sense of direction went with the sense of control I'd thought I'd had, but now realised I'd probably not had during any part of my life. I walked, the London streets passing me by in a blur. The need for a pee seemed to go after a while and instead I felt an inane kind of humour taking over. Logically I knew it was the alcohol and nothing was any better or worse than it had been before, but I felt happier nevertheless.

Tall smoke blackened buildings gave way to elegant architecture and then back to more modern structures. I didn't really notice where I was going. I just kept walking, simply feeling as if my feet would take me where I should go. I brushed roughly past the evening rush of workers making for home or a bar, depending on their view of life. The beep of taxi's and arguing cars punctuated the backdrop of traffic rush, and the grime of the city slipped around me like fog as the evening light darkened to twilight. I'd reached Soho by the time the first rush of the brandy's started to wear off and I went in the next bar I saw open and topped up, downing two cognac's without even tasting them. The burn as they slid down the back of my throat and settled in my stomach like a warm pool was comforting. I wasn't sure now how I'd got there or whether I'd stopped anywhere else along the way first, but after a while the heat in the bar started to make me feel light-headed and prickly heat like tiny red ants crawled over me. I left, still forgetting to pee before I did.

A street vendor was selling fruit and newspapers on the corner of the street as I exited. I giggled at the odd combination and then realised I felt hungry. Drinking always gave me hunger pangs when it's first flush wore off and I decided, going purely on instincts that I wanted four things, more alcohol, food, a pee and probably sex – but not necessarily in that order. The pee was probably more important than the hunger pangs right at that moment but at least the thoughts about Will and Lucy were receding.

Reason said I couldn't just unzip and pee in the street so I went for relieving the hunger instead.

Fumbling in my pocket, I found some loose change and approached the vendor. Hanging suggestively over the edge of the stall, was a bunch of bananas and they caught my attention. I was about to buy a couple when the shape of them registered. Then I couldn't get the shape of a penis out of my head, and how under Will's dress, his was carefully hidden. I reeled back with a shiver of disgust. Next to them were apples, green and waxed to an unrealistic shine, but they looked unblemished, and even better than the ones we'd liberated from old Mother J's orchard as children. The memory brought a desire to feel the crunch of an apple between my teeth, something I could bite hard into – as if I could inflict pain on an object that could feel no pain. I bought two, one for me and one for him, and wandered on, munching on the first one.

The contact of teeth on hard skin and resisting flesh felt good and I chewed vigorously, relishing the tartness of the juice in my mouth and the way the skin of the apple caught between my teeth. I'd reached the sinewy core before I'd got to the next corner without hunger being satisfied at all and tossed the core into the gutter. The pips burst from it as it hit the tarmac and scattered a few inches further on – like seeds onto infertile soil. I bit into the next one and started to chew hard again but something soft squelched as I bit down. I spit the mouthful into my hand and almost gagged. In the middle of the chunk was a once wriggling maggot, now pierced by my

294

teeth. I threw it and the rest of the apple into the gutter after the first core, and breathed out sharply in an attempt to control the convulsion in my guts, before gasping air back in. The sudden inrush of air made my head spin and I staggered against the wall of the building I'd been passing.

'You alright, mister?' The voice was deep but the face attached to it was indistinct, and in shadow.

'Will be.' It was all I could manage, the nausea from imagining the maggot in my throat still swilling through me like ripples of sewerage.

'Here, you don't look too good, come on.' The voice pulled at my arm and the will to resist seemed to have gone with control too. I stumbled along beside them, eyes struggling to focus until we entered the arch of a doorway, lit up with the only word I was interested in at the time. Bar. I'd thought the brandy had worn off, but maybe seven doubles wouldn't go quite as easily as I'd thought they would. Now I felt far drunker than I had on leaving the second bar, or maybe I'd simply not noticed I'd been in others along the way even before what I thought of as the second one. This one was downstairs, like entering a hell hole in the bowels of the earth, but I no longer cared. The anger had dissipated and now I just felt disorientated and lonely. I still needed a pee but I didn't want sex, I wanted love; to be held tightly, to feel important to someone. I was getting maudlin. I needed another drink to perk me up, even though I wasn't sure I could see straight enough to pick up the glass or talk clearly enough to give the order to the bar staff.

'What are you drinking mister?' I couldn't focus properly on the voice, but in the dim light of the bar it looked female now.

'Was on brandy,' I said uncertainly. She turned to the barman and made a small hand signal. The glass was in front of me almost immediately and I guzzled it down. It hit the back of my throat and the burn brought me to life again. The rest of the place was a buzz of music and light.

'Five quid for that.' The barman held his hand out at me. He wasn't friendly like the other one had been. I felt unhappy. The voice next to me shook my arm.

'Can you pay?' She smiled and I felt happier.

'Oh yesh.' I dragged my wallet out and she pulled a note out of it.

'You've got quite a lot in here, Mister. You should look after it better.' She handed it back to me and I shoved it deep in my trouser pocket, managing it on the second go. Concentrating hard I made out some of my companions, pressing close against me at the bar, all interested in the newcomer now. I didn't care about feeling crowded. It made the loneliness feel a long way away and like I was back in the centre of life, not struggling to understand it from the odd perspective of today. The woman next to me turned and smiled broadly at me. I smiled back, feeling crazily happy to be here with these people, all brightly coloured and smiling. She was over made up and slutty with horse teeth but it didn't matter. I laughed stupidly at her and she laughed back.

'Cheers,' she said.

'Cheers,' wondering where my glass was, but it was back in my hand and full again. The woman with the voice who'd led me in there jostled me and I turned my head back to her. It felt like I was moving in slow motion, my head following the rest of my body some seconds later.

'Wanna dance, dahling?' She nudged me with her hips. Yes, I wanted to dance, revel, live life like it would never end in the blur of the noise and heat and colour here. The music throbbed in the background, and it's beat intoxicated me as she moved in closer and her hips ground against mine, automatically creating a sensation of desire where I'd thought I'd lost all sensation until now. I let her lead me hazily onto the dance floor, and clung onto her as we swung from side to side, hands sweating and head whirling. The beat kept me moving, and I sang along to it, 'baby give it up.' The woman, who shouted in my ear her name was Cara, wriggled in closer and followed her name with her tongue. Heat rose in me. The beat pounded in time with my blood and the jaunty lyrics made me think of fun, light-heartedness. God, I hadn't felt light-hearted in such a long time. This was good.

'Baby, give it up,' crooned Cara and I felt her fingers unzipping my fly, prising the material apart and manipulating my cock. The intensity of desire almost made me come there and I knew, even through the alcohol haze, that she must be experienced at this because she sensed the building explosion and stopped it, pinching my foreskin closed so I winced and the imminent eruption dissipated. 'Let's go, shall we baby?' I didn't want love after all, now I wanted sex, and I didn't care who with – just anyone to make me feel like I wasn't useless.

'Les go,' I lurched against her and she steadied me, before stuffing me back together and pulling me by the lapel towards the stairs back to the door.

'Cara, where you goin'?' I heard it clearly above the disco beat. The other woman at the bar; the one with the big teeth was waving at her.

'See ya later alligator. Come on dahhling.' The last was to me. I clattered up the stairs behind her and she'd already hailed a cab when I bumped into her at the top. She took hold of my lapel again as the cab pulled up.

'Where you goin', luv? Oh it's you. Leave the poor prat behind, can't you. You can see he's rat-arsed.'

'Mind your nose, you! Come on dahhling.'

'Hey Mister!' The woman at the bar added to the melee. 'You forgot something.' She was at the door to the bar waving, something small and dark in her hand, but Cara edged me towards the cab.

'Go on you, get going.' She rapped on the cabbie's window as she pulled the door shut after me. I tumbled onto the seat next to her, confused by both the other woman calling to me and the cabbie's prevarication.

'What about Jimmy?' He asked Cara.

'Wass goin' on 'ere?' I mumbled, but forgot I wanted a reply.

'Nothing dahhling. Ignore *her*. *She's* just jealous,' she nodded curtly at the cabbie, 'and he's worrying about getting his fare. You've got money on you, haven't you?' The inference annoyed me. Too many people had already interfered with my life and turned it upside down. I wasn't letting some jumped up little cabbie get involved too.

'I've got money.' I announced and waved my wallet obligingly. There were raggedy bits hanging out the edges. What were they? I couldn't be bothered to work it out and shoved it back in my pocket again. I slumped back in the seat and let the swaying of the taxi lull me into sleep.

'See?' Cara hissed at the cabbie. 'Now can we go?'

'Ok mate, your choice,' he said and slipped the cab into gear. In the vague recesses of my mind I knew that he was warning me off and I guessed she was a prostitute but that didn't bother me. It was nothing new to me; you just had to remember the safety rules. We drew up a few minutes later outside a neo Georgian three-storey place and she relieved me of another fiver to pay the fare then pushed me out of the door and slid after me, skirt rising up her thighs as she exited. I enjoyed the view and made a lunge at her, but she pushed my hand away smartly.

'Greedy boy, wait till we're inside, what kind of girl do you think I am?' The taxi driver snorted and added his parting shot.

'Good luck mate. Rather you than me.' I gave him two fingers and stumbled after her down the iron steps to the basement. It was unlit at the bottom and I tripped, bumping into her as she fumbled with her key in the door.

'Watch it!' She exclaimed sharply and I was struck by how deep her voice sounded, but I wasn't in any fit state to make rational judgements so I let it go. Hearing – yeah, mine definitely played tricks on me.

The room was in darkness and she didn't turn the lights on, just grabbed my lapels again and dragged me towards what I assumed was the bedroom. The alcohol high was just starting to leave me after the doze in the cab and for a brief moment I questioned what I was doing here. Will's hurt face drifted in front of my eyes and I shook my head as if to fling it away from me. Lucy's voice replaced it. *I have Jeff ... Sorry ...* then Will's voice returned. *You're not dumb. We're just different...* Oh Christ, how different we were. Why didn't you tell me before? Why didn't you trust me? The disconcerting realisation that I felt more lost and betrayed by Will not sharing his secret with me than by Lucy cheating on me left me confused. The urge to have sex had gone. I saw now it had only been the need to be close to someone, but Cara wasn't having that.

'Where's it gone? She exclaimed in mock surprise and in the darkness her hands and mouth expertly brought me back to life despite myself. I fell backwards onto the bed and she hovered over me, her head to my toes, sixty-nine style. Her skirt brushed lightly over my face as she moved. Molten lava poured into my stomach as I thrust deeply into her mouth and the feeling of her teeth scraping lightly against the shaft of my cock added a frisson of danger to the delight. She flicked her tongue around my foreskin and then pulled me slowly from her mouth. As I gasped and shuddered, she wormed the end of her tongue into the tip of its head and then rolled it round the rim. The immediate change from depression to desire made me long for more than her mouth round me. I reached for her and found her breasts pressing hard against her flimsy top. It had poppers down the front and as I pulled at it, they burst open, allowing her breasts to swing out, one of the nipples brushing my arm. I grasped it and pinched the nipple, feeling it harden. She had rougher skin than I'd expected. The rush of desire was slowed momentarily as I remembered the safety rules.

'Gotta johnny?' I gasped. She laughed – a deep throaty laugh.

'Don't need that dahhling, just a hand to mouth job tonight.' Her skirt slid up again as I ran my hands up and down her thighs and then pulled her down towards me. My hands felt the ridge of her panties and I slipped a finger inside the top and then froze. The shape was unmistakeable. Suddenly I was stone cold sober and desire left me like someone had thrown a bucket of icy water over my head.

'You've got a cock!' I pulled my hand away as if it had been burnt. This was obscene.

'Oh dahhling, don't tell me you didn't know.'

'Christ!' I pushed her roughly off me and jumped off the bed, head spinning as shouting echoed though the small flat. Was that me? My head reeled, then the door burst open and the shouting was in the room and a fist in my face.

'You bastard, get off her.' It smashed into me again, splitting my eye and grazing my eyebrow. Blood streamed down my face and the room came sharply into focus as Cara snapped on the light. We faced each other, the three of us. Cara – now my alcoholic haze had cleared, plainly not a woman, with a too-heavy jawline, unfeminine brow and squared shoulders like an Olympic swimmer. She stared back at me belligerently. Next to her, arms curled ready for the next blow, was the fist I'd collided with; a heavily-muscled black guy with no neck and a flattened boxers nose.

'Fuck, what are you two?' I clapped a hand to my face, trying to stem the flow from the split eye. I sounded aggressive but inside I knew I was in the shit. There was no way in my still semi-drunk state, and now half-blinded that I would be able to take on just one of them. Even in my army days I would have thought twice about taking the black fucker on. He looked too solid and too stupid. No-neck made a move towards me and I wasn't fast enough to duck. The iron fist crashed into me again, sending me spinning. As he completed the hammering, I slid into the oblivion of night, with just enough wit to work out that Cara was one of those trannys I'd so disparagingly called Will. No-neck must be her pimp and despite my angry denouncement of Will as one of this kind, there were a million reasons why he wasn't, whatever his sexual persuasion. I might now never have the opportunity to apologise for what I'd said to him. Regret was sour in my mouth. The ironic surprise that I could go from stupid drunk to stupid sober and still be stunned by my own blindness almost made me laugh before everything went black.

When I started to come round, it was with a pounding head and a face that felt like it had been rubbed against a cheese grater. My nose was plugged with sodden cotton wool clumps. I tentatively touched the cotton wool and my fingers came away slimy. Old blood. I coughed and a welt of iron-tasting muck slid down my throat, making me reach. In the gloom, a figure moved. My stomach knotted and I tried to rise to a sitting position to defend myself, wincing as my body complained, but failed.

'Ahh, fuck!' I wanted to meet the onslaught head on if there was going to be more. I may be stupid but I wasn't a coward. Wills voice cut through the dark of the room.

'Stay still. You've probably got cracked ribs and your nose has only just stopped bleeding. I've almost run out of cotton wool trying to pack it.' I groaned and fell back onto the bed. Every part of me ached, and my head felt like a truck had run over it. A hangover compounding the injuries from the beating was the least of my worries. I grunted and lay still, praying for the pain to stop, and my head to feel like it was connected to me again. Will got out of the chair and went to the door to turn the light on. Its stark brilliance blinded me and I turned my face away from it, wincing at both the light and the pain of movement. I felt angry, but I wasn't sure whether it was with him or me. I could feel his eyes on me but I kept my face turned in the other direction, even though the position was excruciatingly painful. I resented that he was there, watching over me in the extremes of my vulnerability and stupidity, but I was relieved it was him and I was here, and the night was ending the day. The events of the evening started to fall into place and I felt embarrassed as I realised how naïve I'd been. I didn't want him there in case he could sense my weakness – not the physical, but the mental and emotional confusion.

'It's ok, you can go. I'll manage on my own.' It was more of a croak than a command and irritatingly I felt childish and ungracious as I was saying it, but I just couldn't stop myself. As soon as I'd said it I knew I wanted the security of him being there. The discomfort forced out another expletive I didn't want to say either but it made me feel stronger, and then immediately weaker again. 'Fucking tranny's!'

Will had gone back to the door by then, hand on the door handle. He paused.

'One of those fucking tranny's saved your life. She found the credit cards you were showering everywhere as you left the bar and rang me because she remembered your name.' He clicked off the light and left me in the dark. Christ; was I in the dark. I tried to stay awake to work out in my mind exactly what was going on with me but the after effects of alcohol claimed me. I dreamed mixed up crazy dreams where Will was a girl not a boy and we were children again. I still yelled to her to come on, get a move on, but when I turned to see her racing after me out of the apple orchard, she had skinny girls knees protruding from a gathered dirndl skirt and pigtails bouncing merrily round her cheeks. Her eyes were the same, Wills deep almond eyes, and when she slumped down beside me the camaraderie was the same. But she was a girl, and I felt protective of her. I would never put her at risk, I would never put her in the way of old Mother J's son, and as a teenager I would never walk away from her and leave her on her own in favour of pursuing another girl. I couldn't bear the hurt look, the left out look, which now I knew I'd seen in Wills' boys eyes too. The childish girl Will was replaced by the woman I'd come home to today and rejected. The eyes were the same there too, the hurt look, the left out look. In the dream I encircled the hurt woman in my arms and cradled her close, held her to me and slowly, slowly I found my lips on hers. In my ears, the blood rushed, singing like a choir in the distance and my heart pounded with excitement, anticipation, desire; love. I drew away and the softness of the woman's face hardened to the sharper edge of Wills more masculine features. I reeled away, horrified that I was kissing him so greedily. I woke up with a jump and it was already morning even though the night seemed to have passed in mere seconds since Will had flicked off the light.

I lay still for a while, edging into reality as if testing my footing on quicksand. The gaudy paintwork was the same. The smell of the house was the same, coffee and aftershave and the musky scent that Will used – I'd thought that was aftershave too, but maybe I'd been wrong. It was still the same though. The clock ticked annoyingly in the lounge, and outside, the hubbub of the traffic beeped and buzzed with a normal working day. All my senses were the same; sight, sound, smell – if battered. My head ached dully and one eye was half closed. I imagined the deep purple bruising that probably accompanied the swelling. My ribs gave a complaining twinge like a knife stab whenever I took in a deep breath – at least one was probably broken – but I was here, alive, and otherwise the same. The one thing I'd thought was constant in my life though wasn't; Will. I felt mortified as I remembered the kiss in the dream. I compared it to the rush of desire I'd felt as Cara's hands and mouth had wormed round me but the rush of revulsion that accompanied it was for her, not Will.

Did I have unexplained feelings for him – or her? What was he? Did I think of him as male or female now the secret was out? When I trawled back through my childhood memories, the pigtailed girl impression was more prominent than the boy Will. And the oddities between us were all explained. My best friend had never truly been a boy, but a girl – trapped half way between two expectations – hers and mine. The thought made me question the whole of my previous life, and yet, I was comforted that I now understood it in a way I hadn't before. I found, oddly, that I didn't feel revolted anymore; I felt curious. The very strangeness of him now, the fact that the person I thought I knew was such an enigma, made me curious to know more even as I was repelled. Who was he, this new person? He was a stranger, and yet as familiar to me as I was to myself. I'd recognised him from years before when he hadn't even existed as he was now.

I stayed there until I heard movement which signified Will had got up and was in the kitchen. The coffee smell got stronger. The rib pain made it hard to get up and my head swam as I stood upright, but I made it unsteadily down to the kitchen and sat down heavily opposite him at the worn grey table. He was the same and not the same, but something in me had just accepted that it was OK for him to be like that – despite what I'd felt the previous evening when I'd slammed out of the house in disgust. I'd seen many things in my life already, things that had shown me how everything should be valued, even if it wasn't the way you expected it to be – or even wanted it to be. If it had significance to you, the only way was to accept it simply for what it was. At the moment I didn't know what Will was or what I felt about it or him, but the olive branch was mine to hold out.

'So what shall I call you?'

'What do you mean?' I knew by the way he bristled that he was expecting more abuse.

'Well, Will is a bloke's name, and obviously I can't call you by a bloke's name any more – can I? So what shall I call you?'

'Oh.' He smiled and suddenly I saw clearly behind the covering of make-up, of pretence, of preconception, assumption and prejudice. I saw the woman who I'd known in the boy all along.

'Billie.'

Chapter 14:

The woman, 1982-1983

September 1983

Love never goes the way you want it to, does it? You finally find it or realise it is what you feel and then it all goes to pot. When I answered the door to Tom, it was like fate had replied to my unspoken wishes. The thing I most feared and most wanted was there in front of me – Tom. And now I had to admit to love, but how could I admit that to him? How could I admit anything to him? It was the best and the worst of how anything could be – but that is precisely what unrequited love is, isn't it?

The days and weeks that followed him moving in were both wonderful and terrible. I practised being Will again so I was perfect at it, and yet Will was so not who I wanted to be. I betrayed Billie in my fear of losing Tom as soon as I'd found him. To have Tom there I had to shelve the plans to become Billie and stay Will. I struggled so hard with it and the choice was almost impossible to make. In the end I chose Tom – and therefore of course Will, but inevitably the desire to be what I naturally felt myself to be overcame the desire to be what would keep Tom there. You cannot deny nature, no matter how hard you try. We developed the old boyhood camaraderie but in the moments he wasn't aware of me watching him, I watched with different eyes and thought with a different mind.

I had to keep the Billie me hidden until the times he couldn't see me. I remained his old mate, and the pretty clothes and sweet-smelling make-up was relished when he'd already gone out – to work, or for a drink with someone he'd hooked up with. I had to adjust my working hours to allow for him to leave first so I changed from Will to Billie after he'd gone, and dashing home, changed back again before he returned. Luckily, the library had introduced flexi-time recently so I could shorten my lunch break to almost nothing to allow for earlier or later starts, but as Tom tended to set off early and linger in a bar on the way home, I managed a working pattern for myself that wasn't too different overall after a while, but the pressure was ever-present. The moment when I might walk in and he'd arrived home early by chance always lurked at the back of my mind and the scene that I could imagine, almost word for word that would ensue. Then my stomach would knot and my hands sweat with fear and I had to tell myself over and over that it would be alright, one day – it would be alright. At other times as soon as he went out, the urge to become Billie would take over and I would snatch the precious moments to breathe out. Like the woman I'd first met in the Kings Road shop, I had to take to subterfuge. I remembered her hiding place, behind the bath panel. Early on I pulled out the tool bag under the sink and carefully took the panel off. Underneath was a space where a bag could be stashed but it was dusty and a layer of dead insects and rubbish covered the floor. The idea of having to clear that out regularly and unscrew and then replace the panel made the whole exercise seem underhand. Why should I feel this way? I wasn't doing anything wrong.

I decided to not hide my 'other' wardrobe, but not parade it either – the middle road. If it was discovered, it was because it should be. I wasn't ashamed of who I was. I reasoned that I'd risked that much with the people I worked with – why was I hiding from Tom? But then fear of him stomping out in disgust sent reason reeling again, and so the two sides continued at war for some while. The timid, anxious me only took on my woman's persona when he wasn't around. If I didn't think too hard about it, I squared it with myself by saying he would need time to adjust, and he'd only just arrived, hadn't he? The other side of me knew I was betraying myself and over time pushed harder and harder for recognition. I became gradually more reckless with the time I returned from work, occasionally left an item of women's clothing in the dirty washing, or a stray mascara or lipstick in the bathroom. Tom didn't comment. It was like his eyesight was as defective as his hearing at times – or maybe he made his own assumptions and didn't feel the need to ask.

So I remained undecided, the clothes carefully hidden at one end of the wardrobe and tucked under jackets and shirts that I layered over the top of them. Sometimes determination to be who I wanted to overcame the fear of his reaction and I would rebelliously take out a favourite outfit and determine to dress in it, and parade out in front of him one day. *There, this is the real me.* Then the familiar stomach cramp crippled my inclination to be brave, and instead I would dither, chewing on a finger nail and hating myself. Of course being a figure of fun was a regular occurrence for me. It wasn't that. I knew I was only *almost* a woman. Made up and in female clothes, from a distance I could pass for a woman, but up close, my skin was still too coarse, my shoulders just slightly too square and my hips too narrow. I hadn't yet that softness that personifies, even exudes from a woman. I knew that would only come with the drugs – the hormone treatment, and ultimately surgery. I was aware of the children who openly stared at me on the tube, the women who would nudge their companions and snigger when I looked away. I knew what they called me behind my back – gay, weirdo, tranny. The men were worse – as if my choice to be a woman actually challenged their own masculinity too. Their insults were crueller than the stares and the pointing female fingers.

'Fucking nancy boy' and 'faggot' were common. What was worse – and I was lucky I'd only experienced it a few times – were the beatings when they were drunk and out of control and I was on my own without anyone to back me up. Walking home late at night, or unexpectedly caught in a football crowd were the times I dreaded most. My beatings hadn't been nastier than a black eye, split lip and bruising which had made me walk like an old woman with gout for days. I trawled back in my mind to the time I'd watched Tom be beaten up by Old

311

Mother J's son and the gripping fear I'd felt of feeling that physical pain myself. Maybe it had been a premonition of what would frighten me most as an adult? I'd heard of TV's beaten so badly they'd not walked again, or been cut so viciously their faces would always bear the scars of fear and prejudice. That's all it was – fear and prejudice, but they accompanied every decision I made and every place I went.

That was mainly why I still frequented the gay and TV bars I'd come across before I'd shown the inner me to the world. At least there the risk of physical harm or abuse, for me, was minimised and these people accepted me for what I was without comment or judgement. But more than anything else I wanted to not feel alone and a figure of ridicule and disgust. On the lonely nights when I'd had a particularly bad day, and it felt as if the world would never be a welcoming place for any part of me, I wondered why I was alive at all. Then the memory of the whirling kaleidoscope room and waking to find Fran there after all made me trudge on. And I found Suzanne again; or at least someone who both represented Suzanne to me, and was actually called Suzanne too.

I found her quite by chance not long after my momentous visit home, in one of those clubs in Soho. At first I just noticed a small feisty woman, quite out of place in the day time club. She was facing away from me. I didn't realise she was a pre-op until I'd spent some time talking to her, and looking critically for the signs without even realising that was what I was doing. It was as if I'd now developed an antenna to detect similar species to myself. I thought she might be a lesbian initially but the turning point came when I confessed my situation to her one evening when I was feeling particularly depressed. As Tom's self-confidence grew without Lucy to demean him, or failure slapping him regularly in the face, my sense of self declined, from the pressure of hiding away again. Tom was going out regularly with lads from work – to football matches, for a curry, on a stag night. Funny how we almost naturally put a distance between the matey pair we'd been, and skirted round each other like two birds, as if circling; getting ready to land and engage. I took advantage of the opportunities to go out as Billie in his absence, visiting the TS bars I hadn't been to in a while, and there she was.

The revelation that she was like me was like finding a spark of light in a world perpetually in the twilight. We never became friends to the point of absolute confidences as such – maybe there is an innate rivalry in transsexuals that never quite allows a complete bonding. Or maybe, no matter how hard we try, essentially we retain that tendency to camaraderie that men employ with friends rather than the confidence-sharing women incline to? But we were as close to close friends as we could be. She was pre-op but had been on hormone treatment for a while, so I already knew second hand what to expect when my chance came. It was good being able to joke about the small details of becoming female that somehow you overlook before you have to do them, like remembering to sit down to pee, the routines of taking make-up off, moisturising, shaving armpits, not farting in public; the differences between men and women we take for granted.

The small distinctions took on more significance when she explained them to me. I automatically went to the gents and not the ladies early on in my transformation – but that was like touting for business and legally if I was purporting to be a woman, I had to use the ladies loo. At least that put paid to the indecision about using the urinal or the pedestal next time. The etiquette for a TS is a minefield, as are the legal implications. So many rights I could take for granted as a male didn't exist for a TS. And once I had been gender reassigned, still I would never be fully recognised as a woman. It would be a life still led half in the shadows.

The moment of truth was fast approaching for this Suzanne though. Her final consult was soon. I knew by her tense face the last time I saw her that it was worrying her.

'If they don't agree, it's the end of the road.'

'Of course it's not – you could ask them to reconsider.' I wasn't sure if I was right at the time, but it seemed like the best thing to say. Her tension was now extending to shredding the beermat on the table in front of us in Jimmies.

'Billie, do you really think they'd say yes after they'd said no?' Her expression was incredulous and I felt foolish. I was still living in cloud cuckoo land at times – easier than always facing the harsh realities. The final transition seemed too far away for me to go into its fine details yet – I was finding the fine details of just making the first steps into femininity taxing enough, and maybe laziness played a part too. I was already falling into the trap of thinking that as the trail blazer of the two of us, Suzanne would tell me what to expect. Her expression made me unexpectedly review my opinion of her as trail blazer. Was she strong enough for it after all? I wished again I'd kept the number of the first Suzanne – the woman in the Kings Road shop; the Suzanne who'd set the river flowing. She had the determination to trail blaze for a whole community, not just herself. My Suzanne had started to shred another beermat, leaving small curls of cardboard on the table, rolled into tiny grimy worms as the sweat from her palms bound them together. I put my hand over hers encouragingly, but she jerked it away.

'Sorry,' she said, 'I'm just edgy about it.'

'If they don't agree, what will you do then?' I asked, thinking that talking would help her let off steam. That was the woman's way – not the man's – wasn't it? Women are able to revel in emotions even if they are sad or negative. Men's egos make them shut it away and pretend it's not there.

'Give up and go back to being a bloke.' She paused, 'then probably top myself,' she added. I thought she was joking and started to laugh until I realised she meant it. The laughter drowned in my throat as I took a swig of my drink to cover the faux pas. I didn't know what to say. She looked up from the beermat curls.

'You don't believe me, do you?'

'It's not that, I just don't see how you can ever give up on living no matter how bad it is.' Fran's face loomed in my memory as I said it. *Don't ever do that again…* I was a hypocrite, I knew.

'When you've lived a lie for ten years, been ridiculed, insulted, beaten up by assholes who think they have the right to judge you when they've had too much to drink, been refused jobs and entry to places just because of who you are, lived in dumps and squats where there's no water and no-where even to take a shit other than behind a bush when you're in between jobs, say that again to me.' Her face was angry and set, bitter with the prejudice of years. I'd never seen her like that before. I hadn't known. In all the time we'd talked, she talked of the future and how it would be so much better when she'd had the op. I'd always thought of her as indefatigably positive. It was to be her nirvana, her entry into the state of grace. I wondered if instead it would be her nemesis. 'I'm sorry Billie,' she added apologetically and in a much softer tone. I guessed my face must have registered my shock. 'You're only just starting out and it's so much better now than it was when I did. Maybe it will be easier for you than it has been for me – God knows I hope it will be.' She reached over and touched my face gently with the back of her fingers in the first real caress I'd felt in my life. 'You'll make a pretty lady one day.' She smiled wistfully and then her demeanour changed. 'I'll have to be going – got some stuff to do before Tuesday.' She rose sharply, pushing the bar chair back with a clatter as if she wanted to get away from me as quickly as possible. I felt awkward, hoping I hadn't offended her in my naivety and lack of knowledge about her and her inner emotions. I was also worried about whether she'd meant what she said or not. I couldn't decide. She'd become

316

completely unreadable to me with that snippet of background she'd now let slip. I wanted to call her back, but didn't. The same dithering as I felt over Tom paralysed me and instead I watched her narrow back walk tensely away, alone.

I realised my difficulties had been minor problems so far. The anonymous letters had tailed off after a while. Their author must have got bored and apart from the odd occasion I felt under scrutiny as I walked down the street, nervously imagining the net curtains twitching as I walked past, I hadn't felt under threat in my neighbourhood after that initial problem. Tom there made me feel more secure too. Petty private bullies weren't likely to take on his muscled bulk in a hurry, even though he'd softened considerably since leaving the army. Without knowing it he was acting as a protector for me, a fact which made me laugh ruefully, yet uncomfortably too since I felt uneasily like I was using him because of it. But the confidence it gave me had even enabled me to reach a kind of easy disregard with the building site brickies, who still shouted the rude comments but more out of habit than intent. When I'd had my first crisis of prejudice with them, Sheila had been my saviour. She'd never discussed it afterwards and nor had she said why she'd come round. Maybe she was one of those guardian angels it was claimed we had? I thought about asking her a number of times but didn't. It was like the topic was closed and shortly afterwards she died quietly and without fuss from terminal cancer. None of us had even known. She'd kept it so quiet. I missed her gentle no-nonsense attitude at work, and the sense that she was looking out for me. I placed a red rose on her grave and said a prayer for her, even though I wasn't religious. I knew she had been. Looking up at the stars sometimes I imagined Sheila could be one of the quietly twinkling ones, checking all was progressing as it should. I wished I'd told her how much her small act of kindness had meant to me, but I thought she'd probably known anyway. And from one guardian angel to another; Fran had taken over where Sheila had left off. Many TS's find themselves totally rejected by all their family. From my one small experience of it I knew how empty and alone that made you feel, but as if by a miracle, Fran had made a U turn. Maybe that had been Sheila's doing too? Now my sister – whilst often many miles away – was always metaphorically by my side; my life was charmed compared to many.

I hated myself for simply listening to Suzanne in the past without paying attention to the information beneath the surface level, and enjoying the encouragement she'd represented without thinking of the battles she'd faced. Of course behind all that outward optimism for the future had really been fear. Why hadn't I seen it before? I wanted to comfort and reassure her but by the time the parade of thoughts and realisations had finished she was walking out the door. I started to say something – anything – just to delay her going, but she pre-empted me by turning at the doorway and coming back to add her own final summation.

'You know, sometimes, when you're up against prejudice and dogmatism, it's easier to back off and hide. To go all the way with this, you have to be more than strong, you have to be ruthless. Never give up and always believe. Don't let anyone deflect you or be other than what you are just to conform. If someone cares about you, they'll accept you as you are. I've been trying to do this for ten years but maybe I'm simply not strong enough. You are, Billie, but don't ever think it will be easy. There will be a time when you'll have to sacrifice everything for it. I lost my family years ago because of it. My parents won't speak to me – I don't even exist for them anymore. Luckily I had no children when I was married or they would have been banned from me too. It hurt like hell when my family rejected me. I was only eighteen. A long time ago now, but if you can't rely on your parents to love you whatever, who can you? I don't know about yours, maybe they'll be more able to accept, but there will be some people who never will. Be prepared for that. If you're not prepared to take that hit – and it may be the biggest hit you can imagine, you'll never get there. Get there Billie; get there for all of us, will you?' She clasped my hand so tightly that her nails left small crescent moon indentations across the top of it, like something had bitten me. One even drew the tiniest speck of blood where the skin was pierced. The mark was still faintly there when they told me Suzanne had taken an overdose. They tried to pump her stomach, but unlike me she hadn't been sick. She had absorbed most of the drug before the ambulance even arrived. No guardian angel for her. Her organs just disintegrated and failed one by one from its acid effect. One TV said in a hushed voice that she'd cried blood as she died. I dismissed it as dramatic rubbish but I can't deny the image haunted me for a long time. I cried salt tears just as bitter, for her, for the unfairness of life, for me. It happened seven months into the time Tom came to live with me. As I walked home from the early afternoon funeral, the autumn sunshine filtered weakly through the rain clouds and I decided nothing would stop me becoming a woman, not even Tom.

When he first arrived, after the initial resuming of a semblance of what Tom would regard as normal life, his attention became fixed on finding a better job. His routine was to pore over the Evening Standard as soon as he could get hold of it, spreading it out over the rickety old table in the kitchen and ring the ads that might present a chance of success. Then he'd turn to me, always hovering nearby without seeming to be.

'What do you think of any of those?' That was my invitation to sidle in and stand close by, ostensibly reading the ringed opportunities, but really just relishing his smell and the closeness of him. That just-washed scent of his shirt, and the combination of the shaving foam he used and the aftershave on his skin reacted to produce a particular fresh, warm fruity smell I thought of as peculiarly Tom. His hair curled over the edge of his collar. No matter how often he had it cut, it hardly took any days for the slight curl to regrow and tickle his collar as if teasing it. Under that was the curve of his neck, almost the only place I thought of as vulnerable on him. I'd stand as close looking over his shoulder at the newspaper warranted and read, most of my mind not even registering the words. It was the only time I could be close without seeming inappropriate. We fell easily back into the old friendship but strangely didn't socialise together after a first drink or two out. He went his way and I went mine in the evenings. I would have liked more of his company and yet, if I'd had it, it would have curtailed being Billie so it was a trade-off and I carried on betraying myself for those seven months that way, hating the lies, hating the denial of myself. And yet although we were close but not close, Tom confided everything in me. His thoughts, his feelings, his disappointments, his anger with Lucy, his frustration with his hearing loss and his sense of failure at being unable to father a child. I knew all of the inner man, whilst hiding from the outer one. I felt like a wife without being anything to him. Was this what marriage was like? How could the intensity of love be reduced to mundane routine, with one loving and one not noticing, one trying so hard and one oblivious?

Eventually the frustration if it all prompted recklessness. I wanted Tom to know but didn't know how to tell him. When Tom commented on the state of disrepair of something, I was tired of noncommittally saying I was saving. Why didn't Tom ask what I was saving for? Eventually I positively wanted Tom to ask, wanted him to discover the 'me' that lived part of a life when he wasn't watching. Suzanne's death and the funeral coincided with the day he was called away to see Lucy because she was having problems with the pregnancy and he felt duty-bound to check on her welfare. I welcomed him leaving so I could have space to myself and my thoughts. I dressed for the funeral and went through the motions there as if on automatic pilot. I walked the watery sunshine walk home and let the iron in my soul form. I shut the door behind me with relief that the world was outside and I was in, but the trials of the day hadn't ended there and I lingered as Billie, feeling I would be betraying Suzanne if I changed back into Wills persona now. When his key turned in the door unexpectedly early, I didn't rush to push my bedroom door shut, or tear off my funeral finery to replace them with my normal sweats and t-shirt. I checked how I looked and then stood in front of the mirror and waited.

His face when he burst into the room was funny in one of those comedy sketch routine ways. I almost had to stifle a laugh whilst shivering with the anticipation of knowing life was about to change even more dramatically than when I had told my colleagues who I really was. Strands of fear wound themselves round my intestines, curling up to my heart and then pulled tight, like a snake constricting round prey. Tom's voice preceded him.

'Complications, my arse.' It catapulted him into the room as the door flung back and his stocky bulk filled the opening. Then, 'fucking hell, what are you playing at?' The moment was here. Inwardly I steeled myself for the blows because I knew they would come. I knew Tom too well to expect a sympathetic response. The alpha male would have to speak first. I just hoped my assumption I knew him well enough was right and the gentler man I thought was under the alpha male would eventually displace it and try to understand the real Will; Billie. The force of his reaction drew fear to my face but I took a deep breath and stepped into the ring nonetheless. This was for you, and me, and for the river, and for all of us, Suzanne.

'I'm not playing. This is something I was going to have to tell you about.' The inclination to laugh bubbled up again as his face revolted between comic dismay and classic horror.

'Something you were going to have to tell me about? What, that you dress up like a, like a…' In my head I was re-writing the scene to take the sting out of it. Here I knew I would want to describe him as apoplectic like a stuffy Colonel would be. The bubble of mirth tickled my ribs and fought with the boa constrictor. 'Christ, Will! What are you?'

'I'm me; that's who I am.' At that moment, I'd never felt stronger, braver – which was odd because my adversary was the person I loved most and was most likely to lose. Fear gives you wings to fly as much as love does.

'Me.' The pause was dramatic and very deliberate. 'And is me male or female?' That was easy. The more I admitted, the better I felt, the more real – the more me. The shackles of submission fell away completely. It may hurt but it was better to have truth with pain than be continually in denial.

'Female, I think.'

'Female. Really? Are you a tranny?' I didn't answer. I knew there was more to come and I might as well weather it and deal with the whole string of abuse. I wondered at how calm I was now. Why hadn't I faced this challenge long ago? Fearing loss makes you weak. Facing it – even if you do lose – makes you suddenly strong. Many things fitted into the jigsaw of self-belief in my mind over those passing minutes, like a song coming to a sweet conclusion. There was a long pause, and then the insults hit. 'We had one of those little arses when I was in. He used to let all comers get up his bum too. God knows what they caught off him. Jesus! Are you a bum-fucker too?'

'No!' I couldn't help a sharper response to that. The memory of Freddie came too strongly to mind and the pain of that night. My turn to pause – more to recover equilibrium from the unexpected reaction to the Freddie memory which I'd thought I'd long since stifled. He had his eyes closed like a child would to signify they weren't even there. 'I'm not sick or a homo, if that's what you mean. Nor am I a tranny.' I knew I was talking to deaf ears – and not because of failed hearing. His mind was closed, just as his eyes were. I wasn't sure he even heard the last part because suddenly he lurched off to the bathroom and I could hear him vomiting. I waited, my nerves jangling, but determined to hold it together. The vomiting made me feel bad, partly because of that awful smell that sick always brings with it, but also because it said more to me than any words could. I made him sick. My self-belief wavered. Maybe this had been a bad idea after all. There was no turning back now but the butterfly wings of fear trembled inside me and the eagle wings of courage faltered and flapped ineffectually.

After a while he returned, wiping his face with the back of his hand. He didn't give me the chance to say anything, but launched another attack immediately.

'Then what the fuck are you, then? Dressed in women's stuff and mincing in front of a mirror?' He flapped at my dress as if there was a wasp on it. The flick of his finger stung my leg, but I didn't react.

'I'm a pre-op transsexual.'

'A pre-op transsexual.' His voice was cruel, making fun. 'What the fuck is that?' I explained, using all the correct technical terms whilst he stared at me as if he was looking at a zombie out of a movie. Then he passed judgement. I'd hoped for more leniency because of the time we'd known each other, but prejudice loomed too large for the moment.

'You're a warped fucker who wants to chop his dick off in the mistaken belief that if he sucks it up inside himself, he'll become a bird.' That really stung. I couldn't keep the expression from my face this time, and I knew there was satisfaction for him in having drawn the response.

'I'm out of here before you do anything to me. Dress up all you like, but don't come anywhere near me. You're just a sad, sick fuck.' Then he was gone, barging so hard through the door it flung back and bounced on its hinges before springing back and slamming shut. Its bang almost coincided with the bang of the front door, like an echo. I stood trembling in the silence for a while, wondering what life would be like now. I hadn't wanted Tom to see me react. The trembling stopped after a while, leaving just an empty sadness. Life had changed forever, we had changed forever and I didn't know whether it was good or bad, just that it was different. Still dressed as I had been when Tom flung out; Billie – how I felt I should be, I went out the kitchen and made myself something to eat. I took it into the lounge and sat in the corner of the old settee with the plate on my lap, kicking off my shoes before curling my feet up under me. The TV picture wasn't good and it kept snowing with interference but I persevered. I needed something to do to keep my mind off of wondering what Tom was doing and what his return would be like. 'Coronation Street' gave way to a documentary about hedgehogs and then ultimately moved into 'Blackadder'; far more my taste and I actually found myself laughing at the sarcastic wit. When that finished, I marked time with the news and then wasn't sure whether to go to bed or wait up. The decision was made for me by the phone. I jumped to it because I wondered if it would be Tom, but it was Millie, one of the TV's from the Kings Road shop. She was falling over her words, stuttering – and quite drunk. I eventually calmed her down enough to get sense out of her.

'Tom, your Tom. He's here, been here.'

'Where's here?' My heart was pounding. What could be the reason he was in what could only be a gay or TV bar if Millie was there too? Was he out gay-bashing? That didn't seem him at all despite the abuse he'd fired at me. Even hurt as I was, I knew most of it had been because he felt confused and hurt too. I didn't even know yet what had happened on the visit to Lucy, but it had obviously not gone well as he was back so early and in the light of his opening sentence as he burst into my room.

'I'm at Jimmies place in Soho. We came back here to drink one or two to Suzanne.'

'Oh no.' The groan came from the depths of me. I already knew what was coming next. Jimmies was so-named not only because it was frequented by Jocks but because it was owned by one – a brick-shithouse of a black Jock with no neck or brains and a skull and fist hard enough to crack anyone else's brains with one hit. If Jimmy 'kissed' you, you went home in a box or via the hospital. 'Please don't tell me Cara is in tonight.' Cara, occasional visitor to the Kings Road shop; sexually rampant and on the verge of being a male prostitute with Jimmy as both her lover and pimp, but not quite. Sometimes she mocked the TV's by dressing as one of them and fooling the drunken punters in the bar. My dealings with her had been minimal whilst in the shop, but I knew her fame of old. Millie and Christine part hero-worshipped her for her effrontery and part hated her for her bitchiness and amoral attitude to life in general. Cara was known for regularly picking up drunks and idiots around the bars in Soho and taking them back to her place to shake them down. The routine usually included Jimmy appearing from nowhere and claiming uncontrollable jealousy before beating the poor sucker to a pulp and clearing his wallet of cash and credit cards. The cards got cleaned out before the victim was even conscious the next day, but then he'd also get a warning that more of the same would be coming his way if he complained, so he didn't, even after his jaw was unwired and his teeth replaced. The TV's hated being used as a front this way – but often got inveigled into providing the lure in return for debts being written off or blackmail threats being set aside. Cara and Jimmy were bad news to anyone who tangled with them, whether voluntarily or not.

'Oh Billie, I'm sorry, it happened before I realised it was him. I mean why would I? Why would he come into Jimmies anyway? He's not a gay from what you said.' She was starting to ramble on with more of the same but I still didn't know what Tom had done apart from be there.

'Millie, Millie …' Her torrent of words paused, allowing me long enough to put in the main question. 'What was he doing there?'

'He went back with Cara.' I could feel the tension on the other end of the phone. My blood raced. This was the worst news Millie could have given me.

'When?'

'About fifteen minutes ago. I thought he was just a sap but he'd dropped his credit card – he was showering stuff out of his wallet everywhere because he was sooo drunk – and I picked it up and it said Tom Wilson and I thought that's exactly the same name as the guy Billie loves….' I wanted to say, *whoa there, Billie loves*? *How would you know that?* but then wondered if it had been obvious to everyone but me all this time. I let her ramble continue. '… and he looked the way you'd described him and then I found some other bits he'd dropped with the credit card and one was his wages slip and it had your address on it so I knew then that …'

'Ok,' I interjected. Millie's flow could go on forever in that vein, like a Woolf stream of consciousness but without the consciousness. I knew the most important details – apart from one.

'Where does Cara live?'

'Billie you can't take Jimmy on – he'd kill you!' She sounded genuinely terrified. Defiance surged though me. I'd had enough of being walked over, abused, ridiculed. I'd never liked what Cara and Jimmy did, and now I wasn't going to allow them to do that to Tom, no matter what he'd said to me earlier. Ironically although Tom's rejection fired me up to be his saviour, I'd never imagined myself going to war, or being in the midst of the fight, yet here I was actually starting it. Transformation indeed.

'No, but we all could.' She didn't reply. 'Millie?'

'We can't get involved in no trouble, Billie.' The fear was still in her voice.

'It won't be trouble. Haven't you ever heard how the bully backs down when everyone gangs together to face them? You'd like to break his hold over the bars you go in wouldn't you? You'd like to be able to go in any one of them and not be worried about being threatened into something you don't want to do? Suzanne told me how she'd been beaten up so many times in the past when I last saw her. Let's do this for her too.'

I knew this was a theme amongst the gays. I was ashamed to use it on them but vulnerability creates its own kind of beast. Jimmy was a beast who fed on the vulnerability of the fragile egos that strutted into the Soho gay bars to find companionship, and when he was around, instead found bullying and coercion. It was a common complaint but no-one on their own had the clout to get rid of him or his kind. Getting rid of Jimmy wouldn't mean the end of harassment, but it would be one less hood to be bullied by and one less hustler to use them. She didn't answer but it was the kind of no answer that meant she was thinking about it.

'I'll ask the others,' was all she'd be pushed to eventually. 'Get over here anyway and I'll find out her address.' I didn't need to wonder about anything else then. The path seemed straight and set. I grabbed a coat, as much money as I could lay hands on, raiding the gas, leccy and phone bill tins and emptying my purse. Whether it was by money or force, I knew I had to get Tom out of Cara's clutches. I didn't bother with my car. It was quicker to get a cab – no parking required – and the cabbies knew their way round the smoke quicker and better than I ever would. Millie was waiting outside the bar with a small crowd behind her. I was overwhelmed almost to tears when I saw them. I didn't need to ask their decision. It was all over their hands and faces; hands that clutched bottles with jagged necks, and knuckle dusters and flick knives. I feared the pent up violence it represented and hoped the rallying zeal wouldn't turn into a bloodbath, but I also had to get Tom out. Suzanne had told me to be ruthless. I was only just starting.

As I got out of the cab, Millie rushed forward, tottering on her too-high heels and holding firmly onto my arm.

'I've got the address,' she announced very loudly. 'Shall we go?' I hesitated, uneasy with the mob-hand feel of the group of gays and TV's.

'This isn't a battle, it's a liberation.' I said it as loudly as I could so they all heard. I might as well have saved my breath. The niceties meant nothing to them. Then I thought of Tom, and the niceties meant nothing to me either.

Cara's place was about fifteen minutes away. Millie seemed to know the backstreets of the area like the back of her hand.

'The knowledge,' she explained. 'I was a cabbie in a past life.' She directed us this way and that, like a Mexican wave flowing through the dark alleys of Soho. Our flood swept away the johns and the tarts plastered against walls they were conducting business against, the pimps hovering in their blacked-out saloons and the casual onlooker hurrying for a safe place to watch the show. Cara's place was a seedy looking basement with a wrought iron gate hanging on only one hinge, leading down rickety iron steps to a heavy wooden door like the door to a cell.

"Jimmy's car is here already,' hissed Millie. A sleek black Merc was parked just across the street. My heart turned over. I wondered what horrors were already happening behind Cara's imposing door.

'How do we get her to open it?' I hissed back.

'Easy. There's a code word for the fuzz.' Millie explained. Jake told me it. Jake nodded behind her. I'd never paid much attention to him before, except to remark he seemed too quiet and gentle to be a barman in Jimmies. I wondered what his story was and felt ashamed again that here was another person whose life history was unknown to me. Their miseries and joys had gone unremarked by me in my self-immersion. Gratitude for their willingness to help me in my moment of need even though I didn't even notice theirs almost overwhelmed me then and I felt a lump rising in my throat. It was no time for displays of emotion and I struggled to swallow it.

'He'll believe it if I say it – it's a warning signal.' Jake was softly spoken, with a Irish lilt; from the green stretches of Ireland to the rank depravity of Jimmy's employment. I wondered how that had happened. He stepped in front of Millie, and knocked on the door – an orchestrated tattoo beating out the rhythm of danger. I wondered if it was SOS but doubted that Jimmy would have the wit to know the combinations of beats that signified it. Anyway, for all my criticism of him, neither did I. There was movement behind the door, and Cara's voice questioning.

'Who's that? Whad'ya want?'

'It's Jake.'

'What's up?'

'Pigs.'

'Where?'

'At the bar. Open up, we need Jimmy there. They're going to open the safe.' There were sounds of locks being shot and Cara's voice calling to Jimmy.

'Hey, the filths at the bar and you need to get back there. Come on!' More rattling on the door and it swung inwards fractionally, Cara peering cautiously out into the gloom from behind its edge. Jake gave a hard shove and stepped firmly over the threshold, followed by Millie. The surge behind me pushed me in with them. I heard Cara gasp and start squawking angrily as she was pushed aside and Millie threw a left hook at her that Bugner would have been proud of. Cara stumbled back, blood pouring from her nose and seeping through her fingers.

'You fucker!' she shouted nasally at Mille. Mille gave her the finger and the Mexican wave filled the small basement. I heard her shout once for Jimmy, but it was truncated like a amputated leg. Squeamishness made me not want to know how she'd been silenced, but I lost that when I saw the state of Tom when we burst into the stuffy hell-hole that passed for Cara's bedroom. The bed dominated the room — a big black iron affair with handcuffs swinging from the headboard and manacles from the footboard. On a table off to one side an array of vicious looking instruments of torture awaited use. Tom was spread-eagled on the bed, hands and feet firmly encased in the cuffs and manacles, eyes black and closed, nose swollen and off-centre on his face. His head was lolling as if his neck no longer worked and a thin trail of watery red saliva had dripped from the side of his open mouth onto the pillow. There was already a dirty brown stain where it had soaked in. That meant it was old blood. Christ, how long had he been there and what had they already done to him? Jimmy was in the process of offering him more kind ministrations. A long whip with barbs on the end of the tail was raised behind his head as he perched, one knee firmly pinning Tom's chest to the bed. The spotlights in the ceiling were trained on the scene on the bed as if it was a tableau and it gave the two figures an unreal quality – as if they were waxworks, captured for ever in the moment of exquisite pain and torture. I froze, terrified that Tom was already dead, or dying from other invisible wounds.

The tableau shattered a second later as the mob behind us surged and overwhelmed the two figures on the bed like a throng of hornets, swarming over its prey. The surge took Jimmy's body struggling and shouting curses, holding him up high above their heads as if he was a victor they were parading in celebration. Before I could remind anyone this was a liberation exercise, the mob had gone, as if it had never been there, leaving only Jimmy's vague cries of terror to drift back. I felt shaken by the silent cloud of destruction that had swept in and engulfed him. The urge to retch made me totter dizzily until Tom's prone body came back into focus. Two familiar figures hovered around him now, rattling at the manacles and cuffs to free him. Millie and Jake hadn't followed the mob and intense gratitude replaced nausea. I joined them in trying to undo the locks and tangled chains pinning him down. He groaned as we tentatively shifted him to get better access, and relief he was at least still alive prompted a sting of hot tears from me. The second handcuff lock sprang as Millie jiggled a hairpin rigorously inside it.

"How did you know how to do that?' Curiosity overcame emotion temporarily.

'Bit of moonlighting sometimes,' she said gruffly. I marvelled at the double lives we all led. I watched Jake expertly remove the manacle from one of Tom's ankles.

'And Jake?'

'He used to be a locksmith before Jimmy got his clutches on him.' She pulled the handcuff away to reveal a reddened and grazed wrist. 'Think we'd better get going as soon as we can. Jimmy's got mates.'

'We'll have to take him to the hospital.' I said.

'You mad? Didn't you hear what I just said?' Millie swung round from the bed to face me. I didn't understand. She explained patiently. 'I don't know if they'll actually top him, but he ain't going to be a pretty sight even if they don't and Cara's not going to be too happy with her special cosmetic surgery. We can probably square it with her to keep her mouth shut – especially with this little lot to let the cops know about. She won't want a spell inside for prostitution – but if you go advertising who was on the receiving end of it all, Jimmy or his mates will soon put all of us together and come after us. You'll have to take him home and sort him out yourself. He's only a bit roughed up – I've seen worse. A few broken ribs and his pretty face messed up, but he'll get better. We'll help you get him back, but no hospitals and no chat, huh?' Christ, where had I been all my life, even mixing with and living on the periphery of this life for the last few years? Of course she was right, and I now saw how much she, Jake and all the others had put themselves on the line for my naively optimistic view of rebellion. It wouldn't last long, it was a temporary shifting of power, that was all, but one to be taken advantage of in a world where any advantage was better than none. I started to understand what Suzanne had meant about being ruthless now. We left the flat carefully, after having a serious 'chat' with Cara. I wisely left Jake and Millie to do that since I now saw I knew so little about the politics of Soho. Good as their word, they helped me home with Tom, who I doubted was conscious at all throughout the journey.

I kept vigil in his room until his breathing settled into a regular pattern and was about to leave him to it and snatch a few hours' sleep myself when he stirred. The evenings' events were churning over in my mind as I sat in the dark, listening to the ragged sounds of his breath. The day had encapsulated what the whole struggle was all about to me. Death, grief, bravery, sacrifice, violence, liberation – but it was all at a cost. I now had learnt to accept that there are no actions in life wholly without the potential for blame, malice or pain somewhere along the line. Those actions simply had to be turned to as much good as possible. I was still amazed and humbled by the support shown to me, and Tom, not even one of their own, by the TV's, TS's and gays that Millie, Jake, Suzanne had made an unexpected second family for me. Even if my own rejected me, I had another to look to for support if I needed it. Now it was time for me to stand firmly on my own two feet, speak out for what I knew to be right for myself. If that meant rejection by Tom, then acceptance of that too was part of the route forward I now knew how to walk.

He moved and tried to sit upright.

'Ahh!'

'Stay still. You've probably got cracked ribs and your nose has only just stopped bleeding. I've almost run out of cotton wool trying to stop it.' I went over to the door and flicked the light on so I could see if he needed any more attention. He deliberately turned his face away from me.

'It's ok, you can go. I'll manage on my own.' I felt irritated. How did he think he'd managed until now? I was about to go anyway when he added, 'fucking trannys!' Anger fired me up. No, I wasn't going to be abused by anyone – not even Tom. Suzanne's words reminded me of where I was going, with or without him. I spoke out.

'One of those fucking trannys saved your life. She found the credit cards you were showering everywhere as you left the bar and rang me because she remembered your name.' I clicked the light off and left him. *Manage on your own then, you ungrateful bastard. I need some sleep.*

I was surprised to see him shuffle into the kitchen the next day. I'd dressed as Billie. I was Billie, now and for the rest of my life. I didn't know what to expect, but it wasn't 'what shall I call you?' Mentally I squared my shoulders against the insults to come, but they didn't.

'Will is a bloke's name, and obviously I can't call you by a bloke's name any more – can I? So what shall I call you?'

'Oh.' Reality shifted, and once again in a way I hadn't expected. I shared it with him. 'Billie.'

Chapter 15:

The woman, 1983-1984

That first day with Billie meandered on, with both of us unsure what to do or say. As he stood opposite me in the kitchen, fiddling with the dirty dishes from last night, hanging up the tea towel, finding homes for the now washed and dried crockery, I couldn't help sneaking glances at him when he wasn't looking, trying to decide what I felt. I didn't know. How do you feel when your old school mate suddenly announces they want to be a woman? I felt uneasy with him, that much was sure, yet he was the person I'd known for well over a quarter of a century. We'd scraped knees, suffered detentions and struggled through adolescence together. He'd always been Will, and now he wasn't. It was like the awkward tension you feel when you're waiting for a funeral to start. Small talk, inconsequential phrases said to fill the gaps between the momentous things you want to say but don't know how to. Maybe it was like a death had occurred for both of us?

The table top looked the same as me; worn and ill. The pain from my ribs was the worst – knifing me suddenly when I shifted in my seat or risked a breath deeper than the shallow half gasps that had kept me going until then. I can still quite clearly replay that day – or most of it, in my head. I can even hear the song that was playing on the radio as we negotiated towards an uneasy truce, and wondered what kind of alliance we would make in the future. As the tinny sound of the Eurythmics 'Sweet dreams' filled the kitchen, followed by the gaudy sexual ambiguity of Culture Club's current hit I realised I was right up against another kind of view on the world. I felt like an alien in an alien land, even though the oddity here was Will – Billie, not me. He seemed to feel the oddity less though. He leaned against the sink and looked directly at me.

'You look like you need a brew.'

'I guess.' I wasn't sure what I needed. I placed my hands palms down on the grey table top, like my father used to when he surveyed us at meal times. We were his squad, when home; mother and me. Not much of one, but always waiting on his command. When he sat like that, poised to bark an order at one or the other of us, satisfaction curved his mouth in a half smile under the bristling moustache. Sitting like him had made me wonder for a moment whether I could imagine how he'd felt as he'd watched us. I watched Billie as he moved about filling the kettle, flipping a teabag into one of the blue-striped brickie's mugs he always brewed up in. I knew what my father would have called him, a 'fuckin' freak'. My reaction last night had been my father's too but something in me rebelled at the insulting generalisation. To that extent at least I wasn't my father's son. Now I watched Billie, his movements had the same lithe grace that a woman's had.

'Coffee or tea?'

The smell of coffee made me shiver. The aftertaste of blood had the same sharp metallic tang this morning.

'Tea, thanks.' I compared how he would make tea to how I would. The teabag slipped into the mug with the spoon. That was the same. Then came the kettle, sending off a plume of steam as it bubbled up like a witches' cauldron and the switch clicked off. I'd slosh the water into the mug, letting it swirl up and bring the bloated teabag to bursting point out of the top, before splashing milk in, not caring if it spilled over. The teabag would be plopped onto the drainer and Will – Billie – would tidy it up after me later on. Billie's tea-making was entirely different. He hovered by the kettle until it boiled and flicked the switch neatly as the first swathes of steam wafted into the air. Then he poured the water carefully into the mug, stopping just short enough of the top for the milk to linger under the rim. No spillages, no slops. The teabag went straight into the bin and the counter top remained pristine when the mug was lifted. I caught a waft of Billie's apple smell as he reached across the table to set the mug down in front of me, my hands still outstretched as if bracing myself against the table. My mother had made tea the same way. Perhaps the difference between men and women was as basic in its functionality as breathing, and Billie was as basically different to me – even if outwardly the same – as my mother to my father.

'Thanks.' It was more of a croak than a voice.

'That's ok.' His voice was softer than mine. Not entirely feminine – huskier than Lucy's trill, which had turned to shrill when she'd been impatient with me towards the end of our husband and wife mock-battle. But nor was it masculine either. The cadence was wrong for a bloke. Gentler, more questioning – more inviting of comment. Was that a difference between men and women I'd never noticed before too? I couldn't think myself into my father's mind. He was too alien to me still. For him life was black and white, succeed or fail, male or female. My head throbbed and the steam from the tea made me feel hotter than the autumn morning should. The cold grey table seemed to mock me as my sweating hands now stuck to it. I peeled them off and curled my fingers awkwardly round the mug handle, lifting it unsteadily to drink. It was heavier than I'd anticipated. My weak wrist had only a tenuous a grip on it; like I had on reality at the moment. The mug shook in my hand and some of the tea slopped over the side, scalding the vulnerable skin between thumb and forefinger.

'Shit!'

'You ok?' In a flash I'd gone all the way back to childhood and Will asking me the same thing when Old Mother J's son had beaten me. It was like being yanked back on a string through a kaleidoscope but the kaleidoscope wasn't patterns but situations, all rushing up and then past me until I catapulted into that moment. His face loomed up at me, anxious and pale. I came back to the present to find he was leaning over the table at me and repeating the question. I must have lost it for a moment. Maybe I was concussed. Bewildering feelings followed the abrupt return to the present

– regret, confusion, misplaced memories and blank spots. I wanted to ask him about all the events of last night but didn't want to rely on him to have to tell me them; didn't want to show that I wasn't in full control.

'It's alright.' Hastily I let the mug fall back onto the table and more tea spilt over the side as it made contact too heavily; muddy brown on nondescript grey. That was me. Muddy brown like a splatter of bloody phlegm coughed up on an unwashed pillowcase. Billie by contrast was a peacock of blue, gold and indigo; jeans blue, top indigo and head haloed in gold as the September sun made a sudden showing from behind the morning fug of London and streamed in on us through the window. The sudden splash of colour and light made me wince. Billie leaned in again but I didn't want the proximity yet. I had to get used to this stranger before he got too close to me. I raised my hand, gasping at the sudden stab in my chest the movement caused but determined to stop him touching me. 'I'm just a bit unsure of what I'm doing at the moment.' The significance of it made me purse my lips. From his expression the irony wasn't lost on him either.

'You and me both,' he said quietly, but flashed a smile to go with it. 'Call me if you want help with anything.' He left the kitchen and the colour in it drained away as the sun moved behind a cloud again. It looked like it might rain today after all. I slowly drank the tea, the fluid helping to alleviate the hangover that was the self-inflicted pain. I still wondered how I'd come by the injuries that were causing the rest of it but wasn't going to ask. The warmth from the tea seeped through me like the music on the radio. I lost myself to both sensations, unwilling to move and unable to decide what to do if I did. It was all such a mess. I was such a mess. The tea had gone cold now and a skin had formed over the top of what remained of it in the mug. My fingers were still curled round the handle of the mug, like a clump of raw sausages, the sensation in them as deadened as if they actually were meat. My face had swollen overnight and one eye was completely closed. It left me with a skewed view of the world. That made me laugh ruefully; whose was the skewed view of the world here? Surely it wasn't mine, it was Billie's? So why did everything I did and said feel wrong, whereas he seemed so dignified and calm? I could hear muted movements in the lounge and into the hall. He was tidying away the old newspapers I'd brought home over the course of the week to pore over the football results and then left in a dog-eared pile down the side of the settee. I knew eventually he would make his way back to the kitchen, even if only to make sure I was alright. His departure from the kitchen had been to give me space but I didn't know what to put in it. My mind numbed at the complexity of how life was turning out.

The kitchen door creaked gently behind me and through my dreamy slump in the chair I heard Billie's voice asked tentatively if I needed anything. Moving any part of me hurt. Old age seemed to have taken me over and the awareness that the tea I'd drunk had made it through to my bladder. That part of the mechanics at least was still working.

'I need a slash.' I said it without thinking – the kind of thing I would have said without a second thought before. As soon as I said it now, it felt wrong. I wanted to talk to him like he was my mate, but here he was wavering in front of me like a woman would at that comment.

'Do you need me to help you to the bathroom?' Sound came and went today, but I heard that clearly enough.

'Christ, no, I can do it.' I put my palms flat on the table to push myself up to standing but nothing happened. My legs were jelly, and the movement made my chest roar into action with knife points stabbing indiscriminately. The groan was involuntary but Billie reacted immediately.

'Are you in pain?'

'What the fuck does it look like?' He backed off, looking offended. I felt ungrateful. 'I'm sorry, this is awful.'

'Do you want some painkillers? It might help.'

'Yeah, maybe that would be a good idea.' I relaxed against the chair back and closed my eyes. I felt a light touch on my hand and when I opened them again, he was holding out pills and a glass of water. I took some pills and waited for things to improve.

'We'll give them a few minutes and then I'll help you to the loo. It's ok, I won't come in – I'll wait outside and then maybe we'll get you to the lounge and I'll make you something to eat.' A glimmer of grim humour intervened.

'Ok, Mum.' He looked at me surprised, and then burst out laughing. 'Jeez, no thanks Tom, I may want to be woman, but I don't want to be anybody's mum, especially not yours!' The awkwardness of the early morning tea suddenly melted away. He held out a hand to pull me up and I took it. His eyes were Wills, his smile was Wills, his memories were Wills. I went back to the moment when I'd first woken that morning and the pig-tailed girl had only just been left behind in my dream. We were both aliens in an alien world today, but somehow I knew I had to explore it and learn its ways.

'Thanks,' and I knew he understood it was for the evening before also. The world spun again and another kaleidoscope pattern formed. 'What happens next?'

'How do you mean?'

'Here, you, me, us.'

'I don't know. What do you want to happen?'

'I suppose we're still mates, just a bit different.' He smiled encouragingly at me. 'But I haven't quite got my head round it all yet.'

'Believe me, neither have I and I'm the one who knew about it from the start.' We both laughed again. I was glad to have some part of my mate Will back.

'Oh, do you want me to tell the story till now?'

'Well some of it maybe, if you like?'

'It would be a start.'

***

I stroked the cover of the diary as it lay on the table. The red of its top made a bold statement in the grimy drabness of the cafe. Grimy drabness described too much of my life until then. Grimy drabness was what seemed to have dictated how I'd led

345

my life until then. There had only been one gesture that was bold red and the prison gate had swung shut after it. The red table top now made a backdrop like blood for the battered diary cover. I opened the diary and flicked through the pages again. The writing was close and small. Always neat – even at school. I scanned the open page. Yes this was more or less where it all really started for me. I closed the diary and rested my eyes. They hurt. The glasses they'd given me for reading in the prison were useless, but a gesture they had to make, like the army's hearing aid, which I'd usually left in its box. It hadn't helped much when I wore it and I objected to looking like a cripple. I wanted to read the rest of the diary somewhere private and quiet, but there was nowhere else to go. Another song came on the radio and taunted me, like the DJ was having a laugh. Michael Jacksons 'One day in your life' was followed by 'Killing me softly'. I listened to them both without attempting to stem the emotions. They made me want to cry – pathetic for a man to cry at songs – and I was glad the café was almost empty now. There was still some way to go in the diary if I was to read the part I'd so studiously avoided in life. I wanted to read it all before I left here. The letter nestled in my pocket urging me to decide. *Wait, how can I know yet?*

I signalled to the waitress for another coffee and opened the diary to the right page when she'd gone. It made me smile as the memory hit me like a train. I even remembered saying those words. *Christ you've got a good memory, boy!*

Chapter 16:

The woman, 1984-1986

November 1984

'Christ, it's like male heaven isn't it, being able to cop a feel of tits whenever you want to. What man wouldn't want to be able to handle a pair of them whenever he could?'

'But I don't think of it that way, Tom, they're just part of my body. Do you go round handling yourself all the time?

'Well no, but they're not tits. And playing with your tits beats playing with your balls any day. Come on, you're a bloke – you know what it's like to get hold of a handful.' As he ended the jokey sentence he suddenly looked embarrassed. I said nothing, just watched him steadily. 'But you're not really a bloke any more are you?' I shook my head. 'Christ, mate, Billie – I'm sorry – I'm crass sometimes aren't I?'

'It's ok – it's an odd experience for both of us.'

'No, but I mean, you're almost a woman, and,' he didn't finish the observation, just blushed beetroot red. I continued to button up my blouse, and he averted his gaze.

'Shall I grab something to eat from the takeaway? Kebab?'

'Um, I guess.' He looked for all the world the ashamed school boy and I laughed outright.

'I won't ask you to play with my tits if you won't ask me to play with your balls.'

'What?' He looked shocked but my smile told him I was joking. The ashamed schoolboy's face cracked into a grin.' It's a deal, well – or maybe not – you've got a fine pair there Billie me lass!' He slipped into a comically broad Scottish accent and we both laughed.

I don't know if it's easy with Tom or not. I don't know how he feels. I don't think he knows how I feel. And how do I feel? Up and down. They warned me the hormone treatment would affect me this way. It's the way a woman is, high one minute, down the next.

'Enjoy,' the nurse at Charing Cross had said whimsically as she handed me the next month's medication. It's why some call the menstrual cycle God's blessing and others call it the curse. She looked at me and winked. 'You can't tell me what it feels like because you won't ever have one, and that in itself is a blessing, believe me, but you can tell me what you think about the mood swings later on.' Her Irish accent made the words lilt merrily. It was the first time I really felt like a woman. A woman talking to a woman, accepted as a woman, classified as a woman. I couldn't speak. The emotion was almost too much to keep inside. I just nodded, and turned away to hide the burgeoning tears in my eyes. Everyone outside of the gender reassignment community generally thinks the effects of hormones are purely physical. What they don't realise is that the effect on your mind may not be apparent to some but it is equally as powerful as the effect on the body. In the case of someone on large doses of hormones being used to cause gender change, combine the natural hormones present of the person's original gender too and you can end up with a mental state the equivalent of a bottle of nitro-glycerine ready to blow. I was aware of that and tried, when I felt the pressure rising and the nitro boiling, to step away from anyone who didn't know the bubbles were ready to burst. They bubbled within nevertheless these days, making me jittery and always watching for something to go wrong.

The routine was blood test, checking for hormonal levels and then the medication adjusted accordingly. Sometimes it makes me feel sick, and I have the hot flushes most women of menopausal age are familiar with. One minute I'll be working away quite normally, the next my body has turned into a raging inferno, face red, sweat pouring out of me like I'm sitting in a steam room. Five minutes later, after standing at an open window, the sweat has dried on me like small icicles and my body returns to stability. One part of me asks intellectually if this is not my body rebelling against the influx of alien hormones and another wants to ignore anything which militates against achieving my goal. There are compensations of course; the tits to start with. The socks in the bra are now a thing of the past. I have the start of a womanly shape, angular edges are moulding into curves and my skin is softer and downier. I didn't shave anyway and only had a fine fuzz on my face before, which I removed with depilatory creams, sometimes causing skin irritation. Now, to my satisfaction even the fuzziness is gone and my facial skin is that of a woman's. Tom generally doesn't react, other than the surreptitious – but to me, obvious – visual assessment of pertinent parts of my body. Sometimes when I catch him watching me I can tell from the look on his face that he is intensely curious what is going on beneath the surface, but he never asks. It is like we have a pact. All the while he doesn't know what is happening inside me, I can transform all I like but for him I'll remain Will, and then it's ok.

I could tell him, of course but the more female I become the more I wanted to retain that sense of feminine distance that creates allure: attraction. I could tell him the more hormones I take the less often I got an early morning erection so that is now almost unheard of and my balls have shrivelled to half the size they were but that still defines me as a man, doesn't it? My nipples sometimes tingle and are sore but to me that signifies another exciting development in my body as they respond to the hormones and grow. I suppose given his fascination with tits, they would define me as a woman but as a woman never tells a man she is having her period, nor do I want to tell Tom my most intimate physical feelings. My breasts are tender to the touch but their very presence makes me proud. They represent the very epitome of femininity to me; the way they hang heavily in my cupped hands, the curve of them beneath my clothes and the pert suggestiveness of an erect nipple. They are my favourite part of my body. Standing in front of the mirror, I run my hands slowly over them feeling the nipples rise and the areola pimple up in excitement. I've often wondered what sex would be like as a woman; to be entered and possessed. It's hard to imagine when you have no experience of it apart from the time with Freddie that I desperately want to forget. Caressing my breasts makes me understand how I might react.

Maybe it's psychological, but also the more feminine I feel, the more Tom responds as a man towards me. The tits conversation came early on in the hormone treatment when a rapid growth spurt had suddenly produced a respectable B cup for me, but he hasn't said anything more about my body shape since. That makes me feel like nothing – asexual. I don't like that. The hospital does nothing to help. The battery of checks and tests slowly wind their way towards the final tick on the list. I have now been undergoing voice therapy for five months, learning how to soften my tone rather than raise my pitch. It's only the occasional slip that lets me down when I laugh at a humorous obscenity that Tom makes or let excitement take more control over my body than dignity has. I don't sound forcedly high-pitched like a fishwife anymore; I sound more like a phone-sex siren. I don't know which is better. The phone-sex voice makes me feel dirty, like I have to prove my gender by parading my sexuality. I'm not a call girl or a prostitute. In fact my morals are ridiculously on the prim side given my lurid background. Who would ever believe I'm a pre-op TS and I've only ever had sex twice – and didn't enjoy either experience. The sheer irony makes me laugh, but there's no humour in it.

February 1985

So the routine rolls on every month. I go expecting nothing and everything. Sweaty palmed that my hormone levels haven't co-operated with the drugs, scared that I'm doing so well, the next stage will loom up like a mirage – tantalisingly in my grasp, and then whipped away again when something goes wrong. The consultant was quite matter of fact when he explained the process. He factualised it and depersonalised me. I was simply a body being manipulated from one shape to another, but however impersonal it was, it was the only way to become me. I came to hate those visits. Prodded and measured, samples taken and compared; the results recorded with interest like I was a lab rat. Today my results were so obviously out of the norm that the endocrinologist and the consultant stood aside in the consulting room and discussed me as I waited humbly by the desk, hands folded into my lap and eyes on my feet because I couldn't bear to see the expressions on their faces in case they were negative. Were they going to take me off the programme? I could feel the sweat trickling down under my armpits and sticking my arms to my top. A hot flush started and I cursed it as it made the sweat volume double, treble. I could feel my forehead break out too, and the under layer of fringe stuck to my skin like someone had glued it there. I strained to hear what they were saying but the low murmur was designed to keep me – the only one it really mattered to – out of the discussion.

'Right, we'll keep you on that dose for now.' The endocrinologist sat down dismissively at his desk. The chair wheels squeaked as he pulled himself up close to the littered desk top and started to scribble in my notes; indecipherable hieroglyphics I tried to read sideways but the writing was worse than mine of the pre-exam revision scrawls I'd pored over before my finals. He pushed the notes away from him and flipped their cover shut. 'See you next month.' He waited for me to leave. I wanted to ask what the matter was, was I ok, was it working, but his expression told me I was dispatched to the next part of the process, and the nurse beckoned me out of the room for the next assessment to be made of me. And so the process continued mysteriously, month after month, without ever knowing what would happen next. For once my nerve cracked and I told Tom about the out of earshot discussion when I got home and was cooking tea. I had to tell someone and I wouldn't see Fran for a while as Jenny had mumps. The hospital nurse had warned me to stay well away.

'Not good for men past their teens.' She'd looked apologetically at me as she'd said the word 'men'. She reminded me of Sheila, but it was one time when she couldn't make the charade of being a woman override the reality of still being a man.

'Funny things, hormones. Make you go a bit stir-crazy.' Tom surprised me by responding when he would normally shake his head apologetically and melt away. I looked at him questioningly. It wasn't something I would have expected Tom to know about, or want to. 'They pumped Lucy full of them – or rather I had to,' he gave a wry laugh. 'Only time she showed me her ass once the IVF stuff started.'

'Oh.' I wanted to know more but wasn't sure if I should ask. I risked chipping away at our self-imposed pact. 'How was she on them?'

'Fucking awful.' Subject closed. He shook the paper he was reading and disappeared behind it again. I let my breath out heavily under cover of the racket the pressure cooker was making and stepped back into my own little world of worry, wishing I could talk to Fran. 'You're alright though, aren't you?' Tom asked, unexpectedly reappearing from behind the paper barricade and seeming concerned when I'd thought he'd deliberately put me and my transformation into the box I knew he labelled 'disquieting'. Another hot flush started and I could barely stand being in the kitchen with the steam of the bubbling saucepans and the whistling pressure cooker raising my outer temperature to the same high as my inner one.

'Yes, yes, I suppose.' I breathed a heavy sigh out and blew air upwards at my sweating forehead.

'What did they say then that might have meant you weren't?' The heat from the flush was burning me up like magma from a volcano and I felt light headed. The need to get out of the stifling heat in the kitchen became imperative.

'Tom, I have to go,' was all I managed to gasp before I dashed to the front door and onto the cool street. He must have taken my abrupt departure as an unwillingness to talk as he didn't raise the subject again after I returned when the worst was over. He eyed me awkwardly through the steam and shuffled the newspaper.

'I'll just go and er ...' He made a gesture towards the lounge. I nodded. I knew my comments about the hospital procedures made him feel awkward and worry how he should behave with me. The very ambivalence was frustrating but elating because it meant that even this man saw someone new and different, not the boyhood friend he'd always thought of as the same as he. The little he'd mentioned about the IVF experiences with Lucy indicated he found hospitals and medical details hard to handle too. I didn't know whether to push it by telling him more or not. I cursed the hot flush that had dragged me out of the kitchen just when he might have ventured more. His self-imposed isolation behind the newspaper when I came back suggested it was probably best left now. Anyway, at times I wasn't sure how I felt discussing any of it either.

April 1985

Before I went to bed tonight I stood in front of the long mirror in my room and looked at my naked body. My breasts swung jauntily above the gentle curve of my belly, and the soft line of hair from navel to pubic hair was only faintly visible now the hormone treatment had thinned it to almost nothing. I'd never had a visible Adam's apple so my neck curved nicely to slightly too square shoulders, but careful dressing hid the fault. My face is soft and feminine now, even without makeup, and my hair has grown to a reddish brown cloud tumbling over my shoulders. Suzanne had been right – I would make a pretty lady someday. What disfigured me like a wart on a child's face was the penis and testicles that still dangled from me like some obscenely shrunken pygmy head. I hated that part of me. Sometimes when my balls felt full and bulbous when I was aroused – which was barely at all these days, the drugs saw to that at least, I wanted to take a knife to them and slice it all off. That night was one of those times.

Maybe running my hands over the sleek skin from breast to belly had made me imagine they were someone else's hands caressing, followed by someone else's tongue tracing the same line of skin on skin. Desire surged. My ears sang with the hot pulse of blood, and I longed for the imagined feelings to be real. Then the hateful sensation of penis bloating, filling out, rising, turgid and swollen and balls tingling like electric eels were wriggling inside them took over and I opened my eyes and looked at my responding body with horror. No, no – was this what was wrong? The hormones weren't working after all and I was regressing to masculinity. I smacked my penis hard with my hand, making it bounce down and back up, wanting the sudden discomfort to defuse the ticking bomb of desire that had translated into an erection. It made no difference. It stayed erect and engorged with the blood that had been singing through my ears at the thought of Tom's hands on my body.

'Fuck it, go away, you bastard thing!' I smacked it again and again with my hands, alternating the blows on it and then took a testicle in each hand and squeezed hard, making me dizzy. The pain was excruciating and exquisite. I squeezed more and almost immediately my penis flopped to a flaccid lump as if I'd taken a pin to it and deflated a balloon. 'Ahh.' I almost cried out, hot tears gathering at the corners of my eyes as I slowly released my testicles and the blood flowing back into them brought pinpricks of agony. There was a tentative knock at my door.

'Billie?' Tom's voice sounded diffident. 'Are you ok? I thought I heard you call out?' I held my breath, desperately praying that he wouldn't actually push the door open.

'I'm fine,' I croaked, 'just a nightmare.'

'Ok then.' I heard his feet pad away and I let my breath out again. My attention focussed back on my crotch. The pain in my testicles settled to a steady dull ache. I hoped I had irreparably damaged them. I imagined the feel of sharp blade against skin and then with one quick sweep of it, both penis and testicles were cut off. I was clean, nothing to defile the smooth curve of womanhood. I opened my eyes and it was all still there but deflated and shrunken again.

July 1985

I stood in front of my mirror again tonight like I did that night three months ago, when I had my last erection. It's odd how time can pass so quickly and yet so slowly. I wish away the time when I might move on to the next stage of this tedious process of transformation – and yet also dread that day. Tom will move on and I will long for this time back again. It can only be a matter of time before he starts to look at women and want something more than he has. I kid myself he's starting to see me as a woman sometimes when he's gentle and deferential to me, but then I remember that I'm still only half a woman. He's kind and I know he cares about me – why would he still be living here with me, such an oddity, otherwise. But I'm not a woman in the true sense of the words for him.

I sometimes wonder how he satisfies his physical needs. I can't pretend he doesn't have any simply because he hides them. Tom was always such a tom cat! Are there women he sees without me knowing about them? My stomach knots with jealousy at that thought – and yet, what right have I to be jealous?

My penis and testicles still hang like wizened old men from my soft belly. I've taken to holding them every night to test their weight and size like the nurse did at the hospital check-ups. Of course they haven't gone but after that initial attack I made on them, the hot flushes diminished and my balls shrunk almost daily. They've shrunk to small gnarled walnuts now and that was the last erection I've experienced, whatever heat of passion I imagine

January 1986

The turning point came today. The endocrinologist and the consultant huddled to one side again, like they did that other time. They couldn't be throwing me off the programme, surely? I was doing well – the little nurse kept telling me that. Even my critical self-assessments were becoming congratulatory and I overheard the postman refer to me as 'she' the other day. I can't remember when Tom first used the female pronoun when referring to me, but it was quite a long time ago. That gives me encouragement too.

'She's not up yet.'

'Oh, will you sign for her?'

It was a dress I'd bought mail order. She, she she! That was me they were referring to: she. I said nothing when I came downstairs shortly afterwards, but I couldn't burst the bubble of joy all day. Surely they weren't going to burst it now? They walked back to me, still deep in discussion. I waited meekly by the consultants desk.

'Billie,' the consultant was the one who spoke as the endocrinologist walked away. *Was there a smart-ass joke there? How many medics does it take to tell a TS bad news? Three: one of each gender...* I chastised the irrelevant thoughts away and focussed on the consultant. *Dr Burke. Burke and Hare – they'd robbed graves hadn't they? Rob me a woman's grave or put me out of my misery, Dr Burke. Shut up you idiot; concentrate!* He was talking and I wasn't listening, but they were the most important words of my life.

'... assessed for surgical reassignment.' He waited for my reaction.

'What?' *Stupid, stupid! Why weren't you listening?*

'I said you've done so well, we're recommending that you can now be assessed for surgical reassignment.'

'Oh.' Stupid, stupid couldn't say anything more but I grinned like my face would split. I was still grinning when I got home. I'd grinned at the whole world on the way home, and for once it seemed it grinned back.

Tom arrived home three hours later and the grin was still pinned in place, like I'd taken on a clown's face and couldn't remove the grease-painted smile.

'You're cheesy,' he commented. 'What gives?'

'I've done it.'

'You've done what? Laid an egg?' My grin was infectious. I knew that from the way the world had gone my way today and his end of the week surliness softened into a grin too.

'I've been recommended for surgery.'

'Oh God, Billie – that's fucking amazing! We ought to celebrate. Come on, let's go out and have a curry!' My grin slipped into an open-mouthed village-idiot face. He'd never suggested we be seen out anywhere together before.

'Are you sure?'

'Of course – bloody hell! It's bloody brilliant for you.'

'Ok.' The grin seemed to reach right round my head now. I'd had it there so long my face ached, but now the bubble of happiness that had tickled my ribs earlier grew to engulf my whole body like a giant pink bubble gum globe of sweet sticky joy. 'I'll go and get changed.'

'Bloody women – don't take long. I'm starving,' he yelled after me. He'd never offered for us to be seen out together before. My head pounded with excitement and a tiny glimmer of what Pandora had kept back for me after all: hope. It was a funny thing, this see-sawing relationship between us. He lurched between treating me with kid gloves and talking building site crudity, as if he didn't know which was more appropriate anymore even though he'd never been particularly crude with me even as a teenager. The comment about my tits that he'd made early on in my transformation was typical of the building site crudity whereas the melting away to the lounge with the paper to hide behind was equally typical of the eggshell walk he often teetered across when he didn't know who to be with me again. Gradually the kid gloves have become more in evidence as I've transformed but he and I are two strangers who know each other too well, yet don't know how to be with each other anymore. I wondered how aware of me as a woman he was, rather than as his friend who was becoming a woman. I couldn't ask, and he wouldn't say. We tacitly agreed to say nothing; cowards. Tonight he stood behind me as I struggled to fasten the silver chain I wanted to wear, having dressed in record speed in case he changed his mind about the wisdom of being seen with me. I couldn't fasten the catch and my fingers fumbled nervously behind my neck, tangling in my hair as I stood in front of the mirror in the hall. He came up behind me and loitered awkwardly.

'Your hair has got long.'

'Mmm, yes.' The chain slid from my fingers. I scrabbled to catch it before it fell. 'Where did it go?'

'It's in your hair.' My fingers found nothing.

'Where?'

'Here.' His hands were the lightest of touches on the nape of my neck. The fastened chain slipped through my fingers and the little apple charm on the end of it bobbed merrily in the soft furrow between my breasts where my top displayed my cleavage. Then he was gone, swinging out of the house and the door banging behind him, leaving me buzzing with excitement and drowning in disappointment. He didn't come back until it was dark. It was Friday and everywhere was open, especially his favourite bars. I thought he'd been cured of that. He smelt of whisky, but wasn't drunk. I didn't want to ask, but couldn't bear not to, my hurt at the abandoned curry – but more so, actually being acknowledged, cut too deep.

'Where've you been?'

'Out.' I looked at him and he looked at me from under his eyebrows, shielding his eyes from me with a frown, and then turning away quickly.

'You ok?'

'You asked me that when Old Mother J's son beat me up.' He mumbled it.

'Did I?'

'Yeah.'

'What did you say then?'

'I said yeah thanks.'

'And now?'

'I'm working on it.'

'Ok.'

'Your hair's nice.' I held my breath as he paused and turned to face me briefly, 'and sorry I left like that.' He didn't wait for me to reply, walking swiftly away and closing his bedroom door firmly. I waited in the kitchen for a while, wondering where he'd been and what he'd been doing, but always returning to the last sentence. 'Your hair's nice.'

***

The kid gloves are on again today and we've returned to camaraderie and the odd crude joke. The pink bubble has shattered now but strands of it have remained coiled around me, like a filigree net of hope. Somebody once told me as a kid that if you swallow bubble gum, your body never gets rid of it. It was probably to scare me out of having it, but I didn't care. I don't think the sheer joy of that moment when the consultant made my dream a possibility will ever leave my body in the same way as bubble gum won't, whatever Tom says or does.

And I know there was something else on his mind when he flung out of the maisonette, because he said it again to me today.

'Wear your hair down. It looks nice that way.'

Chapter 17:

The other woman, May 1986

I remember the rain beating down on me as I trudged the short distance from Raynes Park station to home. Home; I called it home whenever I thought of it by then. The idea was heart-warming and enabled me to ignore the rivulets of water that were steadily making inroads down the neck of my jacket and settling on my shoulders like a wet ridge of stodgy material. My shoes were sodden, squelching as I walked. I could see the small bubbles of moisture appearing through the stitching as I placed one heavy footstep in front of the other. They would dry with that white tide line that always appeared on leather shoes after a soaking. The thought irritated me. It would mean several layers of polish to hide it. The layers of polish reminded me of the army, and the thought surprised me – it seemed so long ago now. Polish, spit, polish again to create that high gloss sheen that was necessary to avoid a dose of parade quad cleaning or bog floor scrubbing. I couldn't believe now how I'd accepted it so easily at the time. I must have been such a different person then. The seventeen year old squaddie, wet behind the ears, promised to Queen and country without question, ready to give my life for a social system that imposed its will on others merely because a past history of spurious power tricked it into thinking it still should have a say now. The Empire that was, the little country that thought it was still great. My cynicism was heightened by the uncomfortable sensation of wet clothes weighing me down and hampering me from getting home and in the dry, and behind a door where my world was how I chose it to be, not how society dictated it should be.

My world had become Billie, although she didn't know that, and Billie was all things still frowned upon by societies' great and good, even in these so-called enlightened times. The closer I got to Billie, the greater my disenchantment with the status quo, and yet I baulked at making my feelings public and challenging the hypocrisy in myself. That made me angry at the worlds judgemental attitude because I knew it was mine too. I knew Billie was aware of some of the war that raged in me over truth versus caution, diplomacy versus making a stand, but she attributed it to support of her as a friend, not the disturbing feelings that had overrun me as I'd struggled to fasten a cheap necklace round her neck and found my fingers tangled in her hair. Leaning closer to see why the clasp wouldn't fasten I'd been engulfed by the warm scent of her hair and skin, like plunging my nose into a full blooming rose and breathing in its heady perfume so deep it made my head spin. I'd wanted to taste the skin under the soft sheen of downy hair straggling from the hairline on the nape of her neck as she lifted her hair out of the way for me to find the problem. Stray wisps of fine hair curled in small tendrils against the downy peach of her skin. My head pounded with blood heat, and I felt unsteady. I'd only ever felt this rage of desire before and that had been with Susie Evans. It was madness, like an infection had overpowered me and was pulling me under into a deadly sickness. I sprang back like I'd been bitten by the snake in the Garden of Eden, coiling out from the apple and offering it to me in return for my soul. I remember I mumbled something about her hair. I couldn't remember what until now that I was reading her version of the moment.

Was that the first time Billie was a woman to me, and not the mate I didn't understand but was trying to do the right thing by? I almost ran out the house, I remember, taking the jacket nearest me off the hall stand. Lucky it didn't have much money in it so I could only have two whiskies in the bar I found at the end of another confused and blind walk into the grey oblivion of the London night. Billie knew I was confused, but not how much so. I saw it in the half smile she smiled when I ranted on about this politician's secret life being condoned, or that power icons private misuse of the very people who were vulnerable to abuse of sexual liberty whilst they publicly condemned gays and trans-sexuals. *Private Eye* made it easy to do so, providing me with weekly ammunition, but my description of who Billie was, and what she was to me always remained vague when put to it. The uncomfortable recognition of my own duplicity over honesty and openness made me irritable and I tried to think about anything but her as I fought my way through the driving sheets of London rain.

There were times like today when all of London was grey. Grey pavement, grey buildings, grey rain, grey life. The only thing I couldn't think of as grey was Billie, and my irritation eased again as I pictured the wide warm smile as she opened the door to me, the sensation of falling into those deep eyes, full of lights and mysterious places. She always smelled as fresh and sweet as an early autumn apple, skin smooth and rounded like the curve of it in your hand. I'd never touched or even wanted to touch her before but as she'd changed before my eyes from Will to Billie, quite unexpectedly she'd also changed from the odd mix of male and female into something very essentially alien but feminine. Maybe it was precisely because I'd never approached her in a sexual way that she seemed so wholesome to me, not like the TV's I could see in the gay bars I knew she still frequented from time to time.

'They're still my friends and have always accepted me, never judged'.

I couldn't argue with that, other than to try to show her, without being too blunt about the seedy impression those friends gave, that she was almost normal now. Then I recoiled inwardly at the use of the word *normal*. She wasn't normal, and to classify anyone as normal or abnormal was so offensive I was ashamed the word had even popped into my mind. She wasn't normal, but she wasn't abnormal either. Now she symbolised something unique and beautiful, almost untouchable, yet intimately mine. I had to accept those odd lurching feelings as I'd fastened the apple charm around her neck were desire. I still didn't know what to say when I'd returned home that night. She asked anxiously if I was ok. Noncommittally, I'd replied as brusquely as I could, both nervous of upsetting her and angry with her for producing these disastrously terrifying feelings in me. I wanted to be there with her, but even more so now, I didn't know how to be anywhere else.

The crisis point in the fever had come when she came home with the news that her surgical gender reassignment procedure was now on. Light shone from behind her eyes like she was backlit. I was blinded and overwhelmed with humility for her, both for her outward beauty now she was so more a woman than ever a man could be – even just as she was, but also for the courage that had brought her to there. I knew there had been times when she had been rejected, abused, humiliated. She'd been ridiculed and still went out into the world wearing her hopes on her face and body for all to see, not like the rest of us who hide between the safety of 'normality' and social acceptance. To have a belief, a belief so strong that nothing shook you or deterred you from following it, that was courage. It was then I knew that the courage I thought I'd been finding when I joined the army, when I'd faced Mother J's sons' fist, when the rifle shot had taken Gary in Northern Ireland, hadn't been what courage was really about. Or when the bombs had blown the faces of people and places into blackened wrecks, and when I'd felt the fear gripping at my guts and turning them to water at facing those dangers myself and wondering if I would return from them, but going anyway because it was my duty. Yes that had been courage – a moment of instant courage that sets adrenalin pounding and hearts racing. But Billie's was the daily grind of self-belief against the odds, the sense of loneliness that gnawed the soul, the desperation of utter alienation. She had lived out her life thus far with that as normality. We'd never discussed how she felt, and now I was ashamed I'd shied away from such a basic form of comfort that I could have given her then without risking revealing my feelings and my quivering inner core of cowardice. The only time she'd ever given me any idea of what her experience might be was shortly after I found her in full female clothing when I discovered what she'd been keeping secret from me in all the months leading up to it. She showed me a letter a TS had written once – a personal cry of pain and plea for understanding from an ignorant society. She'd found it in her research and it had struck to the core of what she felt. Then, she said, she knew what she had to do for herself.

Since then, so much has changed. From the moment I identified the feelings I felt for her as my fingers tangled in her hair, I knew she was also steadily weaving into the fabric of my soul. Had I the courage to stand alongside her? I wanted to be that brave, to show the courage I thought I'd found at the end of that fist long ago, and that I'd learnt in the army, but when I returned home that night I knew I couldn't. The weeks that followed were a time when I allowed life to simply slip by, vicariously treasuring the moments of shared company with Billie, but desperately having to hold my words and thoughts in check when we strayed off anything but general discussion.

With her latest news there was no being impersonal or emotionally aloof possible. I knew it had to be celebrated – it was the culmination of her fight, and I jealously couldn't bear the thought of her sharing the celebration with anyone but me. With that in mind I'd finally found enough courage to be seen in public with her, after blowing her out with the original celebration

'Let's go out to dinner to celebrate – a proper posh do. You can dress up in one of those fancy frocks you have but complain you can never wear anywhere.' Her face glowed even brighter. I bathed in it, forlornly acknowledging also that I would have to relinquish her soon if I couldn't find the iron in my soul to stand by her side.

We went somewhere no-one would know us and I knew she'd noticed my careful choice but graciously said nothing, just smiled her thanks that we were going anywhere together. I wanted to explain to her it wasn't her I was ashamed of, it was me and my lack of courage, but she wouldn't have understood. I remember that evening so well. It was a good evening, and I was proud of her. I knew from the looks of some of the other blokes in the restaurant that they envied me the beautiful woman sitting across the table from me, talking animatedly about her plans to travel one day and all the places she would like to go to. Oh, if only they knew, if only they knew.

'Paris is a must though – I've never been there, but it's the most romantic place in the world – and the centre of fashion of course.' I joined in as I was expected, suddenly getting the hang of it with her. Why hadn't I before? She was a woman like Lucy and Susie had been, like all the other women in my past. I knew the right words to say then, why hadn't I ever seen to use them with Billie? Maybe it was the ambience of the place or the illusion that we were a happy couple, admired by the other restaurant-goers, or the sheer joy in her very presence as she leaned vivaciously across the table, challenging me to disagree. The words of man to woman came out as they were meant to at last.

'Typical woman, always thinking about clothes and love – I suppose you want me to take you there?' As the last word of the sentence fell into the gap between us at the table, we both acknowledged the subtle change. My stomach clenched in shocked anticipation at what I'd released. The gremlin in the works was free.

'Only if you want to,' she replied quietly, face suddenly very serious, almond eyes narrowed and intent.

'I don't know why I said that, it's just banter,' I laughed anxiously, but the laughter didn't make it into the next sentence. I owed her some truth after all this time. 'No, actually I do. It's because I don't feel like I used to.' Her eyes remained steadily on my face. I could hear the withheld breath in her eyes as if eyes and mouth were one. I went on because I knew if I didn't now, I never would. It was one of those instant moments of courage I *could* muster and maybe it would lead to the on-going steadfastness of true bravery. 'I feel like – I don't know. I'm trapped by convention. There's a lot you don't know about me Billie. It's complicated, and I'm not just your friend any more. I'm something different and I dare not give it a name.'

'Shall I dare give it a name for you?' She asked softly. Her eyes glinted in the dimmed restaurant light and I knew they were holding tears behind their long lashes. She looked down and the lashes swept her cheeks as if dropping the final curtain on a play. But the final act wasn't played out yet. The twisting chain in my stomach unlinked to free the butterflies that had been trapped in it and they flew frantically round my chest. They flew out of my mouth in the stream of words begging for help before I could stop them.

'What name would you give it?' It sounded harsh because my throat was dry and constricted. I tried to swallow but the saliva caught there, leaving an awkward lump instead. She didn't answer the question directly, and I was confused by what she said to start with, but her intense expression begged me to follow the story.

'In Yugoslavia there is a bridge which has a story linked to it, from before the Second World War. A local schoolmistress named Nada, fell in love with an army officer named Relja. After they'd promised themselves to each other, Relja went to war in Greece where he fell in love with a local woman from Corfu. As a result he subsequently broke off the engagement to Nada, who never recovered and after some time they say she died of a broken heart. Young girls from Vrnjačka Banja took to writing their name and the name of their loved one on padlocks and fixing them to the railings of the bridge where Nada and Relja used to meet. They were supposed to be a kind of lucky charm. They thought their love could be trapped by the lock, but love, and everything to do with love, shouldn't ever be a trap. Love is meant to set you free not imprison you, but it can take immense courage to let the one you love go, to be free to choose, and the courage to choose can also be hard to find. It's not always just a simple boy meets girl and falls in love, is it?' She touched my hand. 'I think the name you want to give it is love, but you are afraid of that name because it means you would have to choose a life quite different to one that it would be conventional to live. So I won't give it that name. I won't padlock you and I won't imprison you. You are the one who has to choose both the name and the life of your future.'

She smiled gently at me. I was relieved that I didn't have to say any more for now. How could I? How could I say anything? I wasn't even sure what I wanted to say, or what to tell her either. Those chain links encompassed so many more things than just feelings, things I didn't want to admit to, definitely not to her.

I never kissed her lips until the moment I thought she'd gone. Not even then – at the end of that evening, because everything snowballed after that. Two days later a letter arrived for her saying her treatment schedule had progressed to being assessed for surgical reassignment and her appointment for the first set of tests was a week later. I watched the fear and hope waft in waves over her face as she read the letter and knew now wasn't the time to make any bold moves. The bold moves were all hers for the moment and

I wouldn't steal her thunder. I bought a padlock during the following week, a small red one, and it sat in my pocket. I bought it partially because it was so unusual to find such a padlock, like the shiny red of the rosy part of an apple. There was also the rush of determination that when the moment was right I was going to show her I could be brave, could say that name and follow it through. I kept it in my jacket pocket, tumbling it over in my fingers whenever I dived my hand in there as I walked. I know in my heart of hearts I couldn't have taken it out and shown her just then but it made me feel as if that bravery was possible one day, it was just that the moment was wrong. Of course now I see I was still making excuses.

It was smooth and soothing in my fingers as I pushed open the garden gate and started up the path to sanctuary – from the rain, from the coarse maleness of the factory floor, from the fear of judgement by my fellow humans, even if they weren't equipped to do so. I could hear the raised voices as I walked up the pathway to the front door. In the rise and fall of the angry words, I could tell one of the voices was Billie's, but who the hell did the other one belong to? I almost ran the last few steps to the front door, cursing the key that stuck in the lock as usual. The voices drifted through the door at me. As soon as the key turned and I pushed the door ajar, I recognised the other one. Lucy. What the fuck was she doing here? The next few minutes were a blur – moving us all from one life to the next. I wondered if Billie's diary would tell the tale clearer than my memory. I turned the pages in her diary to around the time of that day. I wondered if she would have written an entry for it. I was sure she must have. It had been the point of no return in so many ways, how could she not? She had.

***

1st June 1986

I don't know what to write. No, that's not true, I do, but I don't want to. It is two weeks ago that I should really write about. The intervening time has just been a nightmare of people and questions and finally Tom going. She had come up the stairs before I even knew there was anyone in the house. I suppose it must be that sticky latch. I thought Tom had fixed it as it seemed to be working alright recently but maybe the oil had got used up and it needed more, or maybe it was just bad luck. I was in my bedroom, putting away some clean washing. The letter – oh that wonderful letter, with the hospital appointment – was on the dressing table. I read it every day, to just make sure it was real. I thought the clatter on the stairs was Tom, home early for some reason. I called out as I usually did when he arrived home after me.

'Hello there, good day? Anything interesting to report?' I didn't expect the voice that came back, but I instantly recognised it – even though I hadn't heard it in years.

'Oh yes, something very interesting, obviously.' The shockwave ran down my back and into my guts. It was Lucy's voice – Tom's ex-wife. I could still remember it from school

375

and from the wedding, slightly too high, fluting, some would call it sweet but it always had a sharp edge to me, as if the sweet could turn sour at any moment. From what Tom had told me, it had, but I hadn't pried and he hadn't commented. There seemed to be an instinctive agreement between us now, without understanding why or how; when to ask and when to stay silent. I swung round to see her framed in the doorway.

'So you're who he's shacked up with ...' Her face turned comically from catty to exaggeratedly surprised, like a cartoon characters would. 'My God, do I know you?' She struggled with her memory. I prayed it would fail her, but from the expression of dawning light followed by bewilderment, I knew it hadn't. 'You look a bit like Will Robinson. I know he had a sister but she's married to that slob Joe Harris and still living in Wilverton.' I didn't say anything even though I wanted to ask her sarcastically how she got in and why she hadn't already left. That way led to trouble and I couldn't afford that now, more than ever. I didn't have long to wait for understanding to follow the light though. Her sharp features tightened, almost as if she was a small predatory animal and she'd caught the smell of blood. 'Oh no, I know who you are.' Her voice was soft and menacing. 'You *are* Will. I heard a bit of a tale about you and going about as a tranny. Now I see it was right. Well, well, well. And so you're shacked up with Tom then?' She let out a short harsh laugh. I didn't know what to say to not make it worse. 'Ain't that just rich! Mind you, it will cause some fun and games in the divorce court. Imagine what they'll say when

I tell everyone the mental anguish it's causing, having to put up with my husband taking up with a weirdo like you. I expect he'd rather settle out of court than stand up there having fun poked at him, but that will be rather expensive. He won't be buying you any frilly knickers after that. He won't have a penny left after what he'll have to pay me!'

I was furious with the little bitch – as if she hadn't already stung Tom enough with the IVF when she was already shagging the back-up in case it didn't work. That much Tom had told me. The divorce reference confused me. I thought she and Tom were already divorced.

'What happened to Jeff?'

'Oh useless prick, he's gone. Me mam's got Lisa today. I was supposed to be going to work. Why should I? Jeff should have been supporting me, lazy bastard, but of course now I need some money coming in from somewhere.'

'Shouldn't he support you? I thought you got married and he's the baby's father?'

'Married to Jeff? No, I'm married to Tom.' She looked surprised. 'Did he tell you were divorced then?' She laughed at my confused expression. He'd never said they'd divorced but he'd certainly given me that impression – and that she and Jeff were settled in together too. 'Oh dear, he is economical with the truth, isn't he? Did he never tell you about Susie Evans either. Fine old fling they were having when he must have come running to you; can't keep his useless prick in his pants. Haven't you ever wondered who he's shagging now, if he hasn't been shagging you – and I would imagine that's a bit difficult ...' She laughed harshly as her eyes raked rudely over me, as if I was a piece of garbage. 'He's still well stuck into someone, don't you think? I wonder who ...' She paused dramatically, as if she already knew who but wasn't telling. I winced involuntarily at the wound she was creating. In the back of my mind had always lurked the question about Tom and how he satisfied himself physically. I knew from teenager-hood that he wasn't likely to be monk-like, but couldn't bring myself to examine the question further than acknowledging it would need answering one day. She didn't stop there. 'So look at you, don't you look *interesting.* Do you fancy being in the news? I seem to remember you went to university – you must have a decent job, unless this,' she gestured at me like I was a figure of fun, 'has meant you've got the sack.' We surveyed each other icily across the room. I wanted her to go more than I wanted to defend myself.

'I think you'd better go now.'

'Oh no, I'm waiting for Tom to come home. I wrote to him, you see, and he responded. He has a wife and child who need him and *a decent respectable* life he could lead there with us.' She preened herself as she talked, moving further into the room and towards the mirror alongside me. I stepped away from her, the letter she referred to making me uncertain what to think now. Tom hadn't mentioned a letter. She must have read my expression well. 'Ahh, did he not tell you about that either? Seems like he doesn't tell you anything of importance, doesn't it? I think you're being well and truly used here, my dear. Or did he pretend he can't hear you when you ask him

378

about things? He's good at that too.' Her eyes were taking in every part of the room by now, openly assessing my worth, I assumed. 'Well, I can't say I think much of the décor, but you can't be short of a bob or two because those are designer clothes you're wearing.' It was true, my one weakness in saving so religiously towards the costs of the cosmetic surgery I might have to meet had been in the clothes I'd chosen.

'I want you to go. You have no right to be here, and I want you to leave.' I could feel myself trembling with outrage that she could invade my home and my life like this.

'Going to call the police? I will say Tom invited me here, you opened the door and I was just waiting quietly for him, *my husband*, when you started getting nasty with me. Who do *you* think they'll believe? You? Or me?' She was right, I couldn't risk trouble now and of course as someone on what society regarded as the shady side of the law, I would be the least credible whatever the situation. She laughed openly at my vulnerability and moved over to the dressing table. She paused by the letter, in pride of place in the middle of it and lingered over it. 'Oh my. A sex change,' she commented eventually. 'You are ripe for the picking, aren't you? Just about to get your cock cut off and replaced with a false fanny and I could ruin all of that for you. And I bet this place is yours too? Money in the bank!' Before I could reply, she picked the letter up and started towards the door, sniggering.

'Give me back the letter,' I followed her, trying to grab it from her but she eluded me, waving it tauntingly in the air just out of my reach.

'Now you and Tom are going to be good buddies and club together for whatever I want, aren't you – or the both of you will be in the news and I don't suppose you'll ever get your nice new fanny will you? Or that you'll be able to use it. I'll let you have this back when you've paid me the first ten thousand.' The part of the letter that said in block capitals 'BRING THIS LETTER WITH YOU AS CONFIRMATION THAT YOU ARE BEING ACCEPTED ON THE SURGICAL REASSIGNMENT PROGRAMME OR YOU WILL BE DENIED FURTHER ACCESS TO TREATMENT' flipped around as she waved the letter at me, the boldness of its print ramming home the severity of its warning.

'Give it back!' I could hear my voice becoming the high-pitched fishwife squawk I'd so hated. Lucy laughed merrily, as she waved it under my nose and then whipped it back. I advanced on her until she was at the top of the stairs, turning to retreat. There was a sound downstairs and the taunting paused momentarily. I knew it had to be Tom; it was his normal return-home time. My attention focussed on the game again before hers did and I launched myself at her before she turned back to me. I was a split second quicker in my reactions than she was and snatched the letter out of her hand as it wafted mid-air in front of her. The movement and the distraction of the noise downstairs must have sent her off-balance because her foot slid off the edge of the top step and down onto the next. Her other leg buckled under her and she grabbed wildly for the bannister rail for support, missing it by a mile in her panic. Her eyes opened wide in terror as she fell in slow motion backwards into the mouth of the stairs. I could have caught hold of that out-stretched hand trying to grasp the banister rail if I had let the letter slip to the floor, but I clasped it to me, like a precious jewel. I watched her tumble into an elegant somersault as she flipped head over heels into the middle part of the stairs and then thumped hollowly down to the bottom. Over the top of her tumbling body I could see Tom standing at the foot of the stairs open-mouthed. The thump, thump, thump of Lucy's body as it made its journey to his feet marked out the space between life and death. She landed in an unnatural sprawl, eyes still wide open in surprise, mouth in a silent shriek of fear. I hadn't heard her scream – had she? Her head stuck out at an impossible angle to her body. I could see even from where I was that it must be broken. Tom didn't move, just looked at me as if he had been frozen in position.

'Tom.' He made a noise like a strangled animal in response.

'Is she dead?' Still he didn't move, just looked up at me, face ashen.

'Tom, if she's not dead, she needs an ambulance.'

'She's dead.' His voice was flat-lined.

'You haven't checked.'

'I don't need to. She's dead.' He took a step towards her body and the foot of the stairs, still looking directly up at me. 'I heard what she was saying. I could hear it even from here.'

'She may not be. Please check.' He paused but my insistence forced him to kneel down by the side of Lucy's body, and place two fingers to her jugular like a professional. He shook his head.

'Come down, we need to decide what to do.' His voice was quiet but firm. Until then I'd felt angry at Lucy and panicked by her taking the letter, then numb as I'd watched her fall. The trembling that had started when I'd first told her to go had stopped as soon as she took the letter and I'd been preoccupied with getting it back. Now it came back a hundredfold as the reality of what had just happened sunk in.

'Oh my God, Tom there's only one thing to do – call the police!' My teeth started to chatter, the trembling making the words sound distorted like a radio message falling in and out of range.

Tom stepped over Lucy's body as if it was non-existent and strode up the stairs to me. It was the first and only time we embraced. His arms round me were like the security I'd never known before, the surety that I was safe, even though I was not. I put my face against his neck and sobbed, for him, for me, for Lucy, for what may never be now. I felt the chording of his tensed muscles, the hard lump of his Adams apple moving against my lips as he swallowed, the pressure of his arms tightening around me, his hot breath in my hair. For that moment we were free, in a world where no-one could touch us. The radio was still on in the kitchen. I'd not noticed it until then. I'd turned it on when I'd come in and then gone upstairs with the clean washing pile. 'Unchained Melody' floated hauntingly up the stairs, echoing my heart, my mind, my body. *Oh my love. My love.* We stayed entwined until the melody died away and Tom gently disentangled us, like chain links unbent and prised apart.

'We can't call the police. Think about what she was saying to you. How she was going to make us both a public show. Blackmail, I guess. Do you really think they'll believe she fell down the stairs when they find out your background and how we're living here together? What about how your father died too? Far too similar, don't you think?'

'He fell, Mum said he did. We saw it.' I stopped. We hadn't seen it. We'd seen the aftermath of it, and mother standing silently there at the top of the stairs – like I had done. Had she been able to clutch him before he fell, but didn't? Or had she helped him fall? It was a question that had lain buried all these years, but there nonetheless. And now I was part of a repeating pattern. How innocent would they think that pattern was? For me - or my mother, now confused and frail? Tom brushed the hair gently away from my eyes, where it had tangled in our embrace.

'Don't you think they'll come up with exactly the same kind of story that Lucy was going to make up? How do you think they will decide she came to fall down the stairs? Fall or was pushed? Things seem to have a habit of repeating themselves in our families, don't they?'

'My mother and father...'

'I know. It was a long time ago, though, and not your fault. *This* is to do with us, and how Lucy came to fall.'

'But I didn't push her, she fell!' I pushed him away angrily at the inference.

'Billie, Billie, I know you didn't push her, I'm saying what will they think? Don't you see what a story this would make for the papers? And even if we manage to get clear of it, do you really think you'll get your operation then? A figure of scandal?' I felt cold all over. Suddenly I saw exactly what he meant.

'Oh my God; then we have no chance.'

'Yes we do. She can have fallen down her own stairs.'

'But these aren't her stairs …' He smiled reassuringly at my bewildered face.

'I know. For someone so smart and pretty, you're very dumb sometimes.' He chucked me under the chin. Why did a situation like this have to be the time he finally showed his feelings? 'I'll have to get her back to her own stairs somehow, won't I?' He sent me to the airing cupboard to find an old blanket to roll Lucy's body into it.

'Shouldn't we leave her longer? Rigor mortis, or lividity – or, or … something like that?' I was trawling through all the detective fiction I'd ever read to try to think of potential clues to avoid giving away.

'Rigor mortis will make it more difficult to move her without breaking any of her bones and that'll look more suspicious.' He sounded more knowledgeable than I felt so I obediently picked up the corner of the blanket again. I was careful to not look into her face. It made me feel sick and the trembling threatened to start again. We waited until twilight had passed and it was another thick grey London evening. He drove the car we shared round to the back of the house where the end of the back garden was separated from a turning area only by flimsy fencing. He came back in and shut the back door quietly.

'Have you looked in her bag?'

"Why?'

'I need her keys to get back in.'

'Oh no.' Her bag was lying beside the roll of the blanket. I walked over to it and picked it up gingerly, staying as far away from the blanket roll as possible. I was about to put one hand round its handle when Tom surprised me by shouting.

'Stop!'

'What?' I straightened up, panicky and sweaty palmed – were the police here? Was she alive? What? My jumpiness communicated itself to him too. He was breathing heavily even though he hadn't exerted himself.

'Don't touch it.'

'Why?'

'You'll put your fingerprints on it and we can't have you linked to her whatsoever. Have we got any rubber gloves here?'

'Under the sink, maybe?'

'Go and find them and put them on. Only then can you touch the bag, ok? I only need the key out of it.'

'Ok.' I rummaged under the sink and eventually found an old pair of marigolds. Getting them over my sweating hands was difficult but eventually they were on after a fashion and I went back to the bag. I stayed at full stretch to reach the bag so I was as far away from the body as possible. I tried not to imagine her face under its covering, still shocked at the sudden change in fortune. Inside the bag were an assortment of lipstick, powder compact, purse, hanky and right at the bottom a key ring. It reminded me of that game you played as a child when you put your hand into a bag and tried to identify what was inside by sensation alone. This time the marigolds made my fingers seem as if they were made of cotton wool, all feeling deadened; a dead woman's fingers. I shivered. There were three keys on the key ring. Obviously back and front doors, and a car key. A thought suddenly occurred to me. 'Tom, we don't know how she got here – what if she drove?' I held up the car key.

'Shit,' he replied. He sat down on the bottom step of the stairs.

'If she drove I need to get her car back there.'

'We don't even know what it is – or if she did.'

'Is there a fob with it?'

'No, it's just a key.'

'Dammit. I'll just have to go up and down the road and look as if I'm a car thief then.' He took the keys from me and gave me a humourless grin, 'might as well seal my fate as a criminal.'

'Fingerprints,' I reminded.

'What?'

'What about your fingerprints on there?'

'Oh fuck! Well, I suppose I'll have to rely on wiping them off, won't I, as it's done now – and I'd look pretty kinky wandering up and down here trying the car doors with a pair of marigolds on, wouldn't I?' The image briefly broke the spell of doom and we laughed almost hysterically until Tom rubbed his hands over his face and brought them slowly away to reveal a serious expression underneath like a clown miming happy-sad. 'Come on, back to business.' He slipped out of the front door and I lurked behind it, keeping a watchful eye through the patterned glass as he sauntered down the street surreptitiously trying the key in each car door as he passed. I periodically cast a glance behind me at the blanket roll, as if it would suddenly leap back into life and carry me off to hell with it. About an hour later Tom arrived back, cold but flushed with success and the sharp night air.

'She did drive and I found it round the corner. I've driven it round to the back and put our car back. I'll drive it back with her in it. Two birds with one stone.'

I helped with carrying the body to the car and loading it into the boot. She had been a small woman whilst alive and hardly weighing more than seven stone I would have estimated, but dead she seemed to weigh much more. Or maybe it was the burden of our souls that we carried too. Another painful thought struck me just before Tom drove away.

'She said she left the little girl with her mam. Poor kid. Won't her mam be wondering where she is by now?'

'Better get a move on and take her home then, hadn't I?' His face was grim, but he showed no interest in the child. I watched him climb into the car with the coldness of those memories clinging to me.

He came back just before dawn. By then my finger nails were chewed almost to the quick. The grey dawn drizzled in as I heard the click of his key in the front door. My eyes felt gritty from lack of sleep. I wondered if anything would ever look normal through them now. Tom wouldn't allow me to know the details of what he'd done when he got to her place.

'If you don't know and you're ever questioned, then saying that is quite true, isn't it? Old army trick – need to know. It makes you more convincing.'

'Will I need to be convincing then?'

'No, but be it anyway.'

How wrong you were, Tom. Two weeks of police and questions, questions, questions and today the nightmare concluded – or has it start in earnest?

Chapter 18:

Aftermath, 1986

22nd June 1986

We didn't talk about it afterwards. Tom insisted it was better and being cowardly, I didn't argue. I tried to believe it would all be alright and in any case other events caught up so fast a few days later, it almost slipped my mind at one point. The hospital letter was replaced safely on my dressing table and I kept the appointment without further mishap. I was surprised it moved my case so much further forward when I'd thought it was merely another administrative session. Instead I was given a full medical check, coming home so stuck with needles I felt like a pin cushion, and then I settled down to wait. The doctor had said it would be at least another six months before anything happened so my attention returned to Tom and what was happening with him.

There'd been a visit from the police almost immediately telling Tom of his estranged wife's death. He bustled me into my bedroom before opening the front door, telling me to stay as far out of things as possible. I didn't like it but I didn't disagree. I stood at the half open bedroom door indecisively. The part of me that was self-protective more than the part of me that loved took over, objectively claiming that caution was the right course of action now, not dramatic displays of support. I listened at the door nevertheless, ear glued to the dull paintwork, but unable to hear more than the deep rumble of the policeman and Tom's answering sounds. He wasn't there long – maybe twenty minutes and then their voices became louder as I guessed Tom was accompanying him to the front door. I heard Tom reply.

'Yes, of course I will.' I waited impatiently to hear the front door click shut before bursting out and down the stairs with a torrent of questions. Before they could be answered, the doorbell rang again and Tom hurriedly waved me back upstairs, pausing long enough before answering to allow me to get to the top and out of view from the front door step. The bell rang impatiently again and Tom answered, feigning surprise that it was the policeman back so soon.

'I forgot to ask, sir,' the officer asked politely, 'do you have anyone else here with you to corroborate your story?'

'I, er, well I share the house with someone but they're often out and not here right now.'

'And were they here the night your estranged wife died?'

'Well, um, no – why should you need to ask that? She died in her home didn't she?'

'Yes sir, apparently, but we are trying to establish who might have been there with her, if anyone, of course.'

'Oh, I see.'

'Was your housemate here then sir?'

'No.'

390

'Thank you. We may have to talk to you again, sir, but we'll be in touch if we do.' The door clicked shut a second time and I ran back down the stairs to him.

'Why the hell did you say I wasn't here? I could have confirmed you were here that night and then they wouldn't want to talk to you again. Are you mad?'

'No Billie, not mad; aware of what dragging you into this could do. You've just got yourself a place on the surgical list – what would being in the headlines do to that? Imagine it, "husbands transvestite lover claims husband is innocent." That would really keep you low-profile – and me, well, I'd be a figure of fun, wouldn't I?' I was about to agree when the content of the last part of what he said registered. I was angry – both at being referred to as a transvestite. He knew that wasn't what I was. Secondly that he was concerned about looking foolish by being linked to me.

'I'm not a transvestite, and I'm not your lover,' I responded huffily. I took a step back and looked coldly at him.

'Oh Billie!' He burst out laughing. 'Don't be such a, a ...' he struggled to find the words, then laughed even harder, tears crinkling at the corners of his eyes and his head throwing back with the force of it, 'a girl!' I clenched my fists angrily at him, speechless with rage that he was making fun of me, and laughing at this so serious situation where I'd been trying to help, but then the irony of it all got me too. I was being exactly what he said I was – a girl throwing a wobbly, like he'd described the girls at school to be doing so often in the past, and my father had said of my mother when she was being

391

particularly awkward and preening herself haughtily over some imagined slight from one of her cronies. My reluctant laughter was fanned by his uproarious humour until we were both breathless. It was the doorbell ringing again that stopped us suddenly in our tracks. Visit number three from the police, and this time I wasn't able to scramble up the stairs and out of sight in time before Tom was forced to open the door because of the insistence of the doorbell, followed almost immediately by loud knocking on the letterbox.

'Officer?' Tom was all courtesy, and a model of calm.

'Sorry to bother you again sir, just wanted to check if you still had a key to your estranged wife's home – oh and I see your *housemate* is home now too?' It was half-statement, half-question and the smug tone of its delivery made me uneasy. It felt vaguely like a cat playing with a mouse and I wanted to warn Tom of that but couldn't. I lingered in the background.

'She has to go out again any minute, so could you talk to her later, if that's necessary?' I knew Tom was trying to protect me but it made us sound suspicious.

'No problem, Sir, Miss,' the latter to me, with a small inclination of the head and a raised eyebrow. Was the eyebrow recognition of me for what I was, or an assumption of what must be going on between a man and a woman living together? The policeman gave no clue. He just went back to the original tease. 'The key, sir?'

'Oh, no – no I haven't got a key.'

'Then would there be any occasion recently when you visited her? We found some male hand size fingerprints at the bottom of the stairs and on the front door, near the keyhole.' He smiled charmingly, 'just trying to rule people out.'

'Well of course I would have been there at some stage, but not the other night.' Tom shook his head. I thought he looked convincing but the police officer scrutinised him for a moment too long. 'They were very recent prints, sir, so I don't think *some stage* would fit the bill. Never mind we'll probably be taking your fingerprints shortly, and probably yours too, Miss…?' He let the sentence trail off into a question so I was obliged to answer.

'Robinson, Billie Robinson.'

'Ah, *Miss* Billie Robinson.' He addressed himself to Tom again. 'I thought it would be a bloke. We'll be in touch then, sir.' Tom slammed the door shut behind him this time and leaned against it.

'Bastard,' he acknowledged. 'He wanted to catch me out, didn't he?' I didn't respond. We both knew the answer. Our humour was completely gone, replaced by a sense of foreboding. Pigs; now I knew why they got called that.

27th June 1986

Oh my God, amongst the continuing police visits – we've now had a further five – the letter arrived today. It announced that there had been a cancellation and my surgery could take place the day after tomorrow if routine tests confirmed I was in good health. I read it uncomprehendingly to start with, wondering what it was about. I thought I'd had all the routine checks, but then the first sentence started to make sense.

'Tom, Tom.' He appeared at the kitchen door, dishevelled and gut-wrenchingly handsome. We never touched, or talked about that evening at the restaurant, but it was always at the back of my mind. I still didn't know what he thought about it.

'What?' He seemed distracted. I held out the letter to him. He frowned and came over close enough to take it. We had developed a habit of not getting closer than arm's length of each other these days, as if skirting round each other would keep us away from the precipice we so easily could fall into.

'Christ, is this for real?' I nodded. 'That's tomorrow then. He pointed to the date on the letter. In my struggle to get my head round it, I hadn't considered that it would have arrived the day after it was sent.

'Tomorrow? I can't. I haven't got anything prepared. I haven't told work, I haven't got a bag packed; and what about the police? They keep pestering you. What if they come back again?' I could feel the panic rising like the swell of a tidal wave, rolling over me and drowning me in fear. My heart started to bump uncomfortably against my chest, making me feel as if my whole body was throbbing to its beat. It echoed the disco song pumping out of the radio, lively and light-hearted till then – a welcome relief from the need for the anxious check out of the window every time the doorbell rang now.

'Billie, it's what you've been waiting for all this time. A bag can be packed in a few minutes and I can tell work tomorrow.' The disco music changed to the steady beat of Michael Jackson's Billie Jean pulsing through the kitchen. Tom unexpectedly grabbed my hand and pulled me forward, making me step into a high armed spin as he sang with the lyrics. 'Come on … Billie Jean … you're about … to become … the dance queen.' I resisted the first attempt at a spin but his enthusiasm was infectious and suddenly from being scared I was exhilarated. I let him spin me and twist me with the beat as he repeated over and over again, 'Billie Jean … dancing queen … in the round.' The music faded away to be replaced by the next and we slowed into a close embrace. 'Billie Jean.' He breathed it into my hair and the beat of my pulse was the same as the beat of his breathing as we clung together. I don't know what might have happened next but he broke the spell by pushing me away just as suddenly, grinning brightly. 'Come on you've got packing to do.' He grabbed a shiny green apple out of the fruit bowl and tossed it to me. 'Catch!' It spun high up in the air, plummeting too fast towards me. I thought I wouldn't be able to catch it but I did, and it landed firmly in my palm with a soft smacking sound. 'An apple a day … and you're going to have plenty of doctors to contend with now …' The doorbell rang out like a clarion call. 'And I have the police again, no doubt,' he added with a grimace as he slipped out of the door and closed it firmly behind him.

'Officer, what a pleasant surprise,' I heard him say from the front door. I stayed in the kitchen, heart still pounding from a mixture of exertion, being so close to Tom I could hear his heart, anticipation for what came next in the hospital, and fear of what came next with the police. The enquiry was obviously another spurious one as Tom was back within minutes. He motioned to the apple still clasped in my hand with a nod of his head. 'Haven't you eaten that yet?' and winked.

'Tom, what did he want this time?'

'Oh, just another question about the car. Had I ever driven it? Apparently the seat was pushed too far back by a couple of notches for her to drive it.'

'Oh Tom, didn't you adjust it when you got out?'

'Of course I did, they're just trying to spook me. I pushed it as far forward as it would go – until it stuck.'

'Why are they trying to spook you?'

'I don't know.' He looked serious. 'I'm trying to think what I did wrong but I can't – and I'm not telling you either otherwise you'll get drawn in. Go and get packed. I will be fine.'

'Why don't you just let me tell them I was here, and you were too. Then they will have to leave you alone.'

'And start on you? When you are just about to get the break you've been waiting for all this time? Stop worrying. It's all just a game for them and they'll stop playing eventually. I didn't do anything wrong, ok?'

'Ok.' I wasn't convinced and I wished he would tell me the precise routine he'd followed when he'd reached Lucy's house so I could review it objectively but he wouldn't. I packed my bag, got delivered to the hospital the next day and my new life began.

3rd July 1986

It's now two days since the operation, and I've not been allowed to even walk to the loo yet. I don't think I could even if I was allowed to. It's not that there's that much pain. The only real pain comes if one sneezes, coughs, or laughs, but I feel as if I've been run over by a juggernaut. I barely have the energy to shift in bed. There is a catheter in place and apparently it will stay there for several days. I am dreading it coming out and having to try to pee through my newly formed exits and entrances. My stomach feels bloated and lumpy as I haven't been to the loo in days. I have been told I will have the joy of an enema tomorrow to get everything going again.

'Like shifting boulders,' the plump nurse attending me announced gleefully, patting the covers down around me and making me shiver inwardly at the thought of anything shifting out of me – it all feels so fragile and sore. To keep my new vagina fixed in place while it heals in the right position inside me there is a thin surgical wire going through my stomach, under my pelvic bone, through my new vagina, back up around the pelvic bone and out my stomach again. I imagine myself being wrapped with barbed wire. I can hardly bare to think of it laced through me, so much so that it makes me scared to move, even if I could. Inside is a wad of surgical gauze, plugging me like a penis. There is no thought of pleasure there, just an uncomfortable sense of being trussed like a turkey for Christmas dinner. I dislike that image intensely and I think I will stop writing there. I'm so tired.

4th July 1986

I had the enema. It was like being drained of my guts. How undignified this is. I hate myself lying here useless and weak and knitted together. Tom came in after they'd cleared up but I spent the whole time he was here afraid he could smell the stench I was sure still lingered from the enema. I asked the plump nurse, who told me today she was called Katrina, to open the window but she forgot. She came back later when Tom had gone, but she didn't remember then either.

Tom sat gingerly on the plastic chair by the side of my bed, looking everywhere but the cage over my central body where the plastic tubing from the catheter slipped into the bag steadily filling with pale golden fluid that looked like liquid gold, but was in reality the rank foulness of my urine. I was so disgusted by myself, how could he not be?

'What did they do?' He asked, timidly, and obviously without thinking. I was amazed at the question. Irritation bubbled up in me and I wanted to shout at him for his ignorance and for being scared to ask before. He'd never asked me but had he really never made an effort to find out anything that would be done to me? I was shocked and part of me angrily wanted to tell him how they'd slit the skin of my penis lengthwise from the head to the base on the underside and then peeled it away and turned it inside out much like one might turn a sock inside out. Even my desire to rid myself of this thing I'd hated for so long didn't stop me feeling squeamish just knowing that. Then the slit is stitched back together, creating an inverted penis, and the skin and muscles of the lower abdomen is lifted up with surgical instruments, to provide a gap near the pelvic bone. The inverted penis is pushed into the gap, still attached at the base, so that it hinges down and into the proper location for a vagina. Before all this happens, the small stub of penile tissue left behind is threaded through another slit to form a clitoris. A second tiny slit has the urinary tube re-routed through it to create a female urinary opening. Finally some of the abdominal muscles are repositioned around the new vagina so that they can squeeze in on it, to create an orgasm. My belly and thighs are black with bruising which will last weeks. I am abhorrent to look at; swollen, stitched, wired, plugged, caked with blood and crusted discharge and peeing through a tube into a bag that sways on the side of my bed when I move, but I am no longer male. I could have told him all of that, I suppose. I held my tongue.

'They made me completely a woman,' was all I said instead. He smiled and squeezed the hand that didn't have a drip in it. I closed my eyes to the mess of blood and bandages and piss and dreamed.

7th July 1986

Today was the seventh day. The nurse proudly told me I was her seventh reassignment and today is the 7th of July – almost mystical. Maybe I shall be a vestal virgin after all. The thought made me laugh. The spring sunshine was filtering gently through the half opened blinds, making it look as if someone had put ladders all over the building. I could almost climb out. Today in fact I was to be allowed out of bed, but not until someone could walk behind me. The surgeon has snipped the wire lacing me together like a chain mail fence and I'm left, just heavily bandaged to try to walk slowly and cautiously to the bathroom for the first time. Tom was late coming in. I asked if he'd been bothered by the police any more. He changed the subject and I knew there was some kind of problem. Katrina came in to help me make the journey to the bathroom.

'Oh,' she said, seeing Tom. 'Do you want to help her instead?' We answered at the same time. Both of us said no. I looked at him disappointedly, but I was relieved too. He looked down at his hands and I avoided his eyes when he looked up.

'Well, it's a bit scary the first time. Come on.' No concern for my dignity, she just flipped the thin hospital bed covers back and indicated for me to try to slide my legs out of bed. I moved a fraction of an inch.

'It's ok, you won't fall apart.' She laughed merrily. Tom looked away, and cleared his throat. I guessed he was feeling bad being in a hospital given his aversion to them.

'Shall I wait outside?' He asked hopefully.

'Oh really, no.' Katrina positioned herself at the side of the bed. 'Now once you've got out once, it'll be easier the second time. Come on.' She gave me no choice. I edged slowly and painfully off the bed, every part of my stomach and crutch throbbing like someone was beating it. I could feel the stitches pulling tightly and stopped. 'Come on,' she urged blithely, 'no slacking!' and giggled.

'I feel like I'm coming apart.' My voice was harsh and male.

'No, you're fine. If you were going to come apart, you would have done so long before now, me girl.' She nodded encouragingly and I reluctantly completed the bottom shuffle to the edge of the bed. My feet dangled over the side and my crotch felt as if it was pulsing like a spurting artery. I slid further, feeling the cotton sheet crisp under the bare skin of my ass. Belatedly I wondered if Tom could see my naked body from where he was standing. I flushed hot and cold with embarrassment. My feet touched the cold floor and my toes curled against it, desperately tensing to gain a steady hold on its slippery surface. *Please don't let me fall, please don't let me fall.* Katrina stuck a plump pink hand under my armpit and pulled me upright until I was standing, both feet on the smooth cold floor.

'There you are. Easy. Now let's walk.' *Jesus what did they want from me?* I shuffled slowly, foot following foot, across the floor towards the bathroom door. I could feel the pull of the stitches, the chafing of the discharge-hardened dressings as they pulled at the skin they'd adhered to. The throb between my legs intensified and I put my hand between them to stop me falling from out of me. It was smooth and undulating, not defined by a prick and two balls. Suddenly the reality hit home and I sobbed. I was a woman at last. I couldn't move another inch. My feet were frozen to the spot and my body shook like a hurricane was battering the branches of a great tree. The tears ran down my face and made heavy dark splodges on the shabby standard hospital gown. I didn't care if Tom could see my naked behind. I didn't care that Katrina was tut-tutting and trying to urge me on. Or that the upright I thought I was doing was actually bent half double as I caught my reflection in a mirror across the room. Greasy hair straggled over my shoulders and the tip of my nose was reddening from the tears, but the figure in the mirror was unmistakably a woman with a woman's silhouette. Eventually the tears lessened and from the storm of weeping I felt a calm settle over me. I made the rest of the journey to the bathroom in grim silence, managed a teaspoonful of piss down the toilet, waited meekly whilst Katrina showed me how to wipe myself properly with a sterile wipe and let her lead me unsteadily back to the bed. I still felt as if I was losing the middle section of my body from between my legs but I hadn't. I laid my hand briefly on my pubic mound to check as I lay back against the pillows. It felt numb now but it was alright. I closed my eyes to sleep, opening them quickly again as I remembered Tom had been there. He was gone. I hoped he would be back but didn't have the strength left to complete the thought. I slept until they brought the cocoa just before lights out.

9th July 1986

I came home today. Released from my little cocoon, reality kicked back in hard almost straight away. Tom came to collect me, tense and pale, but saying little about what was going on with him. I realised I'd been focussing so hard on coping for myself, I'd almost forgotten about Lucy. Once we'd made the slow transition from hospital to home, and I was perched precariously on my bank of cushions on the settee I waited for him to talk. He sat down in the seat across the room from me, coiled like a spring about to jump. There was a light buzz from the traffic outside, but otherwise it was uncannily still inside, as if waiting for the major drama to unfold.

'You haven't told me if the police have been here much since I went in?'

'A bit.'

'A bit?'

'A few times.'

'Saying what?'

'Asking things.'

'What things?'

'Oh, I can't remember now.'

'Tom.' He shook his head.

'No I really can't. Odd little things. Did she wear high heels? Did she keep her keys in a specific hand bag? Did she drive with the car window down? I don't know why. None of it makes sense and I really can't understand why they are asking. Let's leave it. None of them are anything to do with what happened so whatever they're thinking, they're barking up the wrong tree, aren't they? I haven't seen them for a couple of days now so maybe they're giving up pestering me.'

'You never said what happened to the child.'

'She's staying with Lucy's mother. Nothing to do with me anyway.'

'What about the father?'

'Jeff? He buggered off. That's why she was after me. She wrote to me, asking me to go back.'

'You never said.'

'I wasn't going to so it didn't matter.'

'But you did see her?'

'Once or twice.' He avoided my eyes. I knew he was aware I was still observing him. My heart fluttered like a bird in a cage. He'd put it there. I knew he was lying. It wasn't that Lucy had said otherwise, it was that I knew Tom too well now.

'OK,' he burst out after a while. 'I did go and see her a few times. I'd avoided her and refused her calls for the last few weeks hoping she'd go away. I guess that's why she came here in the end – to find out what I was doing.' He looked at me quickly and looked away again.

'Tom, why don't you tell me these things?'

'I've told you now.'

'But only because I asked.'

'I don't know. You had enough on your mind. Anyway, I wasn't going back and it didn't matter.' He shoved his hands in his pockets and looked me back straight in the eyes his time, defensive, but repentant. 'Why didn't you tell me what they did to you at the hospital all those times you went?'

'I didn't think you wanted to know.'

'I didn't think you wanted me to ask. And I suppose I didn't want to know to begin with. It was all too alien – you were suddenly too alien.'

'Alien.' I considered the word. I'd applied it to myself often enough. Why shouldn't he? The thing was, it was just a word when I used it. When he used it, it hurt. I didn't comment. Instead I asked another question of my own. 'When did you start to want to know?'

'When you came back once and started telling me without thinking – the time they were odd about your blood test results. I started to wonder what they were doing to you, pumping you full of drugs. I wondered if it was dangerous. Lucy's personality certainly changed. I didn't want that happening to you. I was worried.'

'You never said.'

'Weren't you worried?'

'Yes, that's why I talked about it then.'

'You never said either.' The length of the room stretched between us like two lives lived apart. 'You're not Will anymore.' He said at last.

405

'I haven't been for a long time.'

'No, I know. Maybe it's time I got to know Billie properly.' He fumbled in his pocket as if searching for something and then seemed to change his mind. 'You're tired.' He was right, I was. I was exhausted by this transition, this final transition.

15th July 1986

The odd thing about genital reassignment surgery is that whereas the body previously had its own mind map of the area, surgery has completely rearranged this and nerve endings that were once associated with one place are now in another. It is most disconcerting going to scratch an insistent itch to discover that place no longer exists any more – or has been transported to somewhere quite different – like deep inside you. It's a form of the phantom sensations that amputees experience, but how do you explain a balls itch that is now on non-existent balls? The first time it happened I was perplexed until the consultant subsequently explained it to me at my next follow up appointment. I told the tale to Tom and he howled with laughter. I didn't like referring to my now non-existent masculinity to him, but the shared joke lightened the almost embarrassed approach he'd taken with me until then and all of a sudden it went from private joke to the opening of a complete avenue of communication we'd preciously avoided at all costs. Sometimes the exacerbated mood swings resulting from the sudden change in my physiology and how my body reacted because of it caused other extreme reactions, but the private joke seemed to be able to encompass all of them so the tension was always easily defused by a Tom remark like,

'Scratchy or just got a phantom itch that needs scratching?'

The main itch that needed scratching was one I'd dreaded from the first; dilation.

After the various fluid discharges following the initial healing from the operation tailed off, I knew the dilation ritual had to start. It wasn't that it was so terrible, although it was uncomfortable and tricky at first, but it was the dirty way it made me feel. I felt as if I was masturbating whilst the world outside was going on its normal way and that made me feel perverted. It was an absolute necessity otherwise the skin would tighten as it healed, scar tissue would thicken and reduce flexibility and the vaginal depth created with the surgery would shrivel like my penis had begun to after the hormone treatment had taken effect. Lying on the bed with my knees bent slightly, a pillow covered by a towel to soak up the lubrication gel, a dilator inserted for twenty minutes at a time felt not only unnatural, but dirty. It had to be done several times a day and the very frequency of it made it difficult too – how do you dilate when you are at work? In the loo?

I hated this routine more than any other part of the surgery and its aftermath. I became adept at it over the following weeks of course, determining the precise angle to enable quick and efficient insertion, identifying the precise place inside my new vagina to massage the internal muscle to allow the dilator to slip past its spasms and then rotating and applying gentle inward pressure as the tissues stretched. I became intimately acquainted with the shape of a vagina in a way ironically I'd never done as a man. It was like a flower opening, an exotic lily opening to the sun. I learnt how to manipulate the clitoris I now had to simulate desire and make my own mucous secretions mingle with the lubrication from the gel. In fact I became so expertly automatic at it that my first delirious orgasm took me completely by surprise.

It was Saturday and the early afternoon sun was streaming through the window and lying on my bed like a lover. It lay across my body and whilst I liked its feel on me I wanted to get this dilation over before Tom came home from watching the football match he'd gone to. I was anxious that after a long period of silence there had been another visit from the police earlier that day. When he came in I'd decided it was time for him to go through what he'd done on returning Lucy's body to her house that day. It all seemed so long ago but the re-emergence of the police visits had brought it worryingly back into focus. My practiced fingers applied the lubrication to the dilator and on the tips of my fingers, directly into my vagina. I inserted the dilator almost absent-mindedly, thoughts more on what the police had asked about in their several visits now. I'd now teased most of the questions they'd asked Tom from him and they were a motley array. Questions about her clothes, shoes, driving experience, where the child might have been on the day and why, what her choice of bedding was, was she a competent driver or would she have driven the byroads locally. What about her beauty regime? Was she an ardent user of make-up or not? None of it really made sense but they were surely asking the questions in order to create a picture of her for some reason – and why ask Tom, if not to try to place him there at the scene? Without noticing it the sensation from the dilator had changed subtly.

Tom's humorous tease, *got a phantom itch that needs scratching* felt closer to what I was feeling than anything else I could describe. I was aware of the sensation of itching deep inside me, exaggerated by the movement of the dilator as I routinely twisted and dipped it inside me. Far from unpleasant, it made me want more of it. Involuntarily I increased the motions and the sensation intensified with it, drawing a gasp of surprise from me as I felt the pull of the dilator sliding out gently, and then sinking back in. I felt the deep itch radiate out into my limbs like warm wax flowing over them as they sank into a composite languorous ache. The dilator moved deeper and faster, my hand seeming to automatically respond to the desire to slide it in and out, in and out. The questions from the police faded away and were replaced by other words, another voice, muffled but flowing over me like a tongue sliding over my bare skin, tasting the dew of desire in the salt sweat on my breasts, face, lips. I imagined hands touching, caressing, probing; teasing, tantalising my nipples into hard pink buds. I shivered; the tingle of the cold air on bare skin made me ice-cold yet also burning inside. I'd pulled my top away to expose one breast and the hand not sliding the dilator deeper and deeper inside me kneaded and squeezing the bare skin. The molten wax spread up my body to my stomach, turning it to a lava pool. Deep inside, the itch became smoother, like an urgent need to be filled tight with the sensation of thrusting. I twisted the dilator frantically inside me as the lava rose up out of me and into my head until a sweet sharp note of piercing beauty, exploded in my ears, into my brain and then flowed like utter peace over my limbs. I sank back, exhausted. I had never had an orgasm before. The thought made me want to laugh hysterically.

The spell was broken by the sound of Tom banging through the front door, and a voice addressing him almost immediately afterwards.

'Tom Wilson, I am arresting you for the murder of Lucy Wilson on the night of 17th May 1986. You do not have to say anything but anything you say will be taken down and used against you in evidence.'

Chapter 19:

Confessions, July 1986

There were no entries after that – how could there be? But having gone this far, I had to follow through the rest of the story in my own head. Now I had all the pieces of the jigsaw, being able to look at the whole story from both Billie's and my perspective somehow made it seem different. It was more a love story than a tale of failure. I put the diary into my pocket and sat back. The chair dug into my shoulder blades like the chair had in the interview room at the police station. It brought the room and the conversation – the whole day, in fact – back with a jolt. The radio sounds in the cafe faded away, the clink of coffee cups and cutlery on dirty plates, the aroma of coffee and grease – all gone. In their place the sterile hopelessness of the dirty magnolia walls of the interview room with its one small window, high up and covered with mesh. The sounds of footsteps echoing along empty hallways approached and then receded. Silence in between, marred only by the odd hoot of a distant taxi in the melee of rush hour traffic far away from this place of quiet hopelessness. The floor smelt that sickly smell of disinfectant, dirt and wet pile that pervades after it has been swabbed clean by a mop that

411

carries more shit and grime than it clears. I'd thought I was long past noticing it by then, but it obviously stuck in my memory after all.

'You've got a visitor.' The officer had said, beckoning me from the cell. 'A lady, so be nice.' Who did he think he was to assume I wouldn't be? I didn't know who it would be until the door of the interview room swung open and she walked in. Of course it would be Billie. How stupid of me, had I lost my brains as well as my senses? 'You've got ten minutes.' The door slammed shut and she was standing in front of me at the iron grey table, its surface defaced with scrapes and mysterious shaped biro doodles. Maybe they were part of some grand escape plan hatched on the eve of sentencing, or the marks were where nail files and sharp instruments had been smuggled across its top for its miserable occupant, sitting where I was now to stash? I brought my rambling mind back to the present and Billie's sweet perfume. Apples; she still smelt of apples – like the apples in Old Ma J's orchard when we were kids, or the tart sweetness of it on your tongue as you bit into it, teeth crunching through flesh to the juicy innards. She sat down and we were at eye level. Hers, bitter almonds, perplexed.

'I don't understand Tom. You're in the papers. They're calling you her husband-lover, that you were still involved. I thought she was a thing of the past.' Her face was drawn and pained. I knew it was time for my truth.

'I didn't tell you because I didn't know how to – or what to say, or even why I would be telling you.' The truth will out –

412

didn't Shakespeare or one of Billie's other favourites write that once? 'You know she wrote to me a while ago, telling me she and Jeff had split up. He'd been a one-hit wonder and after the child was born, he couldn't take the heat so he got out of the kitchen, literally, and left her. At first she was just nagging about more money. It wasn't up to me to pay her and I told her that. The kid wasn't even mine. She said it was, and that she'd even registered it with my name on the birth certificate. She was lying of course but I didn't know that then. I went to see her, to try to find out the truth. I told you I saw her a few times, didn't I?' She nodded, still watching me intently, that little crease indenting her forehead as if a nagging headache was bothering her. I knew the dent would become deeper when I told her the rest but there was no avoiding it now. 'She was back to being the Lucy I knew when she was a teenager. She was sweet and nice, and I was confused, and...' I didn't know how to say this but it was very much part of it. 'I hadn't had sex in a long while and it was just too tempting. I kept seeing bits of you, half-naked, and although I didn't know why, it was turning me on, you see. That probably makes me sick, but, oh I don't know. It barely took a kiss turning into more than a peck on the cheek and I couldn't stop myself. It became a regular thing after that.

On Fridays I started to work a half day, finishing at lunchtime. I could be there by two o'clock, we'd talk a bit, end up in bed and I'd be back home again by eight, as if I'd just worked a longer shift. I don't know why I didn't tell you when she first wrote to me. Now it feels like betrayal, even though that's an odd word to use.' I looked at her downcast face and knew betrayal was right after all. 'So that's why the police placed me there so easily and assumed I caused her death. My fingerprints were already all over the house, and of course we'd had sex the day before. The stupid thing was it could all have been so simple. I could have got away with all of it because the only reason they started to look into the death first was because the pattern the blood settled in after she died was disturbed. That was because we moved her too quickly. If we'd left it a bit longer, when rigor mortis had set in, like you said to, when I lay her body at the bottom of her own stairs, she would have been in the right position and they wouldn't have questioned further. As it was, well, I'd been spotted going in and out of there a few times, and one of the neighbours said they saw me that night too. I didn't think anyone was looking but maybe they were. I was stupid. They said she was blackmailing me because they found another letter, drafted to send to me just before she visited you.' I couldn't look at her. I was too ashamed. I balled my hands into fists in front of me on the table and stared down at them.

We sat in silence for what seemed like hours but can have been no more than seconds. Ten minutes are a painfully short time to explain away a lifetime of mistakes. My ears were full of the words I called myself. *Stupid fucking bastard; can't keep your dick in your pants and your head on your life.* The kind of things we used to say to Jim when we'd been thrown unceremoniously out of another bar after he'd fingered another of the local girls. I never thought I'd one day apply them to myself. I wasn't sure if when she spoke she was saying some of it or it was just my disability playing me up again and shame filling in the gaps.

'Tom,' eventually her voice cut through my fugue of self-punishment, 'you didn't kill her, whatever else you may have done. If you let me tell them what actually happened, you'll be in the clear.'

'Billie, if I let you tell them the whole story, since the press is already enjoying name-calling, don't you think you'll be included too? And what do you think they'll call you? You'll be a much more interesting target than me. And you're forgetting your father – and your mother... No, too much rides on this. In a few years I'll be out again and then maybe we can both start to live a normal life. You will be established as Billie then, and I will just melt away somewhere – America or Australia, perhaps. Maybe I'll even go into something like security. That should suit a big stupid shit like me.'

'You'd go away?'

'It would be best wouldn't it? I've made too much of a mess of everything here. I'm a failure.'

'We had a conversation once about the names we give to things. I wouldn't call you a failure. There have just been mistakes in your life.' She didn't need to remind me. I was painfully aware how many mistakes I'd made, but they also meant I'd failed everyone – Lucy, her, myself, whatever she said.

415

'I love you Tom, whatever you've done, whatever is in the past.' She reached across the table to take my clenched fists and tried to prise the fingers open to lace into hers. I didn't want to. I didn't deserve it now. I feigned deafness and shook my head.

'I'm sorry, my hearings so bad these days.' I knew she didn't believe me. It was too quiet in the room for me not to be able to hear. My fingers slipped out of hers and back into a fist. She pulled her hand away like she'd been stung, face frozen like an ice queen.

'I've always loved you Tom,' she said softly, the tears sliding slowly down her face and dripping onto her blouse. 'I will wait. Not because I'm padlocked in, but because I want to.' I watched her crying, feeling numb inside, not wanting to hurt her, not wanting to lose her, but too beaten up by what I had to face to be able to give her comfort, to find any hope to look forward to.

'Love sets you free. I'm about to go to prison,' was all I could say. I couldn't face her anymore. The warden appeared at the door.

'Time's up.' Billie looked pleadingly at me. I couldn't do it. I had no courage any more. It was all used up on doing this for her. *Don't you see*, I wanted to shout at her, *this is my way of showing you – this, this is for you; my atonement. Let me go. It's the only way I can be good for you. I'm not strong enough to face the world like you.* That stupid adage about being cruel to be kind crossed my mind. I rammed it home just to make sure I did the right thing this time.

416

'I'm sorry. I don't feel the same. You'll always be my mate, that's all, but I don't want your life spoilt because I was a stupid prick. Go and be happy.' I walked out of the room without looking back. Silence slipped into step behind me. I welcomed it now. Back in my cell, I lay on my bunk facing the wall; the lumpy mattress digging in my side and the pillow smelling of stale breath. The clamour outside only distantly distracted me from misery. I let it fold over me like the dark. The piercing wail of a siren spiralled through the void eventually, and I raised my head to unravel the other noises that mingled with it. Despite myself, the urgency of the drama that was plainly going on outside sparked some curiosity. I went to the door of my cell and rapped on it. A small section of the warden's face appeared at the grille as he pulled the trap door back with a metallic click.

'Yeah?'

'What's all the palaver going on outside?'

'A bird just walked out in front of a car. They said she didn't even look. Some people just got a death wish, ain't they?' He looked meaningfully at me, before sliding the panel back sharply, sealing me in. My breath felt like it left me with a punch. I knew who the 'bird' was without being told. Billie's fresh apple scent taunted me and then as abruptly disappeared, leaving me empty, like I'd never had life at all. I went back to the bunk and curled up like a child, burying my face in the pillow and breathing in its foul mustiness. I wondered what it would be like to be dead.

Epilogue:

1986 and 1995

I laid the small posy of lizzyanthus and gypsophilia on the bed, curling Billie's right hand round its bundle of stems, as if she was holding it. Lying under the cool white of the hospital bed linen gave her the vague appearance of being dressed in white – like a bride; a bride in a shroud. The clock on the wall ticked clinically and the tear off page on the calendar on the wall pronounced the days date, as if I would ever forget it.

They were her favourite flowers. I'd never understood why. Usually women liked roses and the romance of the long-stemmed blooms, the sense of the dramatic gesture. But Billie had never been like that. Maybe it was the split view she had from both male and female perspective that enabled her to see things both pragmatically and empathetically, and that was why she appreciated the simple beauty and grace of the tall blue lizzyanthus and the light froth of the gypsophilia. Both the man and woman's view point. Placing the posy under her hand made her look even more the bride. A hot rush of emotion caught in the back of my throat and almost made me choke. Head aching from withheld emotion and eyes smarting as I struggled to stop the tears welling up and rolling out, I swallowed them down hard. I'd come this far.

Far away in another room, the 'Unchained Melody' song played again – or maybe it was just permanently in my head now? I pulled up a grey plastic hospital chair, scraping the legs slightly. I mentally apologised to her for the noise – I was always clumsy, and she'd always smiled at me indulgently for my awkwardness. I was a man from a man's world, forced to acknowledge another perception of life, alien to me. The scraping chair reminded me of the world I would have to go back into once I'd faced my nemesis.

'They'll all be here soon, Fran, your mam, some of your friends,' I told her, touching her pallid fingers tentatively. 'I'm only allowed a few minutes – persona non grata, you see, and I'm meant to be out only for Mam's funeral, not for you. It's only because one of the guards is secretly a bit of an old queen that they've allowed me to slip in here too.' Her fingers looked cold but they were warm to the touch, as if she was still exuberantly able to take my hand to dance with her or drag me along the tow path of the canal, laughing and teasing as she had the last time we'd been at ease with each other. My apology was full of fine words and yet now I was wordless.

I breathed out, steadying myself. Even thinking of saying the words I needed to say made my heart pound, but I knew I had to say them. I had to say them to her just once. I reached over past the tubes and wires trailing from the monitors to her, slipped the oxygen mask gently from her face – a miracle she could breathe on her own despite the brain damage – but not one that was likely to translate into any further miracles. They'd sadly shaken their heads. Clear of the mask, her face was serene. She was beautiful. I wished I could have one last glimpse of those almond shaped eyes, alive with humour and the light of love, but I knew I would have to dredge up the memories and keep them safe in my head instead. I imagined her eyes behind the closed lids, and my chest tightened.

'Will, Billie – it makes no difference. I will name that feeling now. I'm not ashamed or afraid of it anymore. It is love. I've always loved you too, from the first time we scraped our knees in the playground at Wilverton primary to the moment the light finally leaves your eyes. Oh I know we started out differently, but in the end it is all the same. I should have had the courage to tell you that a long time ago, but I'm telling you now.' I kissed her slightly parted lips, feeling her breath exhale gently against mine. I fumbled in my pocket for the padlock. I'd kept it like a lucky charm but it hadn't brought me luck or courage. It sat shiny and fresh in my palm. I took the keys off its fob and clicked it shut. I tucked it into her free hand, squeezing the fingers round it and slipping both hand and padlock under the clasped flowers to keep them safe. There was no use for the keys so I left them on the top of the bedside locker. A single droplet slipped out of the corner of her right eyelid and dropped onto the white cotton pillow sham, soaking in immediately. It looked like a tear, even though I knew that was fanciful of me. The pause seemed to lengthen between breaths. I didn't want to be there for the last one. She and I had already said goodbye.

I felt as if my heart remained there, but I didn't need it anymore. I took a single stem of lizzyanthus with me as I left. I knew they wouldn't let me take the lizzyanthus back into the prison but I took it anyway. Fuck them. That was nine long lonely years ago; slowly passing time. They say time is a great healer, but not even a surgeon could stitch the gaping hole in my life that she left.

I'd left the café by then, its noise and heat slamming shut behind me with the closing door. The loss of heat reminded me I had a last decision to make now, a cold one. The remaining memories were in my head – no diary by then. She was gone. I'd accepted that and moved on – although God knows there was little enough to move on to in prison, just the next day. That was how I'd spent the last nine years though, one day to the next, each as grey as I remembered the night air to have been in London. Maybe I could have been the courageous man I'd wanted to be if she hadn't been lost to me then, but the fight had all gone. Nine years of prison and lack of hope had dissolved it like it was so much ash into water. The lyrics of 'Unchained Melody' swirled in my head as I reached the canal path and headed for the bridge across it. That could be our Vrnjačka Banja bridge, she'd joked as we walked home from the restaurant the night she'd told me the tale of the love padlocks. It was what had prompted me to buy the little shiny red token I'd never attached anywhere after all. The intention at least had been good.

The envelope that had arrived this morning still nestled in my pocket. It was that and the radio programme that had dredged up all these memories. I had almost reached a sad accommodation of my lonely state over the years, so the news in the letter was shocking, almost unwelcome, yet haunting. Now I had to face the battle I thought I'd avoided long ago. The decision was now mine to make whether to fight or retreat. My sigh echoed the songs sigh. In the song someone came home ... *wait for me.* Could that happen after all this time? Could I go back? Could anyone ever go back? My fingers touched the crease of the letter as it folded in two in my pocket. I could visualise the words now, I'd read them so many times since yesterday.

'*...you probably assumed that she died. I know there was apparently no hope then and the prison advised that you were so depressed no contact from her family was advisable at the time. We had little choice but to let you slip away as you thought she had. It wasn't until sometime later that I decided to risk writing anyway. I always tried to keep my ear to the ground about how you were doing but of course we weren't deemed to be related so it was difficult. When you get out, you may want to simply start afresh and try to forget the past completely, but if you want to get in touch, my phone number is...'*

It went on to give Billie's sister's phone number. The letter had been folded round the diary like it was a gift inside a wrapping. The post mark on the envelope read 16th February 1987. The letter had reached across the eight years it had taken to wind its way through an assortment of post boxes, sorting offices, out trays and 'undelivered' pigeon holes until it finally had been handed to me yesterday, having been kept in the 'pending release file' given my instructions to block out all correspondence from outside the prison. I'd read the letter holding my breath, shocked, and then scared. I reached the bridge over the canal. My first inclination was to throw the letter and the diary into the trash and never have to face those conflicting emotions again. Hadn't it already turned out bad enough? Start a new life like Fran had suggested. But when I went to do it, I couldn't. Nine years had blunted and diminished the hurt and fear and disappointment, but it couldn't dispose of love. Thinking of Billie still brought that sharp ache in my chest. In the end there'd been no contest. I had to see what she'd written, and whether I could face what might come after that. Yet even now, after having relived every part of that journey from childhood to emptiness, still I dithered. Why was I such a coward? I could admit love to the dying but not to the living?

Something colourful on the bridge distracted me. Ridiculously it irritated me, not knowing what it was. I stepped onto the bridge and made my way across as it creaked uneasily under my weight. It had seen better days too. I stopped at the bright object. It was a padlock. A red padlock, intertwined carefully in the iron mesh of the bridge sides, but left open. Not closed. Scratched on it was an inscription, almost unreadable now under the weathering of the years, *T and B, 1986*. I disentangled it gently and it lay in the palm of my hand. It seemed almost too impossible, and yet so had the arrival of the letter and its contents. The rivers in the lyrics flowed on to the sea. Where did the canal waters flow to?

***

My fingers trembled as I dialled the number in the letter. The voice the other end sounded the same as all those years ago.

'Fran, its Tom – Tom Wilson. I've just been given your letter from 1987...'

There was a confused silence at the other end and I wondered if they'd moved and I was talking to a complete stranger after all.

'Tom! My God – I can hardly believe it. Tom Wilson? Really?' Her voice rose a pitch at the end of the final question.

'Yes, Tom Wilson.'

'Oh, my God.' She didn't seem to be able to say anything else, so I pressed on.

'I've only just got your letter from all those years ago, unbelievable though that may seem.'

'Oh my God, oh my God ...' There was a pause then she said, 'about Billie?'

'About Billie.'

'Oh,' she sighed, 'all those years – how on earth ... we thought you didn't want to get in touch ...' she trailed off.

'I ...' I didn't quite know what to say – I wanted her to say it, tell me what had happened since; advise me what to do.

'Do you want to ...' she stopped, 'would you like to ...' and again that hesitancy.

'I need to see ...' I had to just bite the bullet – an odd adage considering what I'd experienced so many years ago in the army, but essentially it told it as it was.

'Yes.' There was a smile in her voice. I could hear it in the timbre and resonance. She gave me an address to meet her at and a time. The place was a sprawling Victorian style mansion, with an efficiently busy staff. Fran had barely changed in the intervening years. I wondered how much I had. She didn't comment, just smiled at me and gently took my arm. That feeling I'd first encountered when looking at Gary's empty bunk bubbled up in my chest. Fear. Fran was talking to me but I was barely listening as my heart pounded uncomfortably, shaking me physically with each step I took along the corridor.

'... it took a long time and there's a lot different but, well, you'll see ...'

She was sitting down, looking far into the distance through the large paned window. Its vista was out over grounds that rolled elegantly away. The rich chestnut hair was streaked lightly with silver and the sunlight streaming through the window turned them into iridescent strands of precious metal. The curls tumbled over her shoulders and flowed down towards interlaced hands resting peacefully in her lap.

'Billie?' Fran said gently, touching the sloping shoulder with her fingertips. The tumbling locks moved sinuously as she turned her head and I looked into the deep brown almond eyes of the woman I loved. Her face had dropped fractionally on the left side – the after effects of the accident. She was partially paralysed. Fran had explained it all on the long walk

425

down the corridor. The accident hadn't killed her after all. After I'd left, assuming – as everyone had – no recovery was possible, Billie had staged her own miracle. As if by sheer effort of will, her eyes had opened first, then she'd struggled against the pipes and tubes pumping oxygen into her, and had eventually breathed alone two months after I'd said my goodbye. A full recovery was beyond her and she was paralysed down the left side. It meant she couldn't walk easily and couldn't live independently, and had eventually become settled here once she'd escaped the confines of the hospital. Her nine long lonely years had been here; a mere 54 miles away from me as the crow flew. Two prisoners; imprisoned. Two links of a chain, unlinked.

'She's never given up,' Fran told me gently,' but she needs looking after.'

Wait for me … was that what the single tear had said?

It was lopsided, but otherwise the smile was the same; warm and gentle, and seeming to know what I was thinking before I did myself. I moved towards her, not sure what I was doing, like drifting in a dream. She held out her right hand to me. It was slim and firm like it had always been.

'Hi?' There was a question in her voice. I turned her hand over and put the open padlock in her outstretched palm, clicking the lock shut. She smiled, and I smiled back. The melody swelled around us, unchained at last.

Bibliography

1.   *Julius Caesar*, W. Shakespeare – Act 3, Scene 1, 273

2.   Somewhat anachronistic, as this was published on the internet in 1990, but applying some artistic license, this is an extract from a moving plea to parents encountering the issue of transgender in their children (or other loved ones):

      http://www.susans.org/reference/gfam3.html

3.   *Hamlet*, W. Shakespeare – Act 1, Scene 2, line 146

The songs from the past include:

'School's out' – Alice Cooper

'Mouldy Old Dough' – Lieutenant Pigeon

'Vincent' – Don Maclean

Suzanne – Leonard Cohen

'Sweet Little Lies' – Fleetwood Mac

'You Wear it Well' – Rod Stewart

'Baby Give it Up' – KC and the Sunshine band

'Killing Me Softly' – Roberta Flack

'One Day in Your Life' – Michael Jackson

'Empty Chairs' – Don Maclean

'Billie Jean' – Michael Jackson

And,

'Unchained Melody' – The Righteous Brothers / Robson and Jerome